TAKING CHARGE

TAKING CHARGE

THE ELECTRIC AUTOMOBILE IN AMERICA

MICHAEL BRIAN SCHIFFER

with
TAMARA C. BUTTS and
KIMBERLY K. GRIMM

SMITHSONIAN INSTITUTION PRESS
Washington and London

Library of Congress Cataloging-in-Publication Data
Schiffer, Michael B.
Taking charge : The electric automobile in America / Michael Brian
Schiffer with Tamara C. Butts and Kimberly K. Grimm. p.   cm.   Includes
bibliographical references (p. 199) and index. ISBN 1-56098-355-8   1. Automobiles,
Electric—United States.   I. Butts, Tamara C.
II. Grimm, Kimberly K.   III. Title.
TL220.S34   1994   629.25′02′0973—dc20   93-49483

British Library Cataloguing-in-Publication Data available

Manufactured in the United States of America.

03   02   01   00   99   98   97   96   95   94

10   9   8   7   6   5   4   3   2   1

∞ The paper used in this publication meets the minimum requirements of the American
National Standard for Permanence of Paper for Printed Library Materials Z39.48-1984.

Cover illustrations: front, Figure 53, detail of Figure 25; *back*, Figures 19 and 54.

FOR MY PARENTS,
LOUIE AND FRANCES-FERA,
WITH ALL MY LOVE

CONTENTS

PREFACE   ix

1.
A SPECTACULAR FLOP   1

2.
AND THEN THERE WAS LIGHT (AND POWER)   5

3.
ON TROLLEYS AND BICYCLES   21

4.
A TECHNOLOGICAL CONVERGENCE   35

5.
THE ELECTRIC AUTOMOBILE GOES TO MARKET   49

6.
GETTING A CHARGE   63

7.
THE WIZARD COMES TO THE RESCUE   77

8.
A DARK AGE DESCENDS   91

9.
THE ROAD TO REVIVAL   109

10.
THE CLASSIC AGE   125

11.
DENOUEMENT   153

12.
PROGNOSIS FOR THE ELECTRIC CAR   175

QUOTATION CREDITS   191
SELECTED BIBLIOGRAPHY   199
INDEX   219

PREFACE

The idea for this book struck me in the spring of 1990 while I was doing research for *The Portable Radio in American Life*. In paging through *Scientific American* and *Electrical World* from the late 1890s, I was impressed by the early promise of the electric automobile in America. It was clear that no one then had a clue as to which kind of car—electric, gasoline, or steam—would prevail. In this, it seemed to me, was a fascinating and perhaps significant question: What happened to the electric car? After completing the radio book in the fall of 1990, I began to investigate the electric car's rise and fall. The present work is the result of my labors, and I hope that it will be of interest to the general reader.

From the *New York Times* to *Motor Trend*, one can hardly pick up a newspaper or magazine today without encountering an article about electric automobiles; even television is lavishly covering "the car of the future." Everywhere, it appears, interest in electric vehicles and their batteries is high. And many people believe we are poised on the threshold of a new era of electric cars.

By drawing on the electric automobile's rich history, which began in the 1830s, we may be able to steer discussions of the electric car's future along fruitful avenues. Indeed, that history is a potent antidote to common views about what caused the early electric car's demise. Surprisingly, the causes are not primarily technical shortcomings in the cars themselves or in their batteries. Rather, a complex and changing constellation of technological, social, and cultural factors were at work. A narrow focus on technical issues today may deflect attention away from the contextual factors that will ultimately determine the reception of the new electrics in the American marketplace.

Because the electric car is quintessentially an *electrical* technology, this book naturally lays stress on that technological context. In previous histories of the automobile, the electric car has usually been treated as a curiosity, a pariah, a deadend along the road to the "modern" car. I redress that imbalance by situating the electric automobile within the evolution of nineteenth- and early twentieth-century electrical technologies. In this way, one can appreciate changes in the technological bases of the electric car itself and in the infrastructure needed for charging its batteries.

Social and cultural contexts must also be understood: how automobiles, and the electric automobile in particular, related to the lives of past Americans. Thus, it is necessary to consider everything from leisure activities to gender and class. Study of such contexts allows us to appreciate, for example, that gender relationships in American families decisively influenced the emergence *and nonemergence* of mass markets for particular kinds of cars. These and other insights from the past may help us to guide intelligently the electric car's second coming.

Obviously, placing the electric car into its past contexts requires the assembly and careful interpretation of a great deal of information, much of it not usually consulted in preparing an automobile history. Like others writing about early automobiles, I did comb through the pages of turn-of-the-century automobile magazines, including *Horseless Age* and *Motor World*, for useful tidbits, but these magazines were mainly written by and for the men who were contemptuous of electric cars. The automobile magazines, then, speak most articulately on behalf of the gasoline automobile, darling of the car enthusiasts. Needless to say, their voices have badly skewed treatments of the electric car in most automobile histories.

To hear other voices, I turned to the literature of the American electrical industry, especially *Electrical World*. This trade journal brought news (of the invention, commercialization, and adoption of all electrical things) to far-flung engineers and executives in power stations and electrical manufacturing companies. Not surprisingly, the electric car was held in high regard by the electrical industry, and its development was documented in detail. During the teens, the National Electric Light Association (NELA), trade group of the electric power industry, and the Electric Vehicle Association held joint meetings. As a result, the *NELA Proceedings* became the main voice of electric vehicle makers, chronicling the activities and opinions of industry insiders. The magazine *Electric Vehicles* furnishes similar information, but, because it was aimed at the motoring public, it has a more optimistic slant. *Scientific American*, which dealt in those years mostly with new technology and patents, was a valuable resource because it represented the views of a larger technical community about various automobile and electrical technologies.

Also pored over were hundreds of articles on automobiling in mass-circulation magazines, such as *Colliers, Literary Digest,* and *Ladies' Home Journal*, to sample the automobile-related activities and attitudes of middle-class men and women. Often searched page by page, these same magazines yielded hundreds of advertisements for electric cars, which reveal much about manufacturers' intended markets.

Countless additional sources were examined for information on the origin of the electric car's component, enabling, and competing technologies. Other histories—on American cities, for example—helped to flesh out the electric car's contexts. Finally, visits to technology archives allowed me to piece together stories of several little-known projects of Thomas Edison and Henry Ford, including an electric car.

In creating a book of this sort one obviously incurs many debts. Above all I am grateful to my undergraduate research assistants, Tamara C. Butts and Kimberly K. Grimm; their fine library skills and enthusiasm contributed immeasurably to the quality of the final product. Oleg Lysyj also assisted with library research.

Financial support for this research came from the Social and Behavioral Sciences Research Institute, University of Arizona; the Laboratory of Traditional Technology, University of Arizona; Pacific Gas and Electric Company; and NIFE-SAFT Battery Company. The latter two firms generously responded to my eleventh-hour plea for funds to help conclude the project.

Off-campus archival and library research was carried out at the Henry Ford Museum & Greenfield Village, Dearborn, Michigan; the Library of Congress; the San Diego Automotive Museum Library; and the Edison National Historic Site, West Orange, New Jersey. In each place I encountered friendly people who were courteous, efficient, and helpful. I would like to single out for special thanks Douglas G. Tarr, assistant archivist at the Edison National Historic Site. The staff of the University of Arizona Libraries, especially Interlibrary Loan, also facilitated my research.

I thank GM Electric Vehicles for furnishing specifications on their electric-car prototype, the Impact, and Solar Electric Corporation of Santa Rosa, California, for providing information about their commercial electric cars. Other assistance and information came from Robert C. Post, Catherine Cameron, Mark Harlan, David B. Sicilia, Judy Brunson, the Vermont Historical Society, Ovonic Battery Company, the Electric Power Research Institute, Arizona Public Service Company, New Mexico Public Service Company, the Salt River Project, and the Azienda Energetica Municipale of Milan, Italy. Alan S. Douglas, electrical enthusiast and scholar, generously gave me source material and guidance in the early literature.

Although the majority of information synthesized for this book came from primary sources, a number of secondary sources were exploited for parts of the story. Special thanks go to the authors of these fine studies (which are listed in the Selected Bibliography at the end of the book): W. Bernard Carlson, Robert Conot, Abram J. Foster, James J. Flink, Robert Friedel (and Paul Israel and Bernard S. Finn), David A. Hounshell, Thomas P. Hughes, Matthew Josephson, Stuart W. Leslie, Carolyn Marvin, S. McCrea, David E. Nye, Sidney Olson, Robert C. Post, Richard Schallenberg, Stephen W. Sears, Robert A. Smith, Philip Terpstra, John D. Venable, and Rosamond Young.

For furnishing helpful comments on various drafts, I thank Chuck Bollong, Tamara C. Butts, Kimberly K. Grimm, Paul Israel, David Kirsch, Mark A. Neupert, Robert C. Post, Ann Ramenofsky, Karen Reeds, Frances-Fera Schiffer, Louie Schiffer, David B. Sicilia, James M. Skibo, Christine R. Szuter, Douglas G. Tarr, Rudi Volti, Dave Vaughn, and William Walker. Other suggestions of merit came from Annette Schiffer and Jeremy Schiffer. I am especially grateful to Robert C. Post for his encouragement and faith in my project.

Doris Sample, the Department of Anthropology's word-processor operator, has once more transcribed my raw, yellow-tablet prose, and endured at least ten drafts of every chapter. Her saintly patience is deeply appreciated.

Friends and relatives—too numerous to mention—sent me newspaper and magazine clippings on electric cars as soon as they learned about my interest. Thank you, one and all.

I cannot begin to express adequate gratitude to my wife, Annette. She has provided emotional support and eased the burdens of everyday life in countless ways to allow me to indulge, with great intensity, one more intellectual obsession.

1

A SPECTACULAR FLOP

The electric automobile—energized by rechargeable batteries—appeared to have a great future nearly a century ago. Twenty-eight percent of the 4,192 American automobiles produced in 1900 were electric. In the New York automobile show of that year more electrics were on display than gasoline or steam vehicles. Some of America's most distinguished inventors, including Thomas Edison, were promoting electrics or taking part in their development. And the first American firm to manufacture cars by the hundreds was churning out well-designed electrics.

At the turn of the twentieth century, electric, steam, and gasoline automobiles competed more or less on an equal footing. Many knowledgeable observers believed that each kind of vehicle would find its own "sphere of action," and that all would co-exist indefinitely. In the end, though, the gasoline-powered motor car conquered the others with a stunning speed and thoroughness. By 1920, the electric car as a commercial product was nearly dead.

What killed the electric car? Americans employ many theories to fashion explanations for unsuccessful products. Three are singled out here: the vested interest theory, the technological constraint theory, and the consumerist theory.

The vested interest theory argues that desirable products can be prevented from reaching the market by the selfish (and often underhanded) actions of powerful corporations. A corporation that feels threatened by a new product will seek to sabotage it by purchasing patents, influencing legislation, tying up distributors, and so on. In this case, Standard Oil or General Motors is typically held responsible for killing the electric car.

The technological constraint theory asserts that products will fail if they rely on technologies having fundamental limitations. Explanations based on this theory point out, for example, that storage batteries have a very low energy density (power per pound) compared to gasoline. Dependent on storage batteries, the electric car was therefore an inferior technology that engineers and entrepreneurs rapidly abandoned.

Consumerist theory, the most generally held of all, assumes that consumers determine a product's fate. A product will not catch on if it has shortcomings in performance characteristics important to the buyer or user. Thus, consumers would have shunned the electric because its top speed and range (on one charge of the battery) fell well short of the gasoline car.

Although having the ring of plausibility, these explanations are wrong or incomplete. General Motors and Standard Oil were not friends of the electric car, but neither had much effect on its early history. They did not, for example, buy up and bury crucial patents; and General Motors for a time even made electric trucks. Vested interests did not prevent good electric cars from reaching the marketplace. In fact, more than twenty companies were making and selling them in the teens.

The technological constraint and consumerist theories are incomplete because they float free, divorced from the product's past social, cultural, and technological contexts. They require us to assume that the electric car arrived and departed in a society like our own (though perhaps a bit quainter). In contrast, building a well-rounded explanation requires us to probe our own ancient lifeway, situating the electric car with respect to the activities and attitudes of various groups of people (defined by gender, class, age, occupation, rural or urban, trend-setter or trend-follower). Only in relation to the activities and attitudes of specific groups of past people do technological constraints and performance characteristics have explanatory value.

We may ask, for example: When the electric car's popularity was at its peak in 1913, did speed matter? The answer is yes *and* no, depending on which group of people we consider. Speed was of transcendent importance to the men who bought cars for the sport of touring, which often involved careening over country roads, barely in control. Other men and women, whose cars were driven around town, had little need for speed on streets clogged with pedestrians and horses and speed limits seldom above 12 mph. Further probing also reveals that the electric car of 1913 was regarded, especially by women, as a highly perfected vehicle. In fact, the reliable, economical, and elegant electric set the standards of performance and style for all town cars. Yet in no year were more than 6,500 sold.

Like many products before and after, the electric car was a technological success that found no more than a minuscule market; it was a spectacular flop. Products that flop spectacularly, like the portable radio in the Roaring Twenties and the picture phone more recently, present intriguing puzzles. In solving these puzzles we must illuminate the complex relationships between past people and things.

The electric car evolved and became extinct in a society unlike any on earth today. In 1900 America was already the world's mightiest manufacturing nation, but factories were powered mainly by water and steam. The electrical age had begun, but only the most affluent families had electric lights at home. The wealthy used horse-drawn carriages for city travel, while merchants and factory workers commuted by trolley and horse-drawn bus. Although the urban middle class was expanding, the majority of Americans still lived in the country.

In this peculiar agro-industrial society, constantly in flux, the motor car first took hold as a plaything for well-to-do men. Afterwards its uses expanded relentlessly, until, by the late 1920s, the car was a cherished necessity for ordinary families that facilitated diverse social, leisure, and practical activities.

In trying to understand the electric's failure to thrive, one must do more than paint charming backgrounds with dabs of social and cultural history. The enterprise of explanation forces us to seek out specific connections between people and their things in concrete activities. In these intimate interactions, moving and changing through time, we are able to discern the causes of the electric car's demise.

In America, the origination of new technology has long been personified by Thomas Edison and Henry Ford. They are fascinating figures in the history of technology because their careers were so improbable. Like countless others, both began as inventors. But, unlike most inventors, both established companies to develop, manufacture, and sell their creations. Both made products that were widely adopted, and these sales gave them sufficient capital to invent and commercialize new products. Few inventors ever enjoy such success.

In the space of Edison's lifetime, the United States underwent the most dramatic transformations of its history. In the year of Edison's birth, 1847, America issued its first postage stamps. California—indeed, much of the greater Southwest—was still part of Mexico, and the Civil War was more than a decade away. Canals, rivers, and railroads were taking shape into vital transportation networks, as manufacturing and commerce began to make big inroads in a mostly agrarian America. But neither in towns nor in the country did any home contain an electrical thing. When Edison died in 1931, nearly all city homes—where the majority of Americans now lived—had electric lights and electrical appliances like vacuum cleaners, irons, sewing machines, coffee pots, and radios. And even working-class families had automobiles.

Obviously, the activities of Edison and Ford contributed greatly to bringing about these transformations, which dramatically affected the technologies and contexts of the electric automobile. More than that, both men believed that the car would be democratized, and they dedicated their energies to bringing this about—Edison working on technology for electrics, Ford on gasoline cars. Thus, both Edison and Ford—who became close friends and collaborated on several projects, including an electric car—are important figures in the following story.

In this book I recount the history of the early electric car: where it came from and where it went. Covering much of the nineteenth century, Chapters 2 through 4 detail the electric vehicle's origins; the focus is on *component* technologies (especially motors and storage batteries), *enabling* technologies (electric power and lighting systems for battery recharging), and *competing* technologies (horse-drawn carriages and wagons, trolleys, bicycles, and gasoline vehicles). Chapters 5 through 11 discuss the first era of commercially manufactured electrics, around 1895 to 1930. These chapters address the deceptively simple question, Why did the electric automobile fail to take hold widely? Building on this historical foundation, in Chapter 12 I offer forecasts about the electric car's future.

2

AND THEN THERE WAS LIGHT
(AND POWER)

Americans were ambivalent about cities. Thomas Jefferson, for one, believed that large cities had a harmful effect on morals, health, and human liberty. Such places were in fact filthy and smelly, filled with depraved and miserable people, and subject to periodic plagues—especially cholera. But, as engines of economic growth, urban places also offered unparalleled opportunities to the ambitious and the lucky.

Before city lights were really bright, industry in urban places began to attract new inhabitants in vast numbers. Manufacturing was at first carried out mainly in small factories, sometimes family owned and operated. In the decades immediately following the Civil War, manufacturing was increasingly taken up by large corporations, which produced goods for a national market. As factories enlarged, their demands for laborers became insatiable. Seeking jobs, young people from abroad and from American farms became unwitting participants in a grand social experiment. Corporations of all kinds, growing in size and number, also needed white-collar workers. These managers, clerks, accountants, secretaries, and so forth swelled the ranks of the urban middle class. Although city-dwellers remained a minority of Americans throughout the nineteenth century, the nation had begun its profound transformation into an urban society.

In the early nineteenth-century city, wealthy Americans were conveyed from place to place in coaches, carriages, and cabs, all pulled by horses. Unable to afford the upkeep of a horse in large cities, ordinary people (working and middle classes) used their feet to get to work, market, and church. Gradually, new technologies would give Americans of all social classes and genders a greater range of choices for getting around town.

Surprisingly, even the mid-nineteenth-century city was congested. In addition to carriages and cabs, the streets teemed with horse-drawn wagons and hand carts that incessantly shuffled goods between the port, train stations, warehouses, and countless shops and small factories. Travelers to New York in the 1850s remarked that city traffic frequently came to a dead stop. Easing traffic jams in the largest cities called for new modes of transport, and America's inventors and entrepreneurs responded.

The first technology of urban mass transit was the horse-drawn car, essentially a large coach or omnibus that ran on rails. Horse cars were designed to carry forty people comfortably through the city's busiest streets for a nickel a ride. During rush hour, however, cars often held more than seventy passengers. With their two-horse motor, the cars could travel at 6 mph, about twice as fast as walking.

In the crowded cities of the East, large amounts of capital were invested in horse-car railways, and by the 1850s they were a common sight. New York, for example, had sixteen lines, with some 800 cars and 8,000 horses. At their peak popularity in 1890, more than 20,000 horse cars carried hundreds of millions of passengers annually, and fostered the beginnings of suburbs and city expansion. Middle- and working-class people no longer had to live near jobs and other activity locations.

Like most new technologies, the horse car created almost as many problems as it solved. Most noticeable was the constant flow of horse litter onto city streets. Equine urine and droppings, the latter pulverized into powder and wafted into homes on dry days, augmented the burden of pollution that the city-dweller endured. Needless to say, advocates of a hygienic environment properly decried horses as a source of filth and disease. Another concern was the high mortality of horses: pulling a fully loaded car was arduous work, and many dropped dead on the tracks. Cruelty to horses was tolerated as a necessary evil, but few people were happy with the situation. Noting that during rush hours it was often quicker to walk, Americans longed for better mass transit.

The immense profits to be made in mass transit led, in the post-Civil War period, to the rapid commercialization of many new technologies from cable cars to subways. One obvious remedy was to replace horses with steam-powered locomotives and raise the tracks above the street. Not surprisingly, the elevated railway (or "L") was the earliest mechanized solution to the urban travel problem, with the first one appearing in New York City in 1870. Elevated railways were expensive to build as well as noisy and sometimes dangerous, for occasionally the train jumped the tracks and plunged into the crowded street below. In addition, the "L" left in its wake a pall of black soot on everything and everyone. In view of these disadvantages, some cities banned steam-powered trains. Although the "L" was successful in a few places like New York, Chicago, and Kansas City, a more universal technology was needed. A train powered by electricity might just be the answer.

Could an electric motor develop enough horsepower to drive a locomotive or coach? Inventors of electric motors had grappled with this question since the early 1830s. Using primary batteries, usually with electrodes of zinc and copper immersed in an electrolyte of sulfuric acid, Thomas Davenport, Robert Davidson, Charles Page, and others had shown that their motors were able to propel wheeled vehicles.

Thomas Davenport, of Brandon, Vermont, was an uncommon blacksmith who, in the 1830s, fashioned the first rotary electric motor. Electric motors, Davenport believed, could create a benign substitute for steam power, whose costs in human lives was great. Although ridiculed by his neighbors as the "perpetual-motion-man," Davenport demonstrated the ability of electric motors to drive drill, lathe, and printing press. In 1835, he built a toy train consisting of a wheeled motor and little else, which ran on a circular track about 3 feet in diameter. A few years later, a Davenport motor on exhibit in London pulled several carriages, weighing a total of 70 to 80 lbs, at 3 mph. Although Davenport received favorable press—the *New York Herald* once described his motor as a "most extraordinary discovery" and went on to predict that "the days of steam power, and animal power, and water power, are gone forever," he had little success in loosening "the purse strings of the capitalist." Davenport died penniless in 1851.

The visionary Davenport had a counterpart across the Atlantic, the Scotsman Robert Davidson. In his earliest experiments of the late 1830s, Davidson installed batteries and an electric motor in a small carriage; running indoors on a wood-plank floor, it was perhaps the first electric car. A few years later he fashioned an electric coach, christened the *Galvani*, which could ride the British rails. Sixteen feet long and weighing 5 tons when fully loaded, the *Galvani* was exhibited in a number of places, often with other electrical wonders (Fig. 1). While in Perth awaiting shipment back to Aberdeen, Scot-

Figure 1. A poster advertising Robert Davidson's *Galvani*. (*The Electrical World*, 18 October 1890)

land, however, the *Galvani* was mysteriously destroyed. Some suspect that steam engineers had done the ill deed, perhaps fearing the new engine would make their skills obsolete. They need not have worried.

The American Charles Page constructed an electric locomotive, measuring 21 feet long and weighing 10.5 tons. Despite countless difficulties on its maiden journey in 1851, the electric locomotive reached a speed of 19 mph on a short run from Washington, D.C., but it never ran again.

Though the experiments of Davenport, Davidson, and Page had shown that electric traction was possible, steam-powered trains were evolving rapidly as an economical means of land transportation. People familiar with both technologies saw no immediate future for electric propulsion because of the incessant—and expensive—refurbishing of the batteries. Calculations of R. Hunt in 1850 called attention to electric power's poor economics. After comparing the costs of coal and zinc (the latter material consumed in primary batteries of that time), Hunt concluded that for an equivalent amount of work, "magnetic power" would be anywhere from 25 to at least 150 times more expensive.

As a result of calculations like Hunt's, electric power was judged impractical. This dilemma is a common one in the history of technology, for it is not inventors or engineers who bestow judgments of practicality, but entrepreneurs and financiers. That a technology works as claimed is no guarantee that it will be commercialized, much less become a successful product. Not until an inexpensive source of electricity became available would capitalists give the nod to electric power.

The quest for cheaper electricity, prerequisite for any electric vehicle, was given impetus after mid-century by electroplating and telegraphy. These applications led to the first commercial dynamos, devices for converting rotary motion into electricity. By coupling a steam engine to a dynamo, factory owners could produce electricity from coal, an inexpensive fuel. Most dynamos were one-of-a-kind machines, custom-built for a specific installation, but a few were sold more widely.

The availability of dynamos in the 1850s and 1860s did not lead immediately to electric trains. The latter would also require dramatically improved motors as well as the generation of electricity on a large scale. These developments came from a surprising source. It would be the construction of electric lighting systems, beginning in the late 1870s, that created technology for "practical" electric traction.

With the promise of cheaper electricity made possible by steam-powered dynamos, many inventors tried to build electric lighting systems that could replace gas, candles, and oil lamps. Moses G. Farmer in 1859 was the first American to illuminate a room in a house with electricity; he used incandescent lamps with platinum filaments. Unfortunately, the filaments oxidized quickly and the bulbs burned out. Other inventors experimented with carbon filaments, but the results were no better. Among those captivated by the challenge of electric lighting was Thomas Edison.

Thomas Alva Edison was born on February 11, 1847, the youngest of seven children, in the small town of Milan, Ohio. Sam, his father, was a lumber and feed dealer, and his mother Nancy was a schoolteacher. Their circumstances were modest but, for a while at least, comfortable. About the time that Thomas approached school age, however, the family's fortunes took an unfavorable turn. In search of new opportunities, the Edisons pulled up stakes and moved to Port Huron, Michigan.

Responsibility for educating Thomas fell mainly to his mother, who tutored him at home. Like most bright children, Edison's curiosity was insatiable, a quality that many adults found exasperating. To Nancy Edison, coping with Thomas's incessant questions was a joy not a burden, and she guided him gently with warmth and understanding through the traditional school subjects. Above all, his mother cultivated his self-confidence, which in the not-too-distant future would grow to be a hubris of legendary proportions.

When Thomas was only nine, Nancy Edison brought home an elementary text on physical science, and he took to it immediately. Not only did he read and reread the book, but he repeated all the experiments. Soon his passion was chemistry, the experimental science *par excellence*. Engaging the material world first-hand, teasing out its secrets through painstaking experiments, was to become the defining style of Thomas Edison's work.

Sam Edison's fortunes continued to founder, and so Thomas at twelve was compelled to seek a job—child labor being common throughout the nineteenth century. Edison went to work selling newspapers and sundries on the train that traveled daily from Port Huron to Detroit and back. Even at this tender age he displayed an entrepreneurial flair, selling fresh fruits and vegetables along the route. Edison also set up a chemistry lab at one end of the baggage-mail car and was able to experiment in odd moments. Only once did he set the car on fire.

An important turning point came in April 1862, when Edison saw an edition of the *Detroit Free Press* that headlined the bloody Civil War battle at Shiloh, where 60,000 casualties were suffered. Appreciating the commercial possibilities, he had the news sent ahead by telegraph in advance of the train's arrival at its appointed stops. Crowds gathered at the depots to await the train and its precious cargo of newspapers. The young businessman had obtained 1,000 copies of the paper, which he dispensed to eager buyers at suitably inflated prices. Edison did not fail to note the crucial role that the telegraph had played in this enterprise. With his windfall profits, Edison learned telegraphy.

From 1863 to 1868, Edison covered much ground as an itinerant telegrapher. Usually his earnings were spent on books, chemicals, and apparatus; experiments and tinkering became Edison's real life, interrupted only by the need to eat and earn a living. Throughout this period his experiments became focused on electromechanical devices for improving the telegraph, and his first commercially important inventions were in this field; he also developed a better stock ticker.

Edison had finally found his calling as an inventor and set up shop in Newark, New Jersey. Soon he turned his attention to one of his employees, sixteen-year-old Mary Stillwell; after a brief courtship, the two were married on Christmas Day, 1871.

From his early work Edison learned that earnings from the sale of patents could be invested in new projects, some of which might also pan out, generating still more money to reinvest in invention. Already wealthy from his stock ticker and telegraph inventions, Edison used his capital to found an "invention factory" at Menlo Park, New Jersey, in 1876. There he would develop the electric light and power systems that made possible electric traction.

The year 1876 was also the one-hundredth birthday of the United States. In a huge Centennial Exhibition at Philadelphia, Americans showed off their industrial achievements, such as finely crafted surgical instruments, tools and machines for agriculture, precision instruments for surveying, and countless machine tools. The centerpiece of the exhibition, prime mover of all equipment, was a 1,000 hp Corliss steam engine. This chugging behemoth represented the motive power that had put the industrial revolution in high gear during the nineteenth century. In a typical factory, the steam engine drove a variety of smaller machines through an impressive-looking series of shafts and belts that roared over workers' heads (and dripped oil on them). Moving that mass of shafting and belts, however, often consumed half the steam engine's power. This poor efficiency was eventually overcome by inventions of Edison and others, allowing electric motors to be put directly on production machines. In 1876, though, electrical technology for light and power was still quite immature, which the Centennial Exhibition itself demonstrated.

In addition to the familiar array of telegraphic apparatus, the exhibits included burglar alarms, electric clocks, and Bell's brand-new telephone. It required much imagination to foresee that the telephone a half-century hence would tie together nearly every home and business in America. Another exhibit, from France, also pointed to electricity's future. This was a

Gramme dynamo, driven by a steam engine, and powering a small pump; the dynamo's current was also used for electroplating and for lighting a little carbon arc. Here was an embryonic electrical system, a model of what electricity might one day become. Compared to the giant Corliss engine, however, the French exhibit attracted little interest among the general public; most visitors apparently concluded that electric power and light remained to be perfected.

Also on display at the Centennial Exhibition was a Brayton internal combustion engine. George B. Selden, amateur inventor, saw the Brayton engine at work, and perceived that it could propel a carriage along with a supply of liquid hydrocarbon fuel. Selden thought this idea worth pursuing, though he built no prototype. Rather, being an attorney, he applied for a patent on the fundamental idea of a vehicle powered by an internal combustion engine.

It is said that for many years Selden diligently sought investors to back the manufacture of automobiles but was unsuccessful. Meanwhile, sensing that much time would pass before automobiles were judged practical and sold commercially, he used a series of legal maneuvers to delay its issuance until 1895 (when it might become valuable).

At the time of the Centennial Exhibition, Henry Ford was a mere thirteen years old. Like most Americans of the mid-nineteenth century, the Fords of Dearborn, Michigan, were farmers, and relatively prosperous ones at that. Henry, however, disliked milking, helping with the harvest, and so on. His antipathy to the agrarian lifestyle reached epic proportions in his hatred for cows, chickens, and—prophetically enough—the horse.

Because working the land involved countless hours of back-breaking labor, the farmer was eager to try out all manner of labor-saving contrivances. By the mid-nineteenth century, the American farm was already a hearth of mechanization. The nation's seeming genius for tinkering found expression in myriad machines for plowing, sowing, reaping, and so on that appeared across the countryside. And, after the Civil War, it was not uncommon for farmers to rent portable steam engines—mostly pulled from farm to farm by a team of horses, but sometimes self-propelled—for sawing wood and other heavy labor (Fig. 2). Farmers, especially in the Midwest, also provided an early market for small gasoline engines, which could be harnessed to sundry labor-saving machines.

Ford saw a portable steam engine as a teen, and it made a deep impression

Figure 2. A self-propelled steam tractor. (Collection of the author)

on him. In fact, he was fascinated by machines of every kind, eager to take them apart and study their workings. As an adolescent he became a proficient mechanic, repairing not only steam engines but also watches. From these experiences with the products of industry—large and small, simple and complex—Ford acquired an uncanny ability to visualize any machine's operation. As a young adult, Henry would apply his mechanical genius to the self-propelled vehicle powered by an internal combustion engine.

In the years immediately following the Centennial Exhibition, European and U.S. inventor-entrepreneurs began to sell complete arc-lighting systems for factories and city streets. Steam-powered dynamos furnished the current to individual arc lamps that burned carbon electrodes. These systems had many defects, as Abram Foster recounts:

[Arc] lamps were more suitable for outdoor use than for indoor use. The carbons . . . lasted only about eight hours. . . . The strong, brilliant light illuminated large areas, but some disadvantages were the necessary high voltages and heavy currents, the difficulty of turning individual lamps on or off without affecting the whole system, the peculiar color of the light, and the necessity of frequent adjustment.

Despite its many shortcomings, many factory owners regarded arc-lighting as a distinct advance over gas. Demand for arc-lighting systems also came from cities wishing to brighten up main streets at night.

As a result of the arc-lighting boom, reliable steam-powered dynamos became readily available in a variety of sizes. In contrast, the electric motor had remained mostly a laboratory curiosity, arrested in development and stalled as a commercial product for want of a cheap source of power. The situation changed suddenly with the advent of commercial lighting dynamos.

Not only did steam-driven dynamos finally furnish inexpensive electricity, but dynamos could also be used as electric motors. That dynamos were reversible had been known for decades and the principle was even patented in France in 1854; however, little significance was attached to it until the late 1870s when investigators realized that dynamo technology had leaped ahead of the electric motor.

All at once, it seems, many people on both sides of the Atlantic began to appreciate that the components needed for electric traction were nearly at hand. That such a technology would be judged practical was assured because systems with steam-driven dynamos did not need batteries. Even if electric traction was still more expensive than steam, it had certain advantages for urban applications, such as no air pollution.

In 1879, a German, Werner Siemens, exhibited in Berlin a tiny electric train consisting of a locomotive and three cars. Electricity was generated by a Siemens dynamo connected to a stationary steam engine. A second Siemens dynamo, operating as a motor, turned the locomotive's driving wheels. Power was transmitted through the rails. With its motor (rated at 2 to 3.5 hp) straining under the load of eighteen passengers, the train could reach nearly 8 mph. Siemens's "electrical railway" was widely publicized and called attention to the new economics of electric traction.

The costs of electric drive had been lowered by more than an order of magnitude. Many electric railway applications appeared eminently practical and attractive, and so European capitalists finally began to loosen their pursestrings. During the next few years, Siemens and Halske built several electric tramways, including a line near Berlin that extended 1.5 miles. Because current losses through the rails were excessive, the company quickly turned to overhead conductors (Fig. 3). And so arose the earliest technology for the trolley (Chapter 4). In not many more years, trolley technology would contribute to the birth of the electric automobile.

Figure 3. Siemens & Halske's electric railway. (*Scientific American*, 26 August 1882, p. 134)

At Menlo Park Edison assembled a team of technicians who assisted in experiments and translated his ideas and drawings into hardware. In a laboratory lavishly equipped for electrical and chemical experiments, Edison and his crew tackled technical problems having commercial potential.

One of Edison's first inventions at Menlo Park was also his most novel. A working model of the phonograph was first constructed in 1877 according to Edison's detailed plans by John Kruesi, who ran the Menlo Park machine shop. The phonograph was an immediate sensation, perhaps doing more to immortalize the first words reproduced, "Mary had a little lamb," than any event before or after. Edison went straightaway to New York, where he demonstrated the remarkable device to Alfred Beach, editor of *Scientific American*. A large crowd gathered, including reporters, and they were amazed. Newspapers the next day announced Edison's wizardry.

Although commercial uses of the phonograph were evident to Edison, such as dictation, he set aside these promising applications to take up a more pressing project: the lightbulb and electric lighting. Nonetheless, the phonograph had made him a public figure—even President Hayes had summoned him to the White House for a demonstration—and established his reputation as the Wizard of Menlo Park.

As Robert Friedel, Paul Israel, and Bernard S. Finn point out in their exquisite book, *Edison's Electric Light,* Edison skillfully incorporated the media into the invention process. Obviously he used newspapers and magazines to publicize his work, which kept Edison-the-Wizard in the public eye. When he or his lawyers came calling on potential backers for projects, no one had to ask, "Who is Thomas Edison?" Less obviously, he made pronouncements, sometimes exaggerated or premature, about inventions in progress. These claims highlighted the immediate research goals for the laboratory, and put his reputation at risk. Man of hubris unbounded, Edison thrived with such an incentive, believing that he and the laboratory crew could accomplish whatever task he set. More often than not, Edison's claims became self-fulfilling prophecies, though success did not always arrive easily or on time.

In the *New York Sun* Edison expounded on his latest invention, the electric light. "I have it now," he claimed in 1878, a light both brilliant and cheap, and went on to predict the eclipse of gas lighting. Edison's "breakthrough" in electric lighting played well in the press. The trouble was, while experiments had begun, as yet there was no functioning light bulb.

When Edison took on the electric light project, most homes in America were illuminated by oil-burning lamps. Only the affluent enjoyed gas lighting, the same technology that for decades had been used in factories and on city streets. Edison and other inventors believed that an electric system could leap ahead of gas, eventually bringing bright light to all American businesses and homes. Although in the late 1870s arc systems were already being commercialized for street lighting and industry, Edison would build a different system, one based on incandescent lamps.

The difficulties in making an incandescent lamp were well known at the time Edison's odyssey began. Invariably, filament materials that gave off a good light (when the passage of current heated them to incandescence) quickly oxidized or melted down. Drawing upon his experience with electro-mechanical devices from telegraphy, Edison built into his first lamps, which had platinum filaments like Farmer's, a regulator that briefly cut off current when the filament was about to overheat. It was just this sort of device that was being patented when Edison announced his "breakthrough."

While experiments to perfect the platinum filament were underway, work also commenced on other components of the lighting system. Edison was well aware from the start that an electric lighting system would require huge and efficient dynamos, underground cables, assorted fixtures, and devices for regulating the system. After much experimentation and redesign, the Edison crew built a large dynamo that efficiently converted a steam engine's mechanical energy into electricity. Other components were also taking shape, but still there was no light bulb.

After a year of fruitless experiments, Edison at last gave up on platinum filaments. Dogged by the press and anxious backers, he returned in desperation to carbon, a material he had regarded as totally unsuitable because it oxidized too quickly. Fortunately, the solution to this problem, an ultra-high vacuum, was already at hand because of the work on the platinum bulb. The latter had been highly evacuated to remove extraneous gases in the metal filament. In an unexpected way, then, research on the dead-end platinum filaments, which led to improved vacuum pumps, paved the way for the ultimate triumph of carbon.

On October 22, 1879, Edison tried out a cotton thread after it had been carbonized in a furnace (Fig. 4). Not only did the carbon filament put out a respectable amount of light, but it lasted more than ten hours—a milestone for that time. The promising bulbs of late October stimulated a flurry of experiments with other carbonized materials, and success followed success.

It was now time to publicize the real breakthrough. Edison arranged for wires to be strung up throughout Menlo Park and announced that there would be a full public display of the new lighting system on New Year's Eve. The event came off without a hitch, as described by the *New York Herald*:

Edison's laboratory was to-night thrown open to the general public for the inspection of his electric light. Extra trains were run from east and west, and notwithstanding the stormy weather, hundreds of persons availed themselves of the privilege. The laboratory was brilliantly illuminated with twenty-five electric lamps, the office and counting room with eight, and twenty others were distributed in the street leading to the depot and in some of the adjoining houses. The entire system was explained in detail by Edison and his assistants, and the light was subjected to a variety of tests.

Visitors were especially impressed by the ease with which motors and light bulbs could be interchanged on the power system. According to the *Herald* account, everyone "seemed satisfied that Edison had actually solved the problem of practical household illumination by electricity."

For Edison, then, the electric light was to be a product that everyone could enjoy; it would become the system of choice for lighting homes, businesses, and factories. To achieve this grandiose goal, Edison believed electric light-

Figure 4. Drawing of Edison carbonizing a filament. (U.S. Department of the Interior, National Park Service, Edison National Historical Site, 14931, neg. 6683)

ing would have to be cheaper than gas. Capitalists could scarcely be expected to build a new system unless it effectively challenged the old on an economic basis. Edison and his crew made comparative cost estimates of the two lighting systems; electricity looked attractive. Impressed, the capitalists furnished additional funds, and so Edison geared up companies to electrify America.

The systems Edison would install were based on direct current (DC), the same kind of electricity supplied by batteries. Direct current was the obvious choice in 1879, but it would come back to haunt the Wizard in the years ahead.

The Wizard's feats from phonograph to electric light were avidly followed by young men like Henry Ford. The mechanically inclined Henry especially idolized the Wizard, fellow Michigander. Before the turn of the century their paths would cross.

3

ON TROLLEYS AND BICYCLES

In Western society, recreational travel to far-off lands had become, at least by the Renaissance, a desirable activity. Many a wealthy—or at least adventurous—Englishman, for example, took his grand tour of the continent, getting from place to place by means of horse-drawn coaches and omnibuses. Beginning in the first half of the nineteenth century, the railroad also became a mode of transportation for touring, both in Europe and the United States. As the railroad network expanded to every corner of the country after the Civil War, lodges sprang up in favorite destinations. Steamships, too, were catering to a wealthy clientele, including the nouveaux riches created by America's explosive industrial capitalism, who at great expense crossed the Atlantic to view for themselves the wonders of the Old World. Railroads and steamships made touring more comfortable and attracted ever larger numbers of leisure-seekers of both sexes.

Travel was glamorized in travelogues, children's books, and popular novels of the late nineteenth century, such as *Following the Equator* by Mark Twain. The coming of mass circulation magazines, beginning in the 1880s, including the travel-oriented *National Geographic* and *Outing*, also contributed to a growing interest in touring. Although few people could afford to tour by train or steamship, Americans of the growing middle class, thumbing the pages of *Harper's* or *McClure's*, hoped that this activity would one day be within their grasp.

In the 1880s as today, traveling was a socially acceptable way for the wealthy to indulge themselves. More than that, tourists upon returning received the admiration of friends and relatives as they dispensed souvenirs and told tales of exotic places and narrow escapes. Traveling appeared to be fun and exciting, and so appealed to novelty-seeking Americans.

While affording freedom to individuals of means, recreational travel relied on public transportation. Not only was this freedom constrained by steamship and railroad timetables, but in going from place to place the urban elite risked contact with strangers of the wrong social class. Trains and steamships rapidly discovered the need for first-class accommodations to maintain the comfort of their well-heeled passengers.

In rural America, recreational travel, though seldom over great distances, was also important. After the democratization of horse-drawn carriages and buggies, beginning in the mid-nineteenth century, even a farm family of modest means could take trips whenever they chose, roads and weather permitting. Country folk did not venture to exotic venues, but they could easily travel to family and friends, church and grange socials, county fairs, and shops in town. Surprisingly, the farmer enjoyed a freedom of movement far greater than the urbanite of comparable class. As more Americans born and raised on farms found themselves attracted by the economic opportunities of the city, they became a vast reservoir of potential demand for vehicles that could provide personal transport, a pattern of activity they already knew intimately. The first technology to meet that demand was the bicycle.

As is well known, the bicycle gave us pneumatic tires, ball bearings, and bloomers, but its legacy is far greater. The bicycle helped begin the process of democratizing both touring and personal transport in cities.

The first machine that might be called a true bicycle emerged in France during the 1850s and was known as a velocipede; it had two wooden wheels with iron tires and a handlebar for steering. In spite of a rocky ride that inspired the nickname "boneshaker," the velocipede during the 1860s attracted a small and devoted following in several nations, including the United States.

Interest in the boneshaker waned with the advent, in the late 1860s, of the "ordinary," a bicycle with a huge front wheel (sometimes called a high-wheeler). Although less bone-shaking, an ordinary's ride was sometimes bone-breaking, since not a few riders fell head first after hitting a small rock. Despite the ordinary's danger to life and limb—or perhaps because of it—the high-wheeler garnered a group of enthusiasts.

Albert A. Pope (1843–1909) was an American entrepreneur who believed in the bicycle's mass-market potential. A Bostonian who had served as a colonel in the Civil War, Pope was in the manufacturing business, making shoes and sundry mechanical parts. He first became captivated by the ordinary at the 1876 Centennial Exposition in Philadelphia. Fresh from the fair, his first move was to import English bicycles. His next move—far more momentous —was to have a mechanic design a bicycle, based on an English model, that could be produced in an American factory. In 1878 Pope launched the Columbia ordinary, a 70-lb bicycle that cost a princely $313.

During the commercial bicycle's first decades, before the craze of the 1890s, bike ownership was confined mainly to young men of means. Because of entrepreneurs like Albert Pope, however, bicycling would soon become more accessible to the middle class.

Albert Pope, above all, was a man who knew how to seize opportunity. The still-growing rail system provided the ideal means for distributing Columbia bicycles nationally, and the new mass-circulation magazines made it possible to hawk his wares throughout America. Pope also orchestrated favorable publicity for cycling, contending that it promoted good health, the risk of broken bones notwithstanding.

One reason for the dangers of bicycle riding was America's dilapidated roads. The earlier coach roads had been allowed to deteriorate with the coming of railroads, and roadside inns that once served long-distance travelers fell into ruins. By the 1880s, roads as such scarcely existed outside cities; the intrepid traveler had to negotiate unpaved and often sandy or muddy tracks across the landscape. City streets were usually in no better shape. To promote their interests, cycling enthusiasts established the League of American Wheelmen, an organization that became a vocal lobby for better roads and bicyclists' rights. The League's good roads campaign, partly financed by Pope and other bike makers, included the dissemination of propaganda booklets and the publication of *Good Roads Magazine*.

Although the price of bicycles had dropped, ordinaries still cost $100 to $150, a sizable sum even for a bank clerk or steam engineer. Although price doubtless deterred many potential purchasers, women especially were at a disadvantage in the new pastime as long as the ordinary prevailed. In *A Social History of the Bicycle*, Robert A. Smith describes the not very feminine act of mounting the "steel steed":

Getting on . . . meant running alongside the ordinary until it got up speed and then putting the left foot on the mounting bar that was welded to the frame. Hoping that momentum would continue to carry the bicycle forward, the cyclist next vaulted into the saddle and frantically tried to get his feet on the pedals, which all this time were turning with the front wheel.

Two new technologies made the bicycle more appealing to women. The first was bloomers. Initially regarded as an outrageous outfit, bloomers nonetheless allowed women to get on an ordinary. The second technology was to replace the ordinary with the safety bicycle—essentially the bicycle of today, with two wheels of identical size, a diamond frame of tubular steel, and chain drive. Safety bicycles were commercialized in the United States with the A. H. Overman Company's Victor bicycle taking the early lead in 1887. The women's style of safety bicycle appeared the next year; designed to allow the rider to mount and dismount easily while wearing a skirt, it enjoyed great popularity (Fig. 5).

Inventors on both sides of the Atlantic discovered during the 1880s that technologies for making self-propelled carriages and wagons had progressed dramatically. Soon sundry vehicles powered by steam, internal combustion engines, and electricity were rolling across Germany, France, and the United States.

The first practical internal combustion engine was built by Étienne Lenoir, a Belgian living in France. Patented in 1860, his water-cooled contraption burned coal gas and was noisy and inefficient; even so, for two decades it had many buyers. Lenoir's engine was a clear proof of concept to other inventors, especially in Europe.

Nikolaus Otto, a German, was one of many inspired by Lenoir's technical and commercial success. Mechanically gifted, Otto sought to improve the Lenoir engine, and in the late 1870s he did. Otto's four-cycle design embodied features that would become standard in gasoline automobile engines.

The Otto engine and the many clones it spawned, though intended to replace small steam engines in industry, inaugurated the era of the gasoline-powered automobile. Clearly, the compact internal combustion engine was a most suitable technology for the self-propelled vehicle.

Karl Benz, also a German, employed his own Otto-type engine to power a three-wheel carriage in 1885. These tri-wheelers, with a one-cylinder engine that developed 0.8 hp, were put on the market in 1887, perhaps the earliest commercial automobiles (Fig. 6). In 1891 Benz added a four-wheel mo-

Figure 5. The woman's safety bicycle. (*The Cosmopolitan*, January 1896)

torized carriage to his company's offerings. These automobiles sold well and were widely imitated. In the early 1890s, for example, Panhard et Levassor as well as Peugeot in France were peddling cars to the public. Henry Ford, however, was still a long way from building automobiles.

Henry Ford became engaged to Clara Bryant in 1886, but her father believed that at twenty she was still too young to marry. So, for two years the

Figure 6. A Benz tricycle, powered by an internal combustion engine. (*Scientific American*, 5 January 1889, p. 9)

persistent Ford courted Clara. As they lived some miles apart, Ford spent much time journeying to the Bryants' home in a buggy. Had he resided in New York or Philadelphia, visits to his sweetheart would have been made by foot or horse car. Like most rural Americans, however, Henry already had personal transport technology, horse-drawn to be sure, but still available for business or pleasure trips. When an American of Ford's background moved to a big city, as many increasingly did in the late nineteenth and early twentieth centuries, they suffered a palpable loss of freedom, for they could not bear the expense of keeping a horse and buggy.

Henry and Clara finally married in 1888, when he made a living by running a small sawmill on his share of the family farm. But the big city beckoned, with its unlimited social and economic opportunities. In 1889, the Fords packed up their belongings, loaded them on a haywagon, and moved to Detroit. On the day of their arrival, Ford found a job with the Edison Illuminating Company (Detroit Edison). By the end of the year he was earning

Figure 7. The dynamo room in Edison's Pearl Street station. (*Scientific American*, 26 August 1882, p. 127)

$50 a month, a decent wage for an entry-level engineer. Ford worked for Detroit Edison throughout the 1890s and eventually became chief engineer. This steady income, not to mention access to the company's tools and workshops, would support Ford's automobile experiments.

Edison's lighting of Menlo Park had been a brilliant show. The next step was to refine the components, scale up the system, and electrify part of a major metropolitan area. Edison believed that cities would be wired step-wise through a series of "central stations," each containing steam engines and dynamos and distributing its power within a territory of a square mile or so. For the first central station he chose an area of lower Manhattan; it was known as the Pearl Street District because the equipment was installed in an old building at 257 Pearl Street (Fig. 7). Not accidently, this demonstration district included portions of New York's newspaper and financial centers.

For more than two years Edison and his team were consumed with the challenge of the Pearl Street District—designing and building new dynamos, making and installing new cables—the works. Edison himself labored long hours in the streets, trouble-shooting and supervising the cable-laying operations. This difficult enterprise tried the patience of the financiers, but Edison came through again. On September 4, 1882, after extensive partial tests of the system, the lights finally went on. The dramatic moment came in the offices of Edison backer J. Pierpont Morgan at the Drexel Building, when at 3:00 p.m. Thomas Edison himself threw the switch. Edison later regarded this event as the most thrilling of his life. The press reported favorably on the lighting system as the electrical age began in earnest.

Though momentous, this beginning was modest. Surprisingly, the building of other central stations took place initially at a very leisurely pace. Even so, the Edison companies that manufactured and sold electric lighting systems did thrive. Right from the start customers anticipated by neither Edison nor the capitalists came clamoring for "isolated lighting plants" to light up ships, factories, and mansions. Henry Villard had seen the Menlo Park display and ordered an isolated plant for *Columbia*, a new steamship owned by the Oregon Railway and Navigation Company, which he headed. The system was put in during the spring of 1880, and it worked well. What is more, the Edison light bulb did not heat up rooms as much as gas or foul the air. Other isolated plants were installed in textile mills, where the risk of fire was so greatly diminished that lower insurance rates made electric lighting very attractive. Although the many isolated plants that came on line following the *Columbia* were profitable, the Wizard of Menlo Park regarded them as a distraction not in keeping with his vision of electric lighting as an inexpensive alternative available to all. Yet, it would be decades before electric lighting was actually cheaper than gas, and many more years before the majority of Americans could summon the electric genie at home.

Not every moment was filled with joy for Edison. In 1884 his beloved wife Mary became seriously ill and died. The eligible millionaire Edison was soon introduced to Mina Miller, of Akron, Ohio. Edison was smitten with nineteen-year-old Mina—nearly twenty years his junior—and she with him. They married on February 24, 1886. As a wedding present, Edison gave Mina the choice of living in the country or in town. She chose the country near West Orange, New Jersey, where Edison bought her the four-story Victorian mansion known as Glenmont.

Like many affluent women, Mina's responsibilities extended beyond raising children to the management of a large home, which often had a dozen or so servants. Practiced in the social arts, Mina was an important link between Edison and America's upper crust. Foreign dignitaries, important people in business, family friends, and even presidents were entertained at Glenmont under Mina's skillful direction. In later years Mina would refer to her role as "home executive."

Less than a mile from Glenmont, in the valley below, Thomas Edison built an astonishing facility dedicated to the pursuit of invention. The West Orange complex, which opened in 1887, cost more than $150,000, and included a library, chemistry lab, and sprawling machine shop. Edison was fond of pointing out that at West Orange he could make anything "from a lady's watch to a locomotive." Among the countless projects he did undertake were perfecting the phonograph, making movies, and building batteries for electric automobiles. Over the years, West Orange grew to include manufacturing plants that employed thousands of people.

Edison's demonstration on Pearl Street that electricity could be generated economically on a large scale was an important stimulus to the commercialization of trolleys (or streetcars, as they are also known) in the United States. At once many inventors, entrepreneurs, and capitalists were drawn to this long-envisioned technology, decades after Davidson and Page had shown that locomotives could be powered by electric motors. The electric railroad, many now believed, was ideal for reducing urban congestion.

Sustained experiments with electric trains began in U.S. cities during the early 1880s. Although many Americans advanced the new technology and built short electric roads, trolleys made a significant stride in the hands of Frank Julian Sprague (1857–1934). In 1885 and 1886, Sprague built several small systems, including one in the Durant Sugar Refinery in New York; their main purpose was to attract financiers who might be pursuaded to invest in electrifying the "Ls." Although Jay Gould and other financiers did not plunge, Sprague acquired valuable experience. The opportunity to take on a full-scale trolley finally came in May 1887, when a New York syndicate commissioned the Sprague Electric Railroad & Motor Company to build a road in Richmond, Virginia. The ninety-day time frame was unrealistic and the $110,000 budget insufficient, but the job got done. With 12 miles of track it was the first major trolley in the United States. But soon there would be more.

Construction of the Richmond trolley had gone way over budget, but it was economical to operate—much cheaper than horse cars—and a quick financial success. Beginning in the late 1880s, then, trolleys proliferated throughout American cities and towns, becoming an instant symbol of urban modernity. Although city pride, humanitarian concerns for the horse, and urban hygiene all stimulated interest in trolleys, it was the decisive economy over horse cars that hastened their near-universal adoption in America, especially in large cities.

Not everyone, however, was enthusiastic about trolleys, for they added to the forest of telegraph, telephone, and fire alarm wires already strung along streets. The blight was so bad that a few cities outlawed or discouraged construction of overhead lines. An elegant alternative, some thought, was to power the trolley with batteries. The bad economics of using primary batteries in this way had not changed since the time of Davidson and Page, but after mid-century a new and appropriate technology had been developed, the *storage* (or secondary) battery. This very same storage battery would make possible the electric automobile.

When the electrochemical power of a storage battery has been exhausted, it can simply be recharged and reused because the chemical reactions that create a flow of current are reversible. Thus, by applying direct current from a dynamo to a discharged battery's terminals, the electrodes are returned to their original chemical state, and the cycle can begin again. Recharging obviously requires a reliable source of DC.

The storage battery was a relative latecomer to the world of battery technology, with a workable design emerging only in 1859. Gaston Planté, a French chemist, was not the first to experiment with storage batteries, but his extensive work with a lead-acid system (electrodes of lead and lead compounds, and electrolyte of sulfuric acid) led to the earliest commercial storage batteries, which were used for telegraphy and scientific instruments.

Planté and other Europeans improved storage batteries during the 1860s and 1870s, but progress was slow. The advent of electric lighting, however, furnished a fillip to battery research as new uses for stored electricity came to the fore. Camille Faure, an itinerant French engineer, had seen dynamos and electric lights displayed at the 1878 Paris Exhibition. It occurred to him that storage batteries could even the flow of current from the then-erratic dynamos. Faure also reasoned that electricity could increase the efficiency of electric lighting systems: when the dynamos were underutilized in the daytime (because few lamps were turned on), the excess power that was being produced anyway could charge the batteries. In the evening, when all the lights were on, the batteries would supplement the dynamo's output. This process is called load-leveling.

Faure, who began his work believing that the new electric lighting industry would provide a growing market for storage batteries, filed for a French patent on his improved battery in late 1880. (Not long afterward he sought a patent on an electrically propelled vehicle powered by his batteries.) The battery used pure lead plates coated with a paste of sulfuric acid and lead compounds (this was the *active material*). A company, S. A. La Force et La Lumière, was established immediately to begin manufacturing Faure's pasted-plate batteries.

The Faure battery was introduced with great fanfare and public demonstrations, even receiving the enthusiastic endorsement of one of England's most distinguished physicists, William Thompson (who later became Lord Kelvin). The battery worked brilliantly, but only for a while. After just a few months of heavy use, the paste began to separate from the plates and the battery failed. The demise of the early Faure battery received as much attention as its introduction; obviously it had been commercialized without adequate testing.

As Edison DC lighting systems spread in the early 1880s, however, demand for reliable batteries soared. With these markets in mind, a number of firms on both sides of the Atlantic began sustained research. Edison himself worked on the lead-acid storage battery but quickly concluded that it had little future, telling one reporter that "just as soon as a man gets working on the secondary battery it brings out his latent capacity for lying." Ironically, beginning in the late 1890s, Edison would spend a dozen years on storage batteries, creating an alternative to the lead-acid system for use in electric vehicles.

In European laboratories, the Faure battery was modified so that it could hold its active material and improved batteries were soon being sold. Not surprisingly, power stations on that side of the Atlantic were first to adopt storage batteries, and by 1890 they were common in Germany and England.

Other markets for storage batteries appeared in these years. They were used, for example, in self-propelled boats on lakes and for lighting systems set up temporarily at political rallies and parties. Among the most important applications was leveling loads in the isolated plants of U.S. trolley companies. And, of course, storage batteries were also employed in trolley cars themselves.

Experiments with battery-powered trolleys began in the early 1880s in France, even before Sprague's success in Richmond, as the new Faure batteries became available. In England, Anthony Reckenzaun built a trolley car

Figure 8. An early battery trolley in New Hampshire. (Rowsome 1956:44)

in 1883 that weighed 5 tons, including 2 tons of batteries installed beneath the seats. It could carry forty-six people at 6 mph, the same speed as a horse car. On the basis of these tests, though, the battery trolley's operating costs were projected to be much less per mile.

During the late 1880s there were many experiments with battery trolleys in the United States (Fig. 8). In Philadelphia, for example, Reckenzaun introduced a battery trolley on the Leland Avenue Railway. The expected savings, however, were illusory. The trolleys ran well, but the rigors of trolley work, such as overloading during rush hours, took their toll on the battery's positive plates. Refurbishing these every six months or so was very expensive. As a result, most battery trolleys died quickly; only in places opposed to overhead conductors, like Paris and Manhattan, did they enjoy greater longevity. With Thomas Edison's help, the battery trolley would briefly revive as an electric bus in the early teens (see Fig. 37).

Research continued on lead-acid storage batteries, and gradually their energy density and life expectancy increased. By the early 1890s, a diligently maintained battery could last several years. However, lead-acid batteries were being designed for applications where handling was relatively gentle, such as sitting sedentary in power plants or resting comfortably—more or less—in a large vehicle. These were the kinds of batteries available to the first generation of electric automakers: batteries not hardened against the rough-and-tumble world of cobble streets and rutted roads; batteries that had a short life without constant maintenance. Perhaps predictably, in the earliest commercial electric cars the battery would be the weak link.

As a result of the trolley boom, technologies easily adapted for making electric automobiles had been commercialized in the 1880s: storage batteries, electric motors of several horsepower, and controllers (electrical switches for changing speed). More importantly, perhaps, an infrastructure to support electric vehicles had emerged—at least in principle. Prior to the 1880s, it was of course possible to create an electric vehicle from scratch, but there was almost no way to recharge its batteries. Thus, the key component of the electric automobile's infrastructure was the central station. In the 1880s, then, a few optimists began to build electrically powered automobiles. Like Edison, they believed that the spread of central stations would democratize electricity, which would enable anyone to charge vehicle batteries at home.

As Americans boarded their first trolleys, technical magazines carried news from Europe about experiments with electric automobiles. One of the earliest to be reported, in *Scientific American* in 1888, was a carriage made by Magnus Volk of Brighton, England. A three-wheeler, Volk's vehicle was powered by a 40-lb motor and a sixteen-cell storage battery. On a macadam road the electric tricycle could attain the dizzying speed of 4 mph, and supposedly it could run for six hours on a charge.

In that same year Camille Faure was issued a U.S. patent for a method to recharge a vehicle's batteries while descending a hill. The solution was simple: use the motor as a dynamo. This important idea, which Faure patented first in France in 1880, would be reinvented many times on both sides of the Atlantic.

Later in 1888, *Scientific American* described another English electric carriage (Fig. 9). An ordinary four-passenger "dog cart," the vehicle was electrified by Immisch & Company of London for the Sultan of Turkey. It had a 1-hp motor connected by chain to a rear wheel. The makers claimed that the twenty-four-cell battery (stored under the seats) could "propel the vehicle at a speed of about ten miles an hour for five hours." In a trial run at a skating rink in Camden Town, "no great speed could be attained, on account of the confined space and the consequent necessity for frequent sharp turns." One assumes that ordinary Turks were properly impressed by their Sultan's electric dog cart.

Figure 9. Immisch & Company's electrified "dog cart." (*Scientific American*, 6 October 1888, p. 215)

Perhaps stimulated by accounts of experiments abroad, American inventors began to play with the possibilities of electric drive. It was about this time, for example, that motor maker A. L. Riker built an electric tricycle. With its 1/6 hp motor, the tricycle was said to be capable of making 8 mph "on good roads." Citing this tricycle, *Scientific American* in 1907 credited Riker with building "the first electric automobile in America." Another electric pioneer was Fiske Warren, a Bostonian, whose eight-passenger vehicle reached the respectable speed of 16 mph. Though breaking new ground, the Riker and Warren vehicles were little known to the American public. In just a few years, however, an electric automobile would achieve modest fame.

4

A TECHNOLOGICAL CONVERGENCE

Strolling amidst the marvelous exhibits of the World's Columbian Exposition in 1893, a visitor intent on seeing everything might eventually encounter the six automobiles on display. Five of the six were from Europe, which already had an automobile industry. The only American automobile, constructed at home by William Morrison of Des Moines, Iowa, was an electric.

Morrison's vehicle was a six-passenger wagon (Fig. 10). The 4-hp motor was "of the ordinary streetcar type," though Morrison had rebuilt it. He also made the battery, which had twenty-four cells and weighed 768 lbs—more than half the wagon's total weight. Unlike the Sultan's dog cart, Morrison's carriage had been tested extensively, in one case running for thirteen hours continuously and reaching a breathtaking speed of 14 mph.

Morrison took his vehicle to Chicago in 1892, where it apparently caused a stir. According to the *Western Electrician*, "a well loaded carriage moving along the streets at a spanking pace with no horses in front and apparently with nothing on board to give it motion, was a sight that has been too much even for the wide-awake Chicagoan." Favorable notice was also taken of Morrison's handiwork in *Scientific American* and *Electrical World*. The latter observed that electric carriages, while "among the many conveniences which novelists and fiction writers have ascribed to future ages," have not received much attention from "practical inventors." Such people, it went on, were apparently engaged in more promising projects, like streetcar work. The implication was not that electric carriages were hard to build, but as yet (unlike streetcars) they had no obvious market. The article concluded on an enthusi-

Figure 10. William Morrison's electric wagon. (*Scientific American*, 9 January 1892, p. 18)

astic note appropriate for a trade journal that relentlessly promoted the application of electricity to all realms of life:

From the satisfactory results obtained from this mode of locomotion the day does not seem so very far distant when carriages as well as other vehicles will be moving around our streets propelled by electric motors that receive their current from concealed batteries, and therefore effect a further emancipation of the millions of animals now performing this service.

In the first reported sale of an American automobile, Morrison's vehicle was bought by the American Battery Company of Chicago. To help advertise the company's products, the carriage was exhibited at various public gatherings, including the 1893 Columbian Exposition in Chicago. Thus, the first U.S. automobile to be shown at any World's Fair was an electric. Perhaps dazzled by the fair's lights and Ferris wheel, some people gathered that the electric carriage would be the horseless vehicle of the future.

If electric automobiles were ever to become more than sideshow curiosities, Edison's DC power systems would have to make significant inroads in American cities. The Edison lighting companies, however, now faced a formidable foe: George Westinghouse (1846–1914) in the late 1880s began to sell competing lighting systems based on alternating current. The attraction of AC lay in the economy of power transmission. To transmit low-voltage DC over long distances was ghastly expensive because of the thick cables needed. With AC systems, no longer was there a 1-mile limit on the service area of central stations. By means of transformers, which work only on AC, a generator's output could be raised to thousands of volts. In this state, electricity could be sent cheaply over many miles of thin cable, then reduced by other transformers to low voltages again. The AC network could grow by the addition of generators and transformers; new central stations were not required as often. In addition, with AC it became feasible to tap distant sources of hydroelectric power.

Alternating current looked very attractive to the new generation of electrical engineers. Even within the Edison organization advocates of AC arose, but the "Old Man"—as he was affectionately known by his crew—would not hear of it. The large investment that Edison and his financiers had already made in DC technology was one obvious reason that the Wizard clung to the old system. More significant perhaps was his notorious distaste for higher mathematics. Understanding DC required only simple algebra, well within Edison's ken, but the mathematics of AC rapidly became complicated. Finally, Westinghouse shamelessly infringed Edison's incandescent lamp patents, among others, and this was intolerable.

The war of the currents began in the late 1880s, as Edison picked up the gauntlet thrown down by George Westinghouse. The battles raged before the public, with both Edison and Westinghouse granting interviews and authoring articles in popular magazines.

Ostensibly, Edison objected to AC because of its dangerously high voltages. To demonstrate that AC posed a hazard to living things, the Wizard had his lieutenants execute large animals in the laboratory. In another infamous episode, an Edison loyalist saw to it that the New York State Prison purchased a Westinghouse AC system for its electric chair.

Because of Edison's prestige, resources, and, above all, tenacity, the war as a spectacle lasted about five years, much longer than it should have. The triumph of AC was sealed at the Columbian Exposition in 1893. Determined to get the lighting contract for the fair, Westinghouse undertook the project at a loss. Twelve enormous Westinghouse generators lighted up 250,000 incandescent lamps, ensuring that everyone who visited or read about the Exposition would associate the name Westinghouse with progress in electric lighting. When the war of the currents was over, Edison, though very wealthy, was no longer a principal in the electric power industry he founded.

Both Edison and Westinghouse were pursuing the same vision: universal electricity for lighting and power. Although Edison sowed the seeds by creating the first practical system, it was Westinghouse, with better technology for building large-scale networks, who finally reaped the harvest. Slowly but relentlessly, AC became dominant in the decades ahead. In the interim, however, AC and DC systems coexisted, with DC dominating central districts of cities and many small towns, while AC held sway in the suburbs. This pattern of infrastructure development would have important repercussions on the electric automobile (Chapter 6).

For much of the remainder of the 1890s Edison threw himself into the construction of an electromagnetic iron-ore separator. Success in this enterprise, he believed, would allow the use of low-grade eastern ores, thus providing an inexpensive source of iron. He bought an iron mine in New Jersey, built a town to house his workers, and constructed ore-crushing machinery of unprecedented size and complexity. It was difficult and heartbreaking work that men less obsessed and less capable would have given up quickly. By the time Edison, at great personal expense, had solved the enormous technical problems with the ore-crushing mechanism, new sources of cheap, high-grade ore from the West had made the whole project obsolete. The Old Man had lost again. Perhaps it was this Edison, the impotent wizard, that L. Frank Baum satirized in his book of 1900, *The Wizard of Oz*. But, as we shall see in later chapters, the Wizard's powers were far from sapped.

Less than a decade after Sprague's achievement in Richmond, horse-car railways were on the retreat. Already in 1890, the United States had 3,000 miles of trolley; a mere five years later, the country boasted 850 trolley systems with a combined mileage exceeding 10,000. Six billion passengers were hauled in 1902 by U.S. electric railways, while horse cars ran on only 1 percent of city tracks. Because trolleys were much faster than horse cars, they could move more people during rush hours.

As David E. Nye has observed in *Electrifying America*, trolleys had a profound centrifugal effect on American cities. "Streetcar suburbs" sprang up wherever trolley lines extended. By 1900, for example, Greater Boston was a metropolis of more than 25 square miles. In later decades, the automobile would simply intensify patterns of city spread established by the trolleys.

To earn supplementary income, trolley companies sold surplus current from their isolated plants to small communities nearby. An even more ingenious money-maker was the amusement park, which many trolley companies built at the end of their lines. Not only did amusement parks with roller coasters and Ferris wheels and garish lighting consume current, but they increased trolley ridership on weekends.

Trolleys made travel to downtown easy, and so the use of the city's core intensified. As land values escalated, so did the height of office buildings. The electric elevator, to which Frank Sprague made singular contributions, allowed buildings to soar skyward as never before. Wealthy corporations waged warfare with masonry and steel, literally one-upping each other with every new building. Colossal corporate icons were replacing churches and civic buildings as the city's most visible monuments. And deep in the canyons that the new architecture created, trolleys labored to carry ever more commuters.

Ordinary Americans found new and sometimes imaginative uses for the trolley. During hot summer nights, for example, the "trolley breeze" cooled off countless passengers. Because interurban trolleys linked many small towns to large cities, rural Americans were able to take the trolley downtown, where they could shop at the new electrically-lighted department stores. The bright lights and cornucopia of mass-produced goods also enticed working- and middle-class shoppers, men and women. By the turn of the century, the civic center was a vibrant mass of jostling humanity. In large cities people of every group—rich and poor, black and white, native and immigrant, Catholic and Jewish—rubbed elbows. Shopping downtown was the one activity in which all Americans could participate. By making movement easier, at a nickel a ride, the trolley partly broke down the social isolation its suburbs had created.

In the large, turn-of-the-century city, expanded first by horse cars then trolleys, the activities of ordinary people—work, shopping, amusements, seeing a dentist, visiting family and friends—scattered into different districts. Americans were becoming accustomed to having a high degree of mechanized mobility in their daily lives.

For middle-class women riding alone, however, taking the trolley was often an unpleasant experience. On trolleys packed to capacity, the violation of personal space was common, as women and men, the latter sometimes dirty and smelly, were thrust together cheek-to-jowl. Germ-conscious to a fault, middle-class women were especially ill at ease with the trolley's chorus of coughing, sneezing, and spitting. The trolley granted mobility to middle-class women, like Clara Ford, but the price was clearly high. As a result, she would be eager to try out new technologies of personal transport as soon as they became available.

The bicycle, of course, was the quintessential technology of personal transport. By the early 1890s, demand for safety bicycles had soared and manufacturers like Overman and Pope expanded their factories. At the height of the bicycle craze in mid-decade, annual sales of bikes, accessories, and repairs amounted to a half billion dollars. An estimated 4 million cyclists, 200,000 in Chicago alone, were roving American roads on bikes made by 500 different manufacturers. Fierce competition and the economies afforded by quantity production brought down bicycle prices. In 1898, when the fad was already fading and Pope was about to build a short-lived bicycle trust, bicycles sold for as low as $35. By this time Pope was already making electric automobiles (Chapter 5).

In the years after the Civil War, wealthy European and American men raced horses and yachts. The bicycle, too, was a technology easily and quickly adapted for sporting activities, and competitions began in the late 1870s. In addition to road and track events, bike racing also had endurance runs. For example, in the "six-day bicycle race," contestants rode twelve hours a day for six days trying to cover the greatest distance. Just a few years later, automobiles would be competing in road and track races as well as endurance runs.

Because of its speed the safety bicycle also found practical applications, especially in cities. Limited by the gait of the plodding quadruped, traffic rarely moved at more than 6 mph. Bicycles were neither confined by the pace of horses nor impeded by traffic jams; after the train, the bicycle was the fastest transport technology on earth. No wonder that, in the Gay Nineties, the

Figure 11. Gay Nineties bicyclists show off their "steel steeds." (Collection of the author)

bicycle was taken up by a few intrepid doctors, ministers, telephone lines-men, postmen, and even policemen. Though the bicycle furnished efficient personal transport (in good weather), most urbanites stayed with the trolley for everyday travel, even middle-class women, who could not easily tote packages and children on the steel steed.

The bicycle's transcendent importance was not in racing or practical affairs but in leisure activities. The bicycle, far more than the train, allowed the middle class to tour. For most people, however, touring was restricted to Sundays, when bicycle herds headed out to the country and back (Fig. 11). (Members of the clergy, however, were not amused, and some sects even condemned Sunday cycling.) Prosperous bicyclists took touring vacations, reinvigorating inns and taverns along well-traveled routes. A long bicycle ride was not exactly like traveling first class on a train or cruise ship, but it was touring nonetheless. The bicycle gave middle-class Americans a taste for touring they would not soon forget.

Among those enjoying weekend freedom on bicycles was the American woman, who by some estimates made up as much as 25 to 30 percent of the bicycle's market. As Robert Smith points out, women had demanded the franchise and some dress reform prior to 1890, but the bicycle craze created the "new woman." More rational clothing, such as shorter skirts, survived the bloomer boom. The bicycle also gave many women first-hand experience in repairing a complex machine, as John Trowbridge observed in *The Chautauquan* and *Living Age* in 1897:

The use of the bicycle has already developed a certain knowledge of mechanics among women. Before its introduction few women could use a wrench or knew the mysteries of cogwheels, washers, and lubricants; now it is not an uncommon sight to see a woman taking her bicycle to pieces and putting it together with the skill which once belonged only to man.

Soon the seeds of liberation planted by the bicycle would be nurtured by the automobile, especially the electric.

By the mid-1890s bicycling had become, in the quickly jaded eyes of America's upper crust, just a little too democratic; with millions of the middle-class now participating, bicycling had lost its luster among America's tastemakers. America's male elite turned, as they always had, to their European counterparts for guidance. In the early 1890s, wealthy Frenchmen and Germans were already buying motor cars. This was the perfect new toy, well beyond the grasp of the middle class—much less women. The sporting and leisure activities that the bicycle had popularized could be easily transferred to the new technology. Wealthy Americans began to buy and play around with European motor cars while others, sometimes of rural origin and rich with visions of motor-powered personal transport, built horseless carriages at home.

The Duryea brothers, J. Frank and Charles E., bicycle mechanics from Springfield, Massachusetts, are traditionally given credit for having put together the earliest American gasoline automobile to run reasonably well. Their vehicle was a remodeled, second-hand carriage having a one-cylinder engine. The Duryeas soon began taking orders for a two-cylinder model, and the first one was delivered early in 1895. And so, it is said, was born the commercial gasoline automobile in the United States.

In that same year *Horseless Age* was founded, a magazine for automobile enthusiasts. Its pages revealed the inventions of countless mechanics and engineers, some of whom would transform the gasoline-powered vehicle into a major American industry. The people tinkering with automobiles at this time included Henry Ford.

Along with countless contemporaries, Ford in the late 1880s became smitten with the idea of building a horseless carriage. His experiments picked up momentum after the move to Detroit. Just before Christmas, in 1893, he made his first one-cylinder gasoline engine, fired up in the kitchen with Clara's help; she was the fuel pump, pouring drops of gasoline into the engine's intake.

His next project was more ambitious: building a two-cylinder engine and a vehicle to house it. With a little help from his many friends, Ford's horseless carriage slowly took shape in the coal shed behind his home. After years of patient tinkering, the automobile was ready for trial on a late spring night in 1896. The first Ford, however, was a bit too big for the shed's door, so Henry took an axe to the brickwork and enlarged the opening. The trial was not without its travails, as a repair had to be effected at a Detroit Edison shop; but the automobile with tiller and bicycle wheels did run (Fig. 12).

Later in 1896, as chief engineer of the Detroit Edison's powerhouse, Henry Ford attended the convention of the Association of Edison Illuminating Companies in Manhattan Beach, New York. Also present at the meeting was Thomas Edison, who had taken time out from the arduous labors of the ore-milling project. Ford, asked if he wanted to be introduced to the Great Man, could scarcely contain his excitement. Who would turn down an opportunity to talk to the man who personified invention in America?

Brought together, Ford and Edison conversed mainly about automobiles, and Henry's in particular. An unusually animated Ford answered Edison's probing questions about his invention. Edison was impressed; pounding the table, he enthused,

Young man, that's the thing; you have it. Keep at it! Electric cars must keep near to power stations. The storage battery is too heavy. Steam cars won't do either, for they have to have a boiler and fire. Your car is self-contained—carries its own power plant—no fire, no boiler, no smoke and no steam. You have the thing. Keep at it.

Ford attached great significance to Edison's encouraging words, remembering this meeting as a turning point. Neither could have suspected that nearly twenty years hence, both would be fast friends, together building an electric

Figure 12. Henry Ford's first automobile. (From the collections of Henry Ford Museum & Greenfield Village, neg. 833-100958)

car (Chapter 11). In the meantime, Henry followed the Wizard's advice, and kept at it. Not until 1903, however, would Ford begin selling automobiles.

While Ford was perfecting gasoline automobiles, electrics from across the Atlantic continued to be reported in American technical and popular magazines. For example, French progress in electrics was discussed in the *Review of Reviews* in 1894, and readers received the impression that commercial electric vehicles were imminent. Similarly, an 1886 article in *Scientific*

American highlighted the efforts of M. Jeantaud, also working in France. Jeantaud's electric carriage (with two passengers) weighed 2,573 lbs, including 925 lbs of batteries. The vehicle could reach a speed of 12 mph and travel 18 miles on a charge "upon a good level road," of which there were many in France but few in America. *Scientific American* readers were advised that Jeantaud's creation was a distinct advance in the art, "a long stride toward the electric carriage." Jeantaud had also driven an electric in the Paris-Bordeaux race, but the racer's 1,875 lbs of batteries had to be exchanged along the route at intervals of 40 to 70 km (25 to 40 miles).

Americans were also at work on race- and street-worthy electric vehicles. Among the most significant figures were Philadelphians Pedro Salom and Henry G. Morris. A chemist, Salom had worked on storage batteries while employed by a battery trolley company. Although a fervent believer in this mode of transportation, he abandoned it in 1894 to devote his energies to the electric automobile. Salom teamed up with Henry G. Morris, a mechanical engineer, with whom he had become acquainted during his trolley days.

The inventors aimed to construct an automobile capable of negotiating the streets in Philadelphia, "irrespective of their suitability for motor-driven traction." This meant making many sacrifices in the vehicle's design, especially in appearance and weight. Their collaboration began in June 1894, and yielded its first vehicle just over two months later. The car was christened Electrobat, the first in a family of electrics with that moniker.

Electrobat 1 was not a dainty carriage—weighing in at 4,250 lbs, including almost 1,600 lbs of batteries—but it performed well, reaching 15 mph. On its wagon wheels with iron tires, the hefty vehicle could travel between 50 and 100 miles on a charge. In the year and a half after Electrobat's debut, Morris and Salom drove it around Philadelphia, accumulating several hundred miles without a breakdown.

To further the development of Electrobats, Morris and Salom set up a manufacturing company, the Electric Carriage & Wagon Company. This firm was loosely linked to the important Philadelphia battery manufacturer, the Electric Storage Battery Company (ESB), which held a virtual monopoly on lead-acid storage battery technology in the United States and supplied batteries for the bats. ESB also owned the Electric Vehicle Company (EVC), which was to become a major player in electric car manufacturing.

Electrobat 2 was a light vehicle constructed to compete in the *Times-Herald* Motocycle Contest. Weighing only 1,650 lbs, Electrobat 2 could easily ride on pneumatic tires, which Salom claimed were "decidedly the best for motor vehicles." The batteries weighed a mere 640 lbs (39 percent of the vehicle's total weight), and could sustain its two 1.5-hp motors for 25 to 30 miles between charges. Surprisingly, Electrobat 2 was front-wheel drive and steered from the rear.

Drawing on trolley technology, Morris and Salom provided Electrobat 2 with a controller. This contrivance connected the batteries and motors in different series and parallel combinations, and empowered the vehicle with three forward speeds plus reverse. Electrobat 2 could reach a swift 20 mph on a good road. To bystanders, a cruising Electrobat 2 had style—for 1895, that is. After all, the body had been built by the Charles S. Caffrey Company, of Camden, New Jersey, a famous carriage maker.

After a lengthy postponement to allow entrants more time to finish their vehicles, the *Times-Herald* race finally took place on November 28, 1895. The course ran a 54-mile circuit from Jackson Park in Chicago to Evanston and back. Unfortunately, a near blizzard visited Chicago a few days before the race, leaving the course deep in snow and slush. As a result, only six entrants showed up, four gasoline cars and two electrics. Along with Electrobat 2 was a heavy Sturges electric—a modified Morrison carriage. Neither electric finished the race, which was won by Frank Duryea at an average speed of 7 mph, but both made a credible showing under the terrible conditions. Electrobat 2 even won a gold medal for excellence of design. The *Times-Herald* race was heavily covered in the press and in technical journals, and is credited by some for energizing the automobile industry in the United States. After all, no horse-drawn vehicle could have averaged 7 mph on the same course.

After the race, Salom and Morris kept building better bats, and completed models 3 and 4 by the end of 1895. These vehicles were even lighter than the Electrobat 2, as they used steel tubing, a bicycle technology, for the frame. Electrobat 4 weighed an astounding 800 lbs, including the 350-lb battery and two 75-lb motors, and was capable of traveling at a top speed of 15 mph; on one charge it would make 20 to 25 miles. Electrobat 4 was not a luxury vehicle, but a spartan wagon; yet it showed what clever design of electrics might achieve.

Electrics fared better the next year in the Providence horseless carriage race, witnessed by 5,000 spectators at the Narragansett Park track, in Providence, Rhode Island. First prize of $900 went to the Riker Electric Motor

Company of Brooklyn, New York; their electric carriage had made the fastest time in a mile—2:13. Breezing along at over 20 mph, a Morris and Salom Electrobat ran the fastest 5 miles (in 11:27), and earned second prize of $450.

In reporting the Providence race, *Scientific American* made a telling comment on the status of electric vehicles:

> The announcement of the success of the electric carriages created some surprise, as it has been thought lately that motors using some form of petroleum were best adapted for horseless carriage use, and the electric motor has been somewhat discounted. The electric carriage has made a record for speed, and the great ease of control and the absence of noise and odor will commend it to those who are anxious to purchase horseless carriages, but whether they are adapted for long runs or not still remains to be proved.

These remarks testify to the importance attached by automobile enthusiasts to race results.

In a talk presented to members of the Franklin Institute (and later published in its journal), Salom discussed in great detail the advantages of the electric over horse-drawn and gasoline-powered vehicles. Salom's assessment (too lengthy for complete presentation here) is that of an electric car advocate, but many of his points were generally appreciated at the dawn of the automobile age.

As Salom stressed, the almost silent electric vehicle is quieter than either horse- or gasoline-powered automobiles. A gasoline engine gets hot and must be cooled by circulating water; sometimes a supply of ice must be carried along. Gasoline engines and drive trains are complex and prone to breakdown, but electrics are simple and reliable. Similarly, gasoline vehicles are so complicated to drive that "it would be absolutely essential to have a skillful engineer and machinist to operate them," and keep them running, "whereas, on an electric vehicle, we can take a boy twelve or fourteen years of age, or a young lady accustomed to driving a horse, and, with ten minutes' practice, they can operate the vehicle perfectly."

Finally, and prophetically, Salom noted that the electric is clean and odor-free, remarking that

> all the gasoline motors we have seen belch forth from their exhaust pipe a continuous stream of partially unconsumed hydrocarbon in the form of a thin smoke with a highly

noxious odor. Imagine thousands of such vehicles on the streets, each offering up its column of smell as a sacrifice for having displaced the superannuated horse, and consider whether such a system has general utility or adaptability!

A cranky *Horseless Age* promptly reprinted most of Salom's comparisons, complaining that they were one-sided and ignored advances in gasoline vehicles. The attempt to refute Salom's points, however, was equally one-sided and sometimes lame. Even at this early date (spring 1896), battle lines had emerged between gas and electric advocates.

Debates about the superiority of gasoline or electricity as motive powers would remain largely academic until both kinds of automobile were commercialized in large numbers. Salom and Morris did not manufacture their Electrobats for sale to the public; they had a different plan in mind (Chapter 6). As we shall now see, other inventors and entrepreneurs did bring electric automobiles to market. Among the first was Albert Pope.

5

THE ELECTRIC AUTOMOBILE
GOES TO MARKET

On May 13, 1897, the Pope Manufacturing Company, makers of the popular Columbia bicycle, demonstrated their latest product to the press. At the Pope factory in Hartford, Connecticut, the assembled journalists witnessed the unveiling of an electric carriage being manufactured for sale to the public. Although Pope's vehicle was not the first electric to reach market, this event was a milestone in the history of commercial electric automobiles in the United States.

Exploiting their bicycle expertise, Pope engineers had built this carriage from the ground up. It weighed only 1,800 lbs, including 850 lbs of battery; the light weight stemmed from the extensive use of tubular steel in the frame. Also borrowed from bicycle technology were metal-spoked wheels and pneumatic tires. A 2-hp motor propelled the vehicle in four forward speeds (3, 6, 12, and 15 mph), and between charges it could run for 30 miles. Pope's machine was easy to drive, as *Scientific American's* favorable write-up observed:

The guests of the company were allowed to run the carriages themselves, and it was found that those who were totally unfamiliar with the horseless carriage were able to manage and turn them with as much ease and success as they would have guiding the gentlest horse.

Marketed as the Columbia Electric Phaeton, Mark III, Pope's automobile remained in production, little changed, for many years.

What most distinguished Pope's electric vehicle from other horseless carriages was that it was built in a factory already familiar with large-scale production. Indeed, Pope's little electric was the first American automobile of any kind to be produced commercially in more than trivial numbers. As one automobile historian recently acknowledged, "Only Pope at this time could rank as a major producer."

The handsome carriage of the Mark III was designed by William Hooker Atwood, who had been borrowed from the New Haven Carriage Company. Its dashboard was the work of Hayden Eames, a Pope executive who would become an important voice in the electric vehicle industry. Mechanical and electrical systems of this landmark vehicle, however, were designed by Pope's young engineer, Hiram Percy Maxim.

Born in Brooklyn in 1869, Maxim was trained in the mechanical arts at MIT and was the youngest in his graduating class of 1886. After graduation he held a succession of challenging jobs designing various devices. While working on torpedoes in 1894, he built on his own time a three-cylinder gasoline tricycle. This effort attracted the attention of Albert Pope, who was able to lure Maxim to Hartford. Although Maxim would have preferred to design gasoline cars because their range was (in principle) unlimited, he and the Pope people agreed that a good electric car could be brought out first. Later, as chief engineer of the Electric Vehicle Company (EVC), Maxim would design both electric and gasoline vehicles.

About the same time as Pope, other inventor-entrepreneurs were also marketing their electric automobiles. One of the most important was the C. E. Woods Company of Chicago, which began selling a line of electric automobiles and trucks in 1896. Less skilled at obtaining publicity than Pope, this firm nonetheless sold their electrics first. Another pioneer was Andrew L. Riker, who had built the early electric tricycle and racers; his cars went on sale in 1897.

When the Columbia, Woods, and Riker electrics were initially offered to the public, nearly fifteen years after Edison's triumph on Pearl Street, progress in realizing the Wizard's vision of universal electric lighting was remarkably limited. An understanding of the odd twists and turns taken by electrification in America can help us to appreciate why, at the end of the Gilded Age, there was nearly no infrastructure for charging electric vehicles at home (or anywhere else).

When a new technology appears, its potential applications are often framed in terms of the old technology it is expected to replace. And so it was with electricity—"replacement" for steam power and gas lighting. Not all such replacements turned out to be immediately feasible, economically viable, or important, and soon electricity in practice came to have uses that no one foresaw.

Throughout the 1880s and 1890s both central stations and isolated plants were built at an accelerating rate. It was civic pride and profit that motivated construction of a central station, which could supply current for street lights downtown. The inauguration of a new electric lighting system was an occasion for celebration that attracted crowds and newspaper reporters. The public reaction to the arc lights placed on Wabash's courthouse was described by the *Wabash Plain Dealer*:

People stood overwhelmed with awe, as if in the presence of the supernatural. The strange weird light exceeded in power only by the sun, rendered the square as light as midday. . . . Men fell on their knees, groans were uttered at the sight, and many were dumb with amazement.

Wabash's central station was the first in the United States to be municipally owned.

City fathers elsewhere immediately grasped that well-lighted thoroughfares were a necessity for a town that wanted to remain competitive in the constant quest for new businesses and factories. A city without a Great White Way—a main street where electric lights (mostly arc lamps) burned brightly white in contrast to the yellowish glow of gas—was simply a backwater, out of the running. In *Electrifying America*, David Nye points out that lighting important public areas and buildings in cities and small towns alike was "more than a mere functional necessity or a convenience; it emerged as a glamorous symbol of progress and cultural advancement." In some of America's smallest towns, in the middle of nowhere, boosters managed to secure a lighting system. The lighting plant for Lander, Wyoming—a town of 1,500 inhabitants —had to be hauled 150 miles by mule over mountain roads from the nearest railroad station, in a round trip that took twelve days. Despite the obstacles and expense, by early 1893 nearly 2000 U.S. cities and towns had central stations. Few cities, however, followed the Wabash model, as central stations became the near-exclusive preserve of private enterprise.

Power from a new central station was also sold to businesses along the main streets. As Nye observed, "merchants immediately discovered that, like moths drawn to the flame, people were attracted to electrically lighted windows." Once one business had lighted up its display windows or one theater its marquee, competitors had to follow suit. Here, then, was a novel and unexpected application of electricity, and it was important. A few lights in the front window were soon supplemented by large illuminated signs; installed on the side or roof of a big building, the largest ones were readable from miles away. On some signs, bulbs going on and off in particular patterns created the illusion of movement. Especially eye-catching was the electric bicycle above the entrance to Madison Square Garden during the 1896 bicycle show. Thirteen feet tall and 20 feet long, the bicycle seemed to be moving—thanks to 2,000 flashing incandescent bulbs. Ingenious mechanical controls, powered by electric motors, created these grand effects, the likes of which had never been seen before. In terms of sheer glitz and wizardry, today's computer-controlled video displays in sports stadiums pale beside their incandescent ancestors of a century ago.

In her captivating book, *When Old Technologies Were New*, Carolyn Marvin points out that electric lights had become a new medium of communication. In addition to the vulgar messages—buy here, buy this and that—Americans were irradiated with an enthusiasm for all things electrical. A technology capable of turning night into day surely could work other wonders.

Entrepreneurs, capitalizing on people's fascination with electricity, quickly brought out a host of new products boasting the "electric" cachet. For example, $3 bought "Dr. Scott's Electric Flesh Brush," which promised to cure sundry ailments (Fig. 13). "Medical batteries" delivered voltage to various places, and were advertised to treat nearly every affliction known to man—and woman. The Venus Electric Massage, only $5, removed wrinkles and "imparts to the skin the vigor and freshness of youth"; the Heidelberg Electric Belt sold by Sears, Roebuck was claimed to restore virility. Even more impressive was Dr. Horne's electric belt "warranted to *cure*" no fewer than nineteen maladies from catarrh to constipation. Like all new technologies, electricity's ability to solve age-old problems was being explored. With a smugness born of the late twentieth century, it is easy to dismiss these efforts as quackery, but they were no different from our own attempts to find technological solutions to all of life's little problems.

Because central stations were still small, they could not yet sell power more cheaply than large users could produce it for themselves. Not surprisingly,

Figure 13. Advertisement for "Dr. Scott's Electric Flesh Brush."
(*Scientific American*, 9 July 1881, p. 28)

isolated plants were installed in factories, office buildings, hotels, and, of course, America's most sumptuous homes.

In Victorian America, steam-powered factories cranked out an unending parade of products, from straight pins to machine tools. Many people were optimistic that factories would be electrified soon, with electric motors on individual machines laying the foundation for a new industrial utopia. This did not happen right away, however, because motorizing old machines was expensive and few new machines came with built-in motors before the turn of the century. Even so, an all-electric factory could be created by replacing the steam engine with a huge electric motor. In the first electrified factories, then, the old belts and shafting remained along with the gross inefficiences in power transmission. But the factory was electric.

Though a few new factories came on line as all-electric, the majority of older factories were slow even to replace their steam engines. Thus, after nearly two decades of electrification in the United States, in 1900 only about 5 percent of factory power was electric.

Many factories did buy isolated plants for electric lighting, both arc and incandescent. Compared to gas, electric illumination was cleaner, cooler, and steadier, and in flammable environments much safer. It was these advantages that hastened the adoption of electric lighting, for the latter was seldom cheaper than gas.

Hotels and the homes of America's elite also put in isolated plants. In New York City the "new" Hotel Waldorf—new in 1893, that is—became an electrical showcase. A set of steam-powered dynamos, deep in the bowels of the building, supplied power for electric lights—6,200 of them. All public spaces and rooms were lit, and the displays were dazzling. The ceiling of the Garden Court was capped with a magnificent dome from whose apex was suspended a gilt chandelier 24 feet high and 8 feet in diameter, luxurious receptacle for 150 light bulbs. Comparably elegant fixtures were found throughout the hotel, including six bronze and glass chandeliers that highlighted the mosaic floors, rugs, and antique furniture of the Turkish room. Behind the scenes, electric motors drove printing press, bottle washer, dishwasher, fans to circulate air during the summer, and a machine for buffing the silverware. Well-heeled guests of the Waldorf and other hotels, each competing to outdo the others in their use of electric lights for decorating and display, must have stood in awed silence upon first gazing at such an ostentatious use of electricity.

In the home, the most obvious use of electricity was also to replace gas in lighting. Installing and operating an isolated plant at home, however, was an undertaking that only the most affluent could contemplate. America's elite, then, took the lead, making electric lighting above all a beacon of opulence. This, of course, was not what Thomas Edison originally had in mind.

Once a handful of homes had been electrified, "mushroom" firms sprouted up selling clever kettles, coffee pots, teapots, chafing dishes, stew pots, plate warmers, and so on. Curiously, like light bulbs they all screwed into "light sockets," for this was decades before the utility outlet and standardized plugs came into use.

The cornucopia of electric appliances created, or so the promoters claimed, new possibilities for domestic life. Manufacturers anticipated, for example, that many of their screw-in products would be used directly on the dining room table, helping to ameliorate the ever-present "servant problem." Electric cooking, observed *Electrical World* in 1893, would lead as well to esthetic improvements "in that dark spot in the household, the present kitchen, with its uninviting interior, unsavory odors and distressing heat."

Factories also supplied sundry electrical things for other rooms of the home. Along with countless styles of lamps, electric fireplaces, sewing machines, and illuminated clocks, the avid buyer could find heating pads, curling iron heaters, phonographs, cigar lighters, and foot warmers. The most popular appliance of this time was the small fan, sometimes battery-powered, already available in dozens of models, doubtless a godsend in the summer. Another important appliance was the electric iron, which really did make ironing quicker and easier. In 1897 J. P. Jackson remarked "that a laundress who had used an electrical iron would be exceedingly unwilling to go back to the old form." He would be proved right a decade later when central stations began pushing appliances (Chapter 8).

There is precious little information on how well most of the electric "conveniences" really performed. Because many lacked effective heat regulators, overheating and burnouts were a constant risk. Though cremated waffles were not too tasty, a shiny electric waffle-maker was nonetheless a potent symbol of the dawning electrical age, there for guests to see, who could be expected to conclude that the family was most modern. After all, in electrical exhibitions (including the Columbian Exposition of 1893) and mass-circulation magazines, electrical appliances had been shown in a very favorable light, certain to be included in homes of the future. The rich, of course, could buy the future immediately.

While entrepreneurs were catering to the public's enthusiasm for electrical things, writers of science fiction had begun to foresee products well beyond the horizon of immediate feasibility, including portable radios and television. Far-out electrical devices even appeared in children's literature, preparing another generation to accept—and create—a future different from the past and present. In 1901, L. Frank Baum, author of the *Wizard of Oz*, wrote the ponderously titled *The Master Key: An Electrical Fairy Tale, Founded Upon the Mysteries of Electricity and the Optimism of its Devotees. It Was Written for Boys, but Others May Read It.* In *The Master Key*, the young protagonist accidently summons the "Demon of the Master Key" while doing electrical experiments. Contemptuous of Edison, whom he regards as "groping blindly after insignificant effects," the demon alone knows how to direct the electric powers. Among the gifts the demon offers the young hero are a stun gun, a wristwatch machine for instant travel, a "pocket automatic record of events" (a combination television and VCR), and an Illimitable Communicator (a wireless telephone). The story's surprising moral is that most people are not wise enough to use such inventions "unselfishly and for the good of the world." Ironically, adult literature expressed few reservations about humanity's ability to cope with the procession of new electrical products.

The ordinary American, who might work in an electrified office or factory, promenade along Main Street, and ride the trolley, saw signs of the new electrical age everywhere. Everywhere, that is, but at home. Even by the turn of the century, electrification was confined mainly to those able to buy isolated plants and a few other affluent families located near central stations. Typical was Muncie, Indiana, which in 1899 had exactly twenty-two electrified homes. Central stations were not enthusiastic about supplying current to every home in America, for it was just not profitable. Extending power lines into older, working-class neighborhoods was expensive, and wiring an existing house could cost between $1 and $4 per light bulb. Even if service had been universally available, not many families could have afforded it: power ran around 10 to 25 cents per kilowatt hour (kwh), and the *minimum* monthly service charge typically was $2.50 to $6.25.

Although a few people, drawing their own conclusions from the Edison-Westinghouse debates, might have feared to have any current in their homes, most Americans were eager for electric lighting. Beginning in the early 1890s and continuing into the new century, a constant stream of articles appeared in mass-circulation magazines, extolling the many—and by then obvious—virtues of the new lighting technology compared to gas and oil lamps. Incandescent lights were easily controlled by a switch, produced neither grime nor excessive heat, did not emit noxious gases, and were unlikely to start fires. As early as the mid-1890s, *Scientific American* was able to proclaim that "The incandescent lamp has been accepted by the public." It was not something to be feared but coveted, for as yet only the elite could bask in the glow of "electroliers" (electric chandeliers), and plug in their electric horseless carriages.

In conventional histories of the automobile, it is said that America's first car show took place in Madison Square Garden in November of 1900. Close to the new year—and new century—it was a splendid affair, attended by the Vanderbilts, the Astors, William Rockefeller, and other members of high society. This exhibition, however, was not the first trade show in the United States to include automobiles.

The earliest show of U.S. automobiles was actually part of the annual Electrical Exhibition held from May 8 to June 4, 1899, also at Madison Square Garden. Along with exhibits on the new technology of wireless telegraphy, the use of electricity in medicine and surgery, and the latest in central-station equipment, was a display area of several thousand square feet dedicated to the wares of the new electric automobile industry. In providing a preview of the Electrical Exhibition, *Scientific American* enthused,

> The prominent feature of the 1899 Exhibition will certainly be automobilism. The exhibit of electric vehicles will be by long odds the largest and best ever seen in America, and second only to the great exhibits of Paris; in fact, in many respects it will surpass the displays of Europe . . . because the vehicles shown will demonstrate the high perfection that the art has already reached in this country.

The electric automobile industry in America had arrived in 1899. In that year a wide assortment of electric passenger cars as well as commercial vehicles was being sold by more than a dozen firms. The name "horseless carriage" aptly described these automobiles since they replicated the traditional array of horse-drawn buggy, wagon, and carriage styles. In virtually every case the electric automobile was an ordinary-looking vehicle driven by motor instead of a horse. Some manufacturers refrained from introducing new body styles, believing that carriage owners were too conservative and would reject the unfamiliar.

Of the standard vehicle types, the runabout was the lightest weight and, usually, the least expensive (see Fig. 19). This was no-frills automobiling, but at $750 and up was thirty to fifty times more expensive than the horse-drawn version (excluding the horse!). Two-seaters with a wagonlike body, runabouts ranged in weight from about 1,200 to 2,000 lbs, of which 30 to 45 percent was battery. Some runabouts had one electric motor, others two (one for each rear wheel), with total horsepower varying from 1 to 2.5.

The runabout was designed, literally, to run about agilely, and most could travel around 25-30 miles (its "radius of action") before needing a recharge. Like most of the lighter electrics, the runabout had a basic complement of three forward and two reverse speeds. The Columbia runabout, for example, moved ahead at 3.5, 7, and 14 mph. There were no intermediate speeds on electric vehicles; if one wanted to travel at 10 mph, it would have been necessary to switch back and forth between 7 and 14 mph.

At the other extreme of size, luxuriousness, and cost was the brougham (Fig. 14). The brougham's body was a closed coach of lacquered wood, and the "coachman" sat outside. Total weight, including 1,000 to 1,400 lbs of

Figure 14. The Riker brougham. (Riker 1900 brochure, on file Library of Congress)

battery, was in the vicinity of 4,000 lbs—little more than today's large luxury cars. Typically, one or two motors gave a combined 3 to 5 hp. Controllers were more complex than those in runabouts, allowing four or five forward speeds. With a range of 25–30 miles, most were designed for leisurely cruising at a maximum of 11–14 mph, though the General Electric Automobile Company's brougham could make nearly 20 mph.

One brougham on display at the 1899 Electrical Exhibition, a Columbia, had been ordered by a wealthy New York physician. In Pope's Hartford plant, artisans fashioned the coach of oak and other fine woods, and applied a lacquer finish of dark green and black that achieved an almost mirrorlike reflectance. The interior was luxurious, with goat skin upholstery and satin roof, both in dark green. Other appointments included an electric reading lamp, hand mirror, pockets and shelves for parcels, and a small clock set in the upholstery. Rolling along silently on its wooden wheels and solid rubber tires, the brougham would have conspicuously advertised its owner's wealth and high standing in New York society.

Only the richest Americans could buy a brougham; its price tag of around $5,000—cash only, please—was at least ten times the annual salary of a factory worker. Like diamond jewelry and ornate crystal electroliers, the brougham was a sparkling symbol of success. When the wealthy sought a horseless brougham, their only choice was electric. Not until late in the following decade would makers of gasoline-powered cars offer a comparably luxurious closed-coach style.

Between the mundane, but by no means inexpensive, runabout and the opulent brougham a variety of victorias, stanhopes, phaetons, dos-a-dos, breaks, surreys, road wagons (Fig. 15), traps, and even tricycles beckoned the

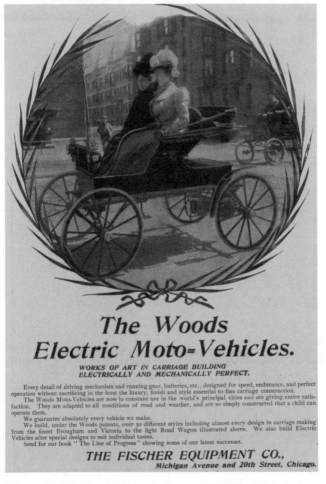

Figure 15. The Woods "light road wagon." (*McClure's Magazine,* August 1899, p. 28)

Figure 16. The Riker victoria. (Riker 1900 brochure, on file Library of Congress)

electric buyer. The break, dos-a-dos, and various surreys were larger vehicles, usually topless (except for the surrey), that could carry at least four people.

The victoria (Fig. 16) was named for the carriage style preferred by Victoria, the English queen; some might say that the victoria's small, low-slung body gave it a certain daintiness. Of all the styles, the victoria was probably the easiest to enter and exit, especially in late Victorian garb. Ordinarily the curvaceous victoria was little more than a feminized runabout; Columbia, however, offered a more luxurious Daumon Victoria Mark VI, which was somewhat heavier at 3,250 lbs.

The stanhope was also a small and agile electric whose appearance was not unlike an overgrown baby buggy (see Fig. 26). This two-seater style implied a playfulness that even today retains appeal. The Waverley stanhope had a 2.5 hp motor and was said to travel 40 miles on a charge. The two-seater phaeton (Fig. 17) was a somewhat more substantial and embellished stanhope or runabout. Columbia's Phaeton Mark III (America's first car produced in quantity) was "superbly finished in black, with panels of green, and upholstered in dark green wulfing cloth"; its three forward speeds peaked at 12 mph. Almost lightweight at 2,570 total lbs, the Phaeton Mark III had a 35-mile range.

Figure 17. The Riker phaeton. (*The Cosmopolitan*, August 1900, p. 5)

In addition to passenger cars, several firms by the end of the century were making business vehicles in styles borrowed from their horse-drawn contemporaries. Most common was the delivery wagon (Fig. 18), but there were also trucks, theater buses, and omnibuses; and in 1900 even electric ambulances were being sold. Although some stores rapidly adopted electric delivery wagons, a detailed study by Robert A. Fliess, commissioned by *Electrical World*, showed that they offered no economic advantage over horse-drawn trucks for relatively light work. In other classes of service, however, business electrics were already cheaper to operate, though the initial capital outlay was steep.

Figure 18. A Riker delivery wagon. (Riker 1900 brochure, on file Library of Congress)

Regardless of how well electrics performed, the slow spread of electrification would be a significant barrier to their adoption. At the turn of the century, even most affluent families lacked electricity. And, outside the home, there were precious few places for an electric vehicle to plug in and recharge. Let us take a closer look at the problems of getting a charge in late Victorian times.

6

GETTING A CHARGE

Glenmont, the Edison mansion in Llewellyn Park, received its power—DC, of course—via underground cable from the laboratory's isolated plant. Even those who had DC power, like the Edisons, found that charging batteries at home was a nuisance. And Americans with AC encountered even greater difficulties.

In homes having DC, it would seem that one could simply "plug in" the electric automobile. Unfortunately, it was not that easy. DC service was generally at 110 volts, though sometimes it was 220 or more volts; in no case was there an exact match to a car's battery voltage. The battery in an electric automobile consisted of sixteen to forty-eight 2-volt cells, the number depending on the car's make and model. When connected in series, the cells could be charged together, but the voltage—say 84 volts for a forty-two cell battery—did not add up to 110. Before the battery could be charged, then, the line voltage had to be reduced with a rheostat, a device that turned the excess power into heat.

In addition to the rheostat, the home charging set-up (which cost $25 to $75) required meters for setting the correct current and voltage and for monitoring the progress of the charge. If the current was not shut off at the proper time, the battery could be damaged by overcharging. Not surprisingly, many people concluded that charging was best left in the hands of a professional electrician.

The nouveaux riches in their suburban homes had an even greater challenge: converting AC to DC. In the late 1890s this conversion was carried out with an expensive rotary converter, an AC motor coupled to a DC generator. Of course, the generator's output voltage had to be matched to the vehicle's battery, which usually necessitated a rheostat. The rotary converter and rheostat together could waste nearly half the precious power. Prior to 1900, when Westinghouse commercialized a rotary converter and control panel for home charging, such devices had to be custom-built by an electrician.

People without power who still wanted to charge their electrics at home could, beginning in 1900, buy J. B. Merriam's tiny (500 watt) power plant driven by a water-cooled gas engine. Designed expressly for automatic charging of automobile batteries, these miniature stations were available as an optional accessory with Baker electric vehicles. These small power plants were notoriously inefficient and did not catch on.

Even if one owned apparatus for charging vehicles at home, the process was vexing. Although by 1901 most cars came equipped with a plug that could be used to charge the batteries without taking them from the vehicle, this practice contributed to less diligent maintenance of the cells (which was more easily accomplished when the batteries were removed for charging). Needless to say, wrestling 500 or 900 or 1,200 lbs of batteries in and out of the car every few days could become tiresome.

Batteries of that time were far more tempermental than today's, and without incessant maintenance, they quickly lost their ability to hold a charge. The condition of each cell had to be checked often by inserting a hydrometer syringe through the vent hole, withdrawing a small amount of acid, and observing the position of the hydrometer's float. To cells showing abnormal readings, the home mechanic had to add water or sulfuric acid. Dripping acid on hands and other precious parts was an ever-present danger. Defunct cells, of course, had to be extracted and new ones wrestled in place. The "mud" that collected at the bottom of the cell jars had to be cleaned out periodically or it would cause a short circuit. And the positive electrodes required washing or replacement at intervals of several months to a year. In describing these travails, one disgruntled electric vehicle owner—Charles Duryea, no less—complained in *Horseless Age* that "a set of batteries was worse to take care of than a hospital full of sick dogs." Battery maintenance could be entrusted to servants, of course, but that had its own risks. Clearly, charging and maintaining batteries at home was not a practical proposition for more than a few masochists.

The "charging problem" was widely appreciated by people in and out of the electrical industry, and various solutions were sought. A few central stations furnished charging facilities at their plants, billing for the power consumed. Traveling back and forth to the electric company was inconvenient unless one lived very close or had servants and carriages to ferry them. It goes without saying that most central stations at this time regarded electric vehicles as little more than a nuisance that occasionally brought in a dollar or two.

It was the fond hope of electric vehicle promoters that the establishment throughout the land of a dense network of charging stations would make even touring practical, the activity most closely identified with automobiling. The idea, as expressed by vehicle maker C. E. Woods in his book of 1900, *The Electric Automobile*, was that after about four hours of travel, which exhausted the battery, the automobilist himself was apt to be tired or hungry, and so would welcome a stop for an hour or two. Automobilist and battery could be recharged at the same time. Woods believed that as soon as sufficient charging stations were available, tourists in electrics would be able to drive effortlessly from New York to San Francisco, much as they could take the train. Only in a very few places outside large cities, however, was it possible for the touring electric to get a charge without making special arrangements. One example was the power station of the Central Railway and Electric Company of New Britain, Connecticut, which allowed visiting vehicles to plug in by the main entrance. Demand was so low in 1899 that the company did not have a regular rate for the service.

Another problem with the scenario of touring electrics was that charging the battery in only one or two hours hastened deterioration of the positive plates; this difficulty was not appreciated at the time, for batteries generally were charged too rapidly. By reducing charging time to the length of a leisurely meal, of course, one kept alive the possibility that electrics could tour.

One creative idea for convenient charging outside the home emerged in 1899 from the mind of John Van Vleck, an engineer in the Edison Electric Illuminating Company of New York. He designed a charging "hydrant" that could be installed curbside at periodic intervals along city streets. Van Vleck envisioned that the operator of an electric vehicle in need would simply park next to a hydrant, plug in, and take a metered amount of current.

In the following year General Electric developed a commercial version of the charging hydrant, christening it the "electrant." For a "25-cent piece" the electrant supplied 2.5 kwh—not an exorbitant price for electricity in 1900. Although the electrant received favorable notice in *Electrical World* and

Horseless Age, and was displayed at the automobile show in Madison Square Garden in 1900, there is no evidence that electrants were actually put into service. Central stations, after all, would have had to buy and install them, and this apparently did not seem like an attractive investment. One reason for this reluctance was that plugs on electric automobiles had not been standardized; of the eight makes of electrics at the automobile show, only three could plug into the electrant.

Assessing the charging situation in mid-1899, an editorial in *Electrical World* observed the rapid development of the "automobile as a factor in the electrical field." It went on to chastise central station managers for failing to address the charging problem, accusing them of having a "Micawber-like attitude." The editorial concluded that central station men should buy electric automobiles to set an example in their communities, and to learn about them from the user's point of view.

Electrical World repeated its plea in November 1900, accusing managers of apathy. One slightly indignant L. R. Wallis of Woburn, Massachusetts, responded in a revealing letter to the editor:

Not unlike many other station managers, I find myself very willing to become the owner of an automobile, but, first, the excessive cost of any of the recognized standard carriages; secondly, the limited distance for which the batteries can be used without re-charging, and, thirdly, the time necessary and the troubles incidental to re-charging the batteries—compel me to await with a considerable exercise of patience the evolution of some plan that will place the same within the means of what might be called a moderately well-salaried official.

Wallis went on to suggest that a "parent battery company" arrange a system whereby car owners could lease batteries and exchange them quickly for fresh ones at every central station. It is clear that central station managers, no less than other Americans, wanted to use the automobile for touring, but this ruled out the electric. When automobiles became more affordable, most station managers would buy gasoline vehicles.

While advocates of the electric struggled with the charging problem, huge amounts of capital began flowing into the automobile industry, enabling dozens of makers of gasoline and steam cars to follow the Duryeas and bring their vehicles to market. The Winton, for example, was already being advertised in mass-circulation magazines in 1898. Also in that year the Locomobile—a steamer—began to be promoted nationally at less than $700. And Ransom E. Olds in 1900 produced 425 automobiles. The one-cyclinder curved-dash Oldsmobile, at the modest price of $650, was the first American gasoline-powered car made in nontrivial quantities. Other gasoline cars, especially French imports, cost as much as $5,000.

Though there was great demand for the first generation of automobiles, the high prices put the horseless carriage beyond the reach of working-class Americans, most of whom earned around $500–600 annually. Members of the middle class made more, as much as several thousand dollars, but for the majority an automobile purchase was out of the question. The automobile, obviously, was a luxury good for the urban elite. Such people already had carriages, carriage houses, and stables; the automobile was simply one more—albeit special—vehicle.

One reason for the automobile's high cost was small-scale production. Before the turn of the century, manufacture of automobiles in truly large numbers was just a fond hope. In most factories, even Pope's, cars were essentially put together by hand. Eventually, Henry Ford would take the lead in replacing highly skilled artisans with mechanized production lines.

In contrast to Winton, Olds, and others, Henry Ford did not rush into making horseless carriages for sale to the public; his experimental vehicle did not yet meet his standards of "simplicity, strength, reliability, lightness." Instead, he continued refining the design, making additional prototypes in the late 1890s. Meanwhile, Ford's reputation as an automobile engineer grew in the Detroit area. As the "horseless carriage fad" picked up momentum, some of Detroit's leading citizens, including mayor W. C. Maybury, began to back Ford's experiments. In August of 1899 they established the Detroit Automobile Company, and a few days later Detroit Edison lost its chief engineer, for Henry Ford was now fulltime in the automobile business.

In a rented factory on Cass Avenue in Detroit, a new Ford vehicle, a delivery truck, took shape. Progress was very slow, too slow for the fledgling firm's backers, and they forced Ford to terminate work on the truck. Next he turned to an automobile. As usual, though, Ford was reluctant to finalize the design before it met his exacting standards. Seeing other automakers take the lead in commercialization, Ford's financiers grew increasingly impatient; unable to compel him to commit the latest design to production, they pulled the plug on the Detroit Automobile Company.

Figure 19. Thomas Edison in his 1901 Baker runabout. (U.S. Department of the Interior, National Park Service, Edison National Historic Site, neg. No. 14.225/29)

Although Henry Ford's work on the gasoline car had the Wizard's blessing, Thomas Edison had already built a tricycle with an electric motor. And soon Mina would be driving a commercial electric carriage. Noting the serious shortcomings of gasoline-powered cars—they were unreliable, dirty, smelly, and dangerous to start—Edison came to believe that the electric would become the practical and popular motorized automobile (Fig. 19).

In the late 1890s, casting about for a fresh challenge after the ill-fated ore-milling venture, and seeing great interest in self-propelled vehicles, Edison seized upon the electric's apparent weak link: the storage battery. What irked Edison most about lead-acid batteries was their short lives, even when scrupulously maintained.

In the Wizard's view, improvement of the storage battery required nothing less than abandonment of the lead-acid system. Apart from the strong prejudices he had formed against lead-acid on the basis of his experiments in the 1880s, there were sound reasons for seeking a substitute. If the heavy metal lead could be replaced by a lighter element, then batteries could have a higher energy density. Abandoning acid might also be the key to simplifying maintenance and lengthening the battery's life. Thus, Edison became committed to building an alkaline battery without lead.

Beginning in mid-1898, Edison's assistants assembled and analyzed the literature on storage batteries; when the Wizard began experimenting, in the spring of 1899, he was thoroughly familiar with the prior art of the alkaline storage battery in America and Europe. As Schallenberg points out in *Bottled Energy*, before Edison, over a dozen inventors had already entered this field. Among the most important was the Swede Waldemar Jungner, who was also inspired to make alkaline storage batteries for electric vehicles.

With a staff of about a dozen chemists and engineers, Edison began to explore various alkaline battery systems. Among those he tried out was nickel-cadmium, which had been pioneered by Jungner. Although this system was promising from an electrical standpoint, the rare metal cadmium was expensive ($1.20 per pound versus 4 cents per pound for lead) and new supplies did not seem likely to turn up; other materials, such as cobalt, were dropped for similar reasons. Thus, the particular system that Edison chose to investigate beyond a preliminary stage had to show good potential for commercialization. As usual, he was thinking about production for the masses, and these thoughts shaped the direction of his experiments. Like Jungner, Edison in 1900 was experimenting with nickel and iron electrodes; soon he would announce a breakthrough (Chapter 7).

While Pope, Riker, Woods, and others plunged into the commercial production of electric vehicles between 1896 and 1899, Salom and Morris held back. They believed that the general ownership of electric cars was not feasible because of the heavy demands of battery maintenance, a lesson learned from the battery streetcars. It was obvious to Salom and Morris that upkeep of an electric car should be the exclusive preserve of specialists.

The ideal solution was to have a fleet of electric vehicles tethered to a charging station where professionals could carry out all maintenance. Vehicles would be housed and cared for there and made available for rental on a monthly or yearly lease. Salom and Morris began to put their plan into action, building their first charging station in Manhattan. When it opened for business (on March 27, 1897), however, the fleet of electric rent-a-cars had become cabs. This change of direction was perhaps related to the decreasing

Figure 20. The Hansom Cab of New York City. (*Scientific American*, 13 March 1897, p. 165)

autonomy of Salom and Morris's Electric Carriage and Wagon Company, which in 1897 was no longer recognizably distinct from the Electric Storage Battery Company (ESB). In any event, ESB took control, and Salom and Morris disappeared from public view.

That the first fleet of electric cabs had been assembled by Salom and Morris is evident from their design (Fig. 20): front-wheel drive, rear-wheel steering, and carriage by Charles Caffrey; Electrobat 2 had undergone a metamorphosis. The elegant cab, whose driver sat in the rear, seemingly above it all, had the sort of appointments that its wealthy clientele would expect, including electric lights and a speaking tube that allowed the passengers to converse with the driver. The ride was described as extremely pleasant, with an unobstructed view. Cruising at its maximum speed of 15 mph, the almost silent cab could warn of its stealthy approach with an electric bell.

The electric cab service in New York attracted the notice of streetcar magnate William C. Whitney. Believing that investments in electric cabs in particular and electric vehicles in general would be as profitable as the trolley business, Whitney, through his Metropolitan Traction Company, began purchasing stock in ESB. After a bruising takeover struggle, ESB yielded to Whitney's control late in 1898. He had grandiose plans for the electric cab business, envisioning franchises throughout the United States. In the opinion of some, Whitney had in mind nothing less than the establishment of an electric vehicle monopoly—though he denied it.

By 1899, there were about sixty vehicles in service, consisting of the original Hansom-style cabs and a newer and more luxurious brougham. Obviously, it was not economical to ground each cab after only three or four hours of service while its batteries underwent a leisurely eight-hour recharge.

To keep the cab fleet afloat, an ingenious system pioneered by the battery trolley companies had been put in place for exchanging batteries. A cab with run-down batteries was backed onto a charging platform and precisely positioned with hydraulic rams. The large compartment under the driver's seat was opened up and the battery removed as one unit by a hydraulic grappling device. An overhead traveling crane took the old battery to the charging room and brought out a fresh one, which was thrust deftly with another hydraulic ram into the cab's battery compartment. The entire operation took just a few minutes, and the cab was again racking up fares.

And the cabs were popular. In its retrospective of 1898, *Scientific American* commented that:

The horseless cab has established itself as a thoroughly practical and popular means of travel with the general public in New York, while its high speed, its ease of control, its comparative noiselessness and its convenience for use in the city in place of the two-horse carriage is rendering it increasingly popular with the wealthier classes. The electric cabs of New York are standing the test of winter work, and, during the recent snowstorms, they ran under conditions which discouraged even the horse cabs.

As the cab operation scaled up, it turned to a new supplier of electric vehicles, the Pope Manufacturing Company. In 1899 Pope and Whitney joined forces, pooling their patents and forming two new firms, the Columbia Automobile Company and the Electric Vehicle Company, to preside over their electric car empire. The Riker Company was also absorbed in 1900 by the Whitney interests. New cabs were ordered, transportation companies established, and ambitious goals announced to the public; it was even claimed that 15,000 cabs would soon be conveying American urbanites.

Whitney made another move, this one far more curious: he bought the Selden patent, the basic U.S. patent on a gasoline-powered motor vehicle. Having bet a bundle on electrics, perhaps he was hedging just a bit, or maybe he was trying to monopolize the entire automobile industry. According to Hiram Maxim, however, purchase of the Selden patent allowed the Whitney-Pope companies to commercialize, without fear of lawsuits, the gasoline cars he was designing. In any event, the Whitney interests soon signed up as licensees most manufacturers of gasoline cars.

Just as Whitney was beginning to exact royalties from gasoline vehicle makers, word began leaking out in mid-1899 that the cab business was operating in the red. Once the bad news spread, stock prices tumbled and the Lead Cab Trust—as the press called it—began to reel. *Horseless Age* published a series of scathing attacks, accusing the Whitney syndicate of being "loud-lunged, brazen-throated hucksters," intent on profiting only from "stock-jobbing schemes." Soon *Horseless Age* claimed that "the Lead Cab Trust has at last given up the ghost, electrically speaking." It was not unsavory financial dealings that shook the cab companies, however, but failing batteries.

The cabs' batteries, made by ESB, were essentially small load-leveling batteries, similar to those used in battery streetcars. Designed for stationary use, such batteries lacked sufficient mechanical durability for the rough-and-tumble world of automobile work.

The sorry state of automobile batteries was highlighted by a well-publicized report issued in early 1900 by the Automobile Club of France. Six brands of battery were tested for endurance, including one nearly identical to ESB's; despite careful maintenance by the manufacturers, none lasted more than six months. Needless to say, *Horseless Age* aired the French findings prominently, which in their view constituted proof that storage batteries were unsuitable for motor vehicles.

If the electric automobile (its battery in particular) was such a conspicuous technological failure, why did people continue to buy them? As *Motor World* pointed out in 1901, the electric was actually a fine automobile, and testimonials from satisfied owners demonstrated that electrics had their advocates. Henry Garrett, for example, enthused in *Horseless Age* in 1902 that his electric car "never breaks down, never leaves me out on the road, never refuses to pull and utterly defies the weather; it is just as reliable as a street car."

In his view, "the electric [is] the only real pleasure vehicle of them all." Dr. Frank Dowe used his electric for making calls, and found that "for physicians' use in city streets nothing can take its place." It is clear that a privately owned electric, whether used for light business or pleasure, did not exhaust batteries at the same prodigious rate as New York City cabs.

The cab operation was an extreme test of battery technology. Each battery could have undergone several charge-discharge cycles daily, and suffered mechanical maltreatment on the road at the hands of poorly paid cabbies. As a result of the battery's repeated deep cycles, the active material on the positive electrode, weakened by alternating contraction and expansion, was more easily shaken loose by a bumpy ride. It is obvious today that a battery's lifetime depended mainly on how many deep cycles it underwent as well as the amount of mechanical abuse it received, rather than its age per se. That is why a well-maintained stationary battery (as in central stations) or one seldom used could last many years.

In view of this discussion, perhaps we can provide an alternative perspective on the troubles that befell Whitney's electric cab empire. Following *Horseless Age's* line many assume that Whitney's expansion plans were put in place even as the battery failures were coming to light. Richard Schallenberg, the most sympathetic writer of modern times toward the Whitney syndicate, concludes in *Bottled Energy* that the battery problem could not have gone undetected until 1899, but must have been skillfully covered up, perhaps for several years. It is possible, I believe, to offer a more benign interpretation of the events, imperfectly known as they must remain today.

When did the Whitney people find out about the battery problems? This question cannot be answered definitively, but one can compose a scenario in which they learn the bad news in 1899. Let us recall that Salom and Morris, both with experience in battery streetcars, were in the beginning intimately involved in the cab company. Knowing that batteries could deteriorate quickly with intensive use, and perhaps believing that batteries, like people, needed adequate rest after strenuous exertion, they may have allowed batteries to sit for a time before being reinstalled in cabs. Such a regime would have required a generous oversupply of batteries, which also would have allowed adequate time for maintenance and more leisurely handling and charging. Under these conditions, cab batteries could have survived several years.

As the number of cabs expanded dramatically, especially in late 1899 and early 1900, and with Morris and Salom out of the picture, the proprietors of the Electric Vehicle Company (EVC) may have regarded a high ratio of batteries to cars as inefficient and uneconomical, especially as the growing fleet pressed upon the depot's limited space. Seeking economies, then, the Whitney operatives perhaps drastically reduced the ratio of batteries to cabs. The result would have been disastrous, as batteries began to fail after only a few months in service. Clearly, the battery problems—and knowledge of them—could have come very late.

There is one suggestive bit of evidence that fits: because of a severe shortage of space, the cab depot was moved to a new 3-acre station in late 1900 or early 1901. In describing the new station, which could control a thousand batteries (vastly greater than the number of cabs), *Scientific American* in April 1901 concluded that the new station "represents the possibilities of the practical use and application of electricity on a large scale as applied to transportation." In a 1902 article in *Electrical World*, W. H. Palmer, an official of EVC, acknowledged that in the company's crowded old station, "the batteries did not receive the attention necessary to satisfactory results, and for a time deterioration was rapid."

That the reputation of the Whitney syndicate be rehabilitated is in no way essential. It does appear, though, that the picture of a shady stock operation, paper companies, and fatally flawed technology painted so vividly by the press, especially *Horseless Age*, was an exaggeration. The batteries of that era were not irredeemably bad, though they did give out quickly under the most strenuous labors. As the testimonials show, people who employed their electric cars casually *and properly maintained the cells* apparently received satisfactory service.

While the battery travails of the New York cabs began to tarnish the reputation of the electric vehicle, the automobilists—nearly all wealthy men—were exploring the capabilities of the gasoline car. An obvious status symbol for wealthy engineers, merchants, and so on, the gasoline automobile also furnished a new technology for indulging in old activities, like racing and touring. *Horseless Age* and mass-circulation magazines, like *Literary Digest*, began to cover particularly heroic tours in horseless carriages. In these vivid and captivating accounts of man's persistence in the face of endless adversity, the touring automobilist was portrayed as a hero. Road and track races were also described in detail in the automobilist magazines, and even in *Scientific American*, which generally frowned on racing.

These well-publicized contests helped to establish the standards for automobile performance; vehicles that could not compete in track races or survive 800-mile endurance runs were no longer considered worthy by the automobilists.

In the earliest track competitions, when all entrants were quite crude and slow, electrics had held their own. For example, the first American track race, held in 1896, sported five gasoline-powered cars and two electrics. A Riker electric won all five heats. In that same year a Riker ran the mile at the then breathtaking speed of 26.8 mph. In not too many years, however, steam and gas vehicles would go faster than their electric cousins.

As for endurance runs, the electric was hobbled from the outset since it could go no more than 20–40 miles without a lengthy recharge. Not surprisingly, even the earliest American endurance runs were won by gasoline cars or steamers. By 1898 the runs had reached many hundreds of miles, pushing out the electrics entirely.

As an article in *Overland Monthly* made clear, endurance runs were an appropriate means for evaluating the "merits of the various makes of automobiles for the service which they will be called upon to render to the average user." Long-distance runs did set a realistic performance standard because most cars then were not used for business or commuting to work but for touring. It was known at that time, appropriately enough, as the pleasure vehicle, and was employed for recreational outings, on weekends to be sure, but mostly in the summer. In a debate with Riker in early 1897, Charles Duryea made a telling point: most people would not buy electrics because bicycles and even horses could take them farther in a day. The gasoline automobile, unlike the electric, represented real progress in personal transportation; and, in a gasoline car, one could challenge the train.

In the eyes of automobile enthusiasts the electric had no appeal because of its limited range. Henry Sutphen's summary dismissal of the electric car, in a 1901 article in *Outing* magazine, was typical: "Electricity is manifestly out of the question for touring purposes." Such people would not have bought an electric car even if its batteries had lasted a century. Thus, within just a few years of the commercial introduction of the horseless carriage in the United States, the electric was no longer considered by auto aficionados to be a serious car. This judgment was based almost entirely on its poor performance in the play activities of elite males—racing and, especially, touring. The voices of the male automobilist, pointing with shrillness to the manifest imperfections of the electric car, drowned out those of its satisfied—sometimes female—owners.

|7|

THE WIZARD COMES
TO THE RESCUE

On the basis of thousands of experiments, Edison was confident that he had solved the storage battery problem. The nickel-iron alkaline battery, he believed, could be the salvation of the electric automobile.

Because the materials that went into the new battery were relatively inexpensive, its commercial prospects seemed bright. With capital from Herman E. Dick, a new firm—the Edison Storage Battery Company—was organized on February 1, 1901, and incorporated a few months later. Edison and his team could now develop the nickel-iron battery in earnest.

Within weeks of the new company's founding, the Wizard was back to his old tricks, publicizing successes in the laboratory and promising that a near-miraculous product was imminent. In an interview in the *New York Sun* on May 23, Edison exulted that the nickel-iron battery's energy density was more than twice that of the lead-acid battery, and it could be charged in half the time. The following year Edison authored an article in *North American Review,* in which he took credit for nothing less than "The final perfection of the storage battery." Field tests of the new battery had in fact produced encouraging results:

Twenty-one cells made in the factories, weighing 332 pounds, were placed in a Baker automobile, the total weight with two men in the vehicle being 1,075 pounds. The vehicle made a run, on one charge, of sixty-two miles over country roads, containing many grades, some as steep as twelve feet in a hundred. At the end of this run the vehicle was making eighty-three per cent of the original speed. The average speed over the entire distance was 11.2 miles per hour. On a comparatively level country road a little heavy from a recent rain, the same vehicle on one charge came to a stop at the eighty-fifth mile.

These were impressive numbers for an electric automobile, an apparent doubling of its range. Ever the optimist, Edison prophesied that an electric automobile could perhaps be sold for around $700 and up, bringing it "within the reach of the man of moderate means."

Despite the generally favorable press, particularly in scientific and engineering journals, some magazines were ridiculing Edison for promising the impossible. R. G. Betts in *Outing* poked fun at "one of the world's most renowned wizards" who has asserted the need for "a featherweight and inexhaustible battery, or one which may, by the twist of a wrist or the pass of a hand, draw power, and be recharged from the skies or the atmosphere or the whatnot, and lo! all problems are solved! The ideal automobile is at hand." A less irreverent assessment appeared in *Overland Monthly:* "Edison is reported as saying that he has invented a battery. . . . which will revolutionize automobiling, but little faith is placed by automobilists in the statement." Indeed, *Motor World* in 1901 and 1902 mercilessly pummeled the Old Man.

To insure that the new battery could withstand the rigors of automobile travel, Edison subjected prototypes to numerous abuses. In the laboratory, machines jolted the cells up and down, 24 hours a day; and test automobiles were sent thousands of miles over bumpy back roads. Packages of the batteries were also dropped out of second- and third-floor windows, often to the amazement of onlookers. These tests convinced Edison that the nickel-iron battery was nearly indestructible. In early 1903, Edison proclaimed the battery finished, and exhibited it at the New York Automobile Show.

Edison was not alone in working on better batteries in the new century. From 1901 to 1909, Edison and ESB were in a grueling race to create storage batteries that could propel the electric vehicle to a place of prominence in American life.

To retain its leadership of the American battery industry and doubtless to recoup lost good will, ESB embarked upon a conscientious effort to develop more durable lead-acid batteries. Early in 1900 ESB brought out the first Exide battery. Its electrodes were specially shaped to hold the active materials tightly; as added insurance, perforated rubber sheets were secured around the positives. This first Exide, according to Richard Schallenberg, broke little new ground in battery design, but was credible as a stop-gap measure.

By the close of 1901 at least nine brands of improved lead-acid batteries were being sold for electrics. The immediate problem facing the industry was to convince people that the new batteries could last a decent interval. The earliest data on battery performance under realistic conditions of use were supplied by none other than the New York Electric Vehicle Transportation Company, subsidiary of EVC—the very same firm whose vicious epitaph had been penned by *Horseless Age*. But EVC was far from moribund in the new century.

Even though sales of stock in the New York cab operation had been below expectations (only $2,355,100 had been raised), by mid-1901 EVC had built a new central station, established three substations, and added an outpost in Buffalo. The new station, using scaled-up hydraulic technology, was said by *Scientific American* to be the largest in the world; it could charge 600 batteries at once, and business was brisk. In addition, EVC had equipped the Fifth Avenue stage line with electric buses and put in 18 miles of new routes. The company was aggressively expanding and, under the Columbia brand, still making electric cars. It was not yet profitable, however, nor were all of its enterprises thriving. The New England Electric Vehicle and Transportation Company, for example, had to be dissolved in mid-1901. Complaining that its hundred cabs were disadvantaged by Chicago's bad roads and hobbled by a strike, the Illinois Electric Vehicle Company in 1901 also expired.

The EVC began selling gasoline vehicles in 1901. This move reflected the realization that, while electrics might yet have a bright future, gasoline vehicles were already a big growth industry. A firm with as much expertise in automobile manufacturing as EVC could not afford merely to sit back and watch other firms profit from the boom.

Not surprisingly, the first Columbia gasoline runabout, the Mark VIII, resembled its electric cousin; both, after all, had been designed by Hiram P. Maxim and William Hooker Atwood. In a fair turnabout, the style of Columbia's new electric "tonneau" model of 1901 mimicked gasoline cars. Depending on the seat configuration, it could hold four to six people. The battery, claimed to allow a 40-mile radius, was distributed in compartments both at the front and rear to provide a better weight balance, an arrangement that would become standard in electric cars. San Francisco's fire department ordered a Columbia tonneau with a red headlamp and an 11-inch gong.

In 1902 EVC heavily publicized some good news about the batteries in its cabs. Data from over 300 vehicles left no doubt about the practicality of the improved lead-acid cells. Not only did the average mileage reach 28.5 to 42.7

per charge, but maintenance requirements had been greatly reduced. Batteries were also lasting longer. For example, of the seventy-five Exide batteries that had been put into service about a year earlier, only thirteen had to be replaced; the average mileage on the sixty-two still-functioning batteries was 3,742. Some Chloride-Manchester batteries had already served for 5,000–8,000 miles. Without question, the new batteries could perform well even under the most demanding conditions. As a result, the electric vehicle, according to EVC's Palmer, "has been developed to the point where, in reliability, radius of action and operating costs, it meets all the requirements necessary to commercial success."

Hayden Eames, now employed by Westinghouse, summed up the battery situation in a talk to the Automobile Club of America in New York in January of 1903: "The technical and mechanical problems of the storage battery have been so overcome that it is wholly practicable; the difficulty now in the way of their introduction is the misapprehension of those who should be purchasers." However, in a telling response to a question, Eames remarked that "The Edison battery in its present form costs a great deal more than others, and even if it is better—which I very seriously doubt—there is nothing revolutionary about it."

Regardless of improvements in storage batteries, there would still be people calling for better batteries on the basis not of practical considerations but of abstract calculations. For example, a good lead-acid battery of 1903 contained enough potential energy to raise itself 5.75 miles. Impressive as that seems, it pales next to the 2,000 miles yielded by the potential energy in a lump of coal. Although only 5 percent of the coal's energy would be available to power a vehicle, the difference in energy density was still substantial, about 20 to 1. Such numbers loomed large to some engineers, giving rise to what I call the "better battery bugaboo." These technical people insisted, despite the evidence around them of successful electric vehicles, economical to operate, that battery design needed a breakthrough. According to this view, not until a much better battery was available could the electric claim its rightful place among transportation technologies.

Ironically, Thomas Edison's incessant attacks on lead-acid batteries did much to perpetuate the "better battery bugaboo." How practical could the electric automobile be, people must have wondered, if—as Edison insisted —its battery was worthless? On the other hand, with the Wizard hard at work on a better battery, hopes were raised that the electric car's ills might be remedied soon. Confused about batteries and entranced by touring, Americans in the first years of the twentieth century turned decisively to gasoline cars.

Makers of gasoline cars could scarcely keep up with demand for their steadily improving product. Attracted by a seemingly limitless market, many new firms joined the fray, but like Ford's Detroit Automobile Company, most were short-lived. Henry Ford, however, was able to rebound after the demise of his first company because some early backers continued to furnish support in his time of great uncertainty. With modest funds he immediately resumed work on the automobile.

Suddenly, though, Ford changed direction: he would join Alexander Winton and others in the quest for speed. Regarding Ford's decision to build a race car, Sidney Olson has observed that "A racing car meant perfect ignition, combustion, steering, endurance, cooling, power, and more endurance and reliability in all parts, all tested under the excruciating conditions of all out speed." Racing was clearly a crucible for better design, as even *Scientific American* acknowledged, but it was more than that. Because the race was a public display of technological virtuosity, Ford felt that builders of successful racers would have an edge in attracting financiers for their less visible automobile ventures.

Through much of 1901 Ford and his assistants toiled on the racer, and by autumn trials were underway. The night before Detroit hosted its first major auto race Ford declared the racer done. More than 8,000 spectators in fall finery gathered at Grosse Pointe to take part in this important social event. The occasion was marred by dull preliminaries, in one case a heat of electric cars uneventfully cruising the 1-mile track at around 15 mph. To rouse the crowd before the main event, Alexander Winton of Cleveland put on a demonstration of speed, covering 3 miles in less than four minutes.

For the 10-mile main event, the number of contestants had dwindled; it was Ford against the experienced Winton. Ford had never raced before, and was wary around the turns, slowly losing ground. But in the sixth lap Winton's engine began to falter and belch smoke; Ford took the lead and the crowd went wild. Michigan's native son crossed the finish line unopposed, and for his efforts gained a crystal punch bowl. It was a glorious victory for Ford and for Detroit.

Almost immediately after the race, Ford's backers regrouped and, on November 30, 1901, formed the Henry Ford Company. Bitten by the racing bug, Ford wanted the new company to build more powerful machines; his backers, however, desired to sell expensive automobiles. Four months after its founding, the Henry Ford Company foundered. The ever-impatient capitalists moved their support to a more compliant Henry Leland who, in that same Cass Avenue building where Ford had toiled on truck and racer, created the first Cadillac.

Because of Ford's renown, he was able to cobble together the wherewithal to continue building better racers. In 1902 he assembled the 999, a monstrosity that looked to be all engine, and four cylinders to boot. Afraid to race the 999 himself, Ford enlisted the services of bike racer and daredevil Barney Oldfield who, it was said, would try anything once (Fig. 21). On October 25, 1902, Barney Oldfield drove the 999 in the 5-mile race for the Diamond Trophy. Against Winton and three others he achieved victory in 5:28, setting a new American speed record.

Americans were also setting speed records in electric racers. Before leaving EVC in late 1901, A. L. Riker gave racing with electrics a final fling. The company prepared a special machine, designed by Riker himself, that

Figure 21. The 999 racer. (From the collections of Henry Ford Museum & Greenfield Village, neg. 833.2908-1)

weighed only 1,850 lbs complete. As *Scientific American* put it, the racer was "an electromobile reduced to its lowest terms, a wheeled frame and a battery," the latter consisting of sixty light-weight cells. Of course it also had motors, two of them at 2 hp each, that in spurts could exceed 7 hp. Sponsored by the Long Island Automobile Club, the race took place on a section of Coney Island Boulevard. Riker drove the electric racer over the 1-mile course, completing the run in 1:03, a world's record for an electric. His run would have been faster had he spent less time dodging pedestrians who, lulled into complacency by the quiet electric, had strolled onto the track. Creating a "frightful din," gasoline cars announced their presence long in advance, and did better. Several gasoline cars also set records, breaking the minute mile. Soon Riker would be racing gasoline cars.

The most ambitious electric racer of this era was built by the Baker Motor Vehicle Company of Cleveland. Dubbed the "road torpedo," the Baker racer was America's first completely aerodynamic car (Fig. 22). To save weight, the wood-frame body had an oil-cloth covering; the car and batteries tipped the scales at around 3,000 lbs. With Walter C. Baker driving and C. E. Denzler on board to report the tachometer readings, the revolutionary racer was set to compete in a speed contest on Staten Island on May 31, 1902. Anticipation for this event was high, for rumors had it that the torpedo in early tests had exceeded 70 mph. Many important personages in the electrical industry were assembled that Saturday afternoon for the assault on the speed record, including Thomas Edison, who had been using a Baker runabout in testing his new batteries (see Fig. 19).

Figure 22. The Baker "road torpedo." (*Scientific American*, 14 June 1902, p. 419)

Baker had built the torpedo (for $20,000) with the intention of not merely breaking the speed record but also of convincing others that, by reducing wind resistance and mechanical friction, an electric vehicle could achieve high speed with minimal horsepower. Although Baker's design concepts had considerable merit, the racer regrettably did not turn out to be the ideal showcase for his ingenuity. After gradually accelerating, the torpedo topped 70 miles an hour as anticipated, but stumbled on streetcar tracks and went out of control to the right. Baker overcompensated, and "Like a flash she swung away to the left and bored a bloody path into the shrieking crowd, dealing death and terror even before anyone could realize what had occurred." The carnage left one onlooker dead, another dying, and six injured. Baker and Denzler, both strapped in, emerged from the wreckage largely unharmed, but were immediately arrested. The Grand Jury issued no indictment, however, and so a day later they were set free. Street racing did not fare as well after the tragedy: the Automobile Club of America sanctioned no more such races. Baker, by the way, continued to take part in track events with improved torpedos, and by the end of 1902 he held all the American racing records for electric vehicles but one.

Beginning in the new century, endurance and reliability runs took on added importance in demonstrating the fitness of cars to tour. Of course, in these long runs electric cars played no role. For example, in the New York-Buffalo endurance test, organized by the Automobile Club of America, eighty cars embarked on a 465-mile journey, but not one was electric. Curiously, Riker was at the wheel of a 16-hp gasoline touring car built by EVC, one of several gasoline cars entered by that company. Because of the death of President McKinley, the race was called off at Rochester after 394 miles.

In races that could be completed, gasoline and steam vehicles were doing much better. In a 1902 reliability run from New York to Boston and back, sixty-eight of the seventy-five vehicles finished in good shape. This was an enviable record, given the pathetic roads between these two important cities, scarcely more than sand or two ruts in the mud. American car makers evidently were gradually learning how to design reliability into their vehicles regardless of road conditions.

The rigors of long-distance runs also helped to hone the distinctive touring-car style, which would prevail for more than two decades. The touring car above all was an open-air vehicle that let in everything from hail and dust to the oily mist wafting back from the engine. Exposure to the elements, of course, was part of the touring mystique. Even so, enthusiasts sometimes donned goggles and special garments for protection.

The absence of electrics in endurance and reliability runs sent the unmistakable message to prospective car buyers, striving to emulate the leisure activities of the wealthy, that electrics should be shunned. That electrics could not, and probably would not, tour was acknowledged in an *Electrical World* editorial of July 1902:

[T]he lack of proper charging facilities outside of the larger cities and towns is discouraging to those who are fond of touring. Gasoline is available everywhere, and the supply can be promptly replenished, while charging a battery is always a slow job.

The editorial went on to demolish two common proposals to remedy this difficulty: sending charged batteries ahead of the touring car and creating facilities for distributing charged batteries. Neither seemed to have promise for the simple reason that "in touring the country [one] wants to have a certain liberty of action which a journey fully prearranged does not and cannot give." At the heart of touring, then, was complete freedom.

Although electrics in the new century participated little in racing and not at all in endurance runs, in other realms they sometimes came in number one. Appropriately enough it was an electric vehicle that was first to carry a car radio. Called Wireless Auto No. 1, it was built by the American De Forest Wireless Telegraph Company and contained not a receiver, but a transmitter. The curious car, with a special "glass showcase cupola" that allowed the operator to see and be seen, parked along Wall Street in New York and transmitted stock quotations to all brokers equipped with American De Forest receivers. Service began on February 7, 1903—several years before Lee De Forest invented the vacuum tube—and reportedly attracted much attention. Wireless Auto No. 1 was displayed at the St. Louis Exposition later that year (Fig. 23), its far-from-indispensable service presumably having ended.

An even more unusual electric vehicle of this period was the bus manufactured by the Fischer Motor Vehicle Company of Hoboken, New Jersey, that generated its own electricity. Under the hood, so to speak, was a 10-hp gasoline engine that turned a 5-kw dynamo. Two 5-hp electric motors usually drew their power directly from the dynamo, but in overload situations a fifty-cell battery kicked in. In one test of the bus on a snowy day, it ran a total of 54 miles and consumed 12.5 gallons of gasoline.

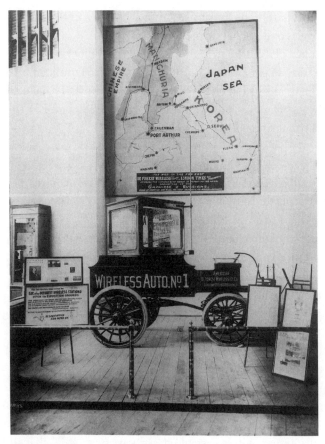

Figure 23. The first radio-equipped car. (Smithsonian Institution, neg. 90-10146)

An interesting feature of the Fischer hybrid omnibus was its manner of starting. To bring the gasoline engine to life the driver simply threw a switch that converted the dynamo—already connected by shaft to the engine—into a motor. Not until another decade passed would electric starters begin to appear in gasoline cars (Chapter 10).

Like other vehicle makers, the Fischer Company exhibited at the automobile shows, which took place annually in most large cities of the East and Midwest. The big shows—at Madison Square Garden, for example—were more than trade exhibits, for they had become gala affairs, attended by America's most wealthy (if not always most illustrious) citizens, crowding in to see the latest horseless wonders. The popular press and automobilist magazines lavished much attention on the shows, taking the offerings as barometers of technical progress and fashion; even *Electrical World* and *Scientific American* covered them in detail.

The growing momentum of the gasoline automobile was thoroughly in evidence at the 1903 show. Observers remarked that the displays of the eight electric vehicle companies were dwarfed to insignificance by the profusion of gasoline vehicles, especially the heavier touring cars, many of which had four-cyclinder engines of 25 hp or more. The electric was clearly losing visibility, outnumbered 168 to 51 by gasoline vehicles. Even so, new models of electrics were being introduced, especially lightweight runabouts and stanhopes selling for $750 to $1,000. Another model growing in popularity was the coupé, a small brougham with inside drive. Somewhat surprisingly, new manufacturers of electrics were entering the field, some focused on commercial and industrial vehicles. Among the newcomers was Studebaker, the nation's largest maker of wagons (Fig. 24).

One noteworthy new-car introduction of 1903 was the "combination surrey and tonneau" built by the Kammann Manufacturing Company, perhaps the first electric vehicle to have an aluminum body. To assist the springs in smoothing the hard ride of solid rubber tires, the car's seats were equipped with "pneumatic cushions."

Though diminished in relative numbers, the electric did inspire some respect. As *Motor World* put it, "That the electric vehicle is no passing fancy and is an art in vehicle construction which is here to stay and grow to unusual proportions is amply indicated by this year's show." Indeed, a few Americans were discovering that the electric car could be used for leisure activities in town (Fig. 25).

Back in West Orange, the Old Man and his minions were ready for real-world trials of the new nickel-iron battery. Although Edison may have wanted to move quickly into large-scale sales, fearing that lead-acid batteries might capture the vehicle market for good, the Wizard proceeded cautiously, bringing out the Type E cell only in small quantities. It may have been offered only to selected customers whose vehicles could be carefully monitored.

First sold early in 1903, Edison's Type E cell was not exactly revolutionary (as Hayden Eames had noted), for in gross features of construction it resembled Jungner's. The positive electrode consisted of a mixture of nickel oxide

Figure 24. Studebaker's first electric. (*The Motor World*, 7 August 1902, p. 540)

powder and graphite flakes (the latter to improve conductivity) placed into a grid of small pockets made of nickel-plated steel. In the grid pockets of the negative electrode went iron powder, also with graphite. Not surprisingly, in Europe the Jungner interests filed patent-infringement suits against Edison, but in court the Wizard would prevail.

The frenzy of publicity surrounding the nickel-iron battery, which Edison fed with exaggerated claims, raised expectations to a high level. Edison perhaps began to realize that even if the battery performed well, it would fall short of his promises. The battery did have virtues, such as a modestly higher

Figure 25. A herd of Buffalo Electrics roams a New York park. (*The Automobile Review and Automobile News*, 15 August 1902)

energy density than lead-acid and an immunity to rough handling. And, already it appeared to have a long life, for no chemical changes were occurring in the active material. But the nickel-iron battery also had drawbacks. For example, an Edison cell's voltage was 1.2 versus 2.0 for lead-acid. In addition, because Edison batteries took up more space for a given amount of stored power, car companies would be obliged to design their vehicles with enlarged battery compartments. Moreover, the battery that was supposed to be trouble-free suffered serious troubles if the water level was not right on the mark. Perhaps the most devastating drawback was cost: the Wizard's wares, at $15 per cell, were more than twice as expensive as a lead-acid equivalent. This, of course, profoundly jeopardized Edison's vision of a $700 electric car that all families could afford.

More ominously still, in April 1903 *Horseless Age* announced that Edison batteries were developing problems. Indeed, reports to Edison on batteries in use disclosed a litany of breakdowns, from the caustic electrolyte eating through the cases' soldered seams to cells that exploded. Even worse, some cells gradually lost capacity. As word of these difficulties spread, officials at ESB breathed a sigh of relief. And makers of gasoline automobiles no doubt gloated, for the electric car had suffered a humiliating defeat. Many Americans would conclude that even the Wizard with all his resources could not make a good battery for electric cars.

Appreciating that his battery's serious woes admitted of no immediate solutions, on December 1, 1904, Edison laid off most workers at the battery factory, leaving only a skeleton crew to assemble cells. The near-total shutdown allowed retooling of the factory and gave Edison the opportunity to concentrate, in the laboratory, on finding and fixing the problems.

It is fortunate that Edison could continue to perfect his battery without having to obtain the approval of several layers of bureaucrats. In today's large corporations, an Edison, apparently past his prime, would probably be invited to retire. After all, many years of work and countless thousands of dollars had already been invested in a project that promised no payoff. Though now in his late fifties and nearly stone deaf, Edison's boundless confidence had not waned; he believed that the battery—and electric car—could be saved. With profits from his prospering phonograph factory and film studio, he redoubled his efforts, even as a pall settled over the electric car industry.

8

A DARK AGE DESCENDS

Queen Victoria's death in 1901 ended the lengthy era that still carries her name. In the years immediately following Victoria's death, many believed that the electric car had followed suit. Greatly outnumbered by runaway sales of gasoline cars, the electric automobile had suffered dramatically reduced visibility on American streets. Ordinary Americans (especially men) were concluding that the car they wanted was gasoline, obvious winner of the motive power sweepstakes among the affluent.

Perhaps emblematic of the diminished status of the electric was the miniature car used at the 1901 Pan-American Exposition in Buffalo by Chiquita, "the little 26-inch morsel of humanity." Crafted by the Jenkins Automobile Company of Washington, D. C., this electric car was, according to *Scientific American*, "The smallest automobile ever built." The message that a cruising Chiquita silently conveyed to thousands of fair visitors was that the electric car, after all, was only a toy.

By mid-decade electrics had almost vanished from car enthusiast magazines and the annual automobile shows, and they were seldom advertised in mass-circulation magazines. The latter sometimes judged the electric car a failure, as in *Overland Monthly's* 1902 appraisal:

At present gasoline and steam are the popular and most successful machines, electricity being "almost nowhere." The last named is without doubt the most beautiful power if it could be suitably installed in the vehicle, but it cannot, and the many drawbacks to such machines to-day are the small radius of action, slow speed, weight of batteries, and cost and time taken to recharge the same.

In another article, *Overland Monthly* gave summary rankings on the basis of twenty-one "desirable points" to the three automobile types. The electric came in last. *Outing* chimed in by noting that the battle of the motive powers is now "between steam and gasolene. Electricity is merely a dignified spectator." According to *Munsey's Magazine,* in a 1903 piece on the automobile's future, "The automobile of today is practically a gasolene vehicle, and from present indications it is likely to remain so for years to come." Once at the front of the pack, the electric car had stumbled, and was bringing up the rear.

Even in the electrical industry, some persons admitted that the electric car had been a failure. Hayden Eames remarked at a 1906 meeting of electric car manufacturers that "The electric vehicle business has, up to date, been a rather sickly baby." Looking back on this period, R. M. Lloyd in 1914 referred to it as the electric car's "dark age." In the history of Western civilization, the Dark Ages was a time of significant technological innovation that laid a foundation for the future. And so it was, too, in the dark age of the electric car. Edison and ESB were improving batteries and car makers were perfecting more energy-efficient drive trains. In not too many years, people in the electrical industry would come to believe that the electric car, with new batteries and new running gear, was poised for a renaissance. Significantly, when electrics revived, they challenged not the gasoline car but the city horse.

After the triumph of the 999, Henry Ford's fortunes took a turn for the better. As he had hoped, the 999's fame led to several business offers, among which he had the luxury of choosing. Ford retired from racing and selected as a partner the aggressive and ambitious Alex Malcomson, Detroit's coal baron. Over much of the next year, Ford labored on a new passenger car, the first Model A, while Malcomson button-holed friends, relatives, and business acquaintances, cajoling them to invest in Henry Ford's automobile. From time to time, Ford's work was interrupted as he dutifully showed potential investors his handiwork. By the spring of 1903, the Model A had begun to attract attention on its merits, which for the time were considerable. Wary investors, their arms twisted by Malcomson, began to plunge.

It all came together on June 13, 1903, in Malcomson's office. A dozen stockholders hammered out an agreement establishing the Ford Motor Company, with Ford and Malcomson owning 51 percent of the firm—though neither put in cash. The company's total capital of $150,000 was meager, inadequate even then to build a full-fledged automobile factory, so Ford farmed out much of the Model A's manufacture to the Dodge brothers, owners of Detroit's most modern machine works (who were not yet producing their own car). The Ford Motor Company in its tiny factory simply put the pieces together. But the Model A was unmistakably a Ford, built to Henry's impeccable specifications. It was a moderately priced car—$750, or $850 with a tonneau—not yet the cheapest, but an excellent value in comparison to its competitors, most of which were heavy and unreliable touring cars that cost between $1,200 and $5,000 or inexpensive buggies with a one-cylinder engine that performed poorly.

The treasurer of the Ford Motor Company was James Couzens, a brilliant financial strategist, who had been borrowed from the Malcomson organization. Like others connected with Malcomson, he became a true believer in the Ford enterprise. With $100 from his sister, $400 in life savings, a $1,000 bonus from Malcomson, and $1,500 borrowed at high interest from a bank, James Couzens bought twenty-five shares. (In 1919, when Ford bought out the other investors, each original share of the Ford Motor Company would be worth a cool quarter million dollars.) One of Couzens's contributions was to rein in Henry's constant tinkering, forcing him to freeze a design for production. More importantly, he put together—almost instantly—a national sales organization. In not too many years, seemingly every small town in America would have a Ford dealership.

The company's first car, the Model A, was a light (1,250 lbs) two-seater, vaguely reminiscent of the tiller-steered Olds. Unlike the Olds, however, the Model A had a two-cylinder engine that developed 8 hp and propelled the almost dainty vehicle at 30 mph; and the Model A had a steering wheel—on the right. Advertised in mass-circulation magazines as the Fordmobile, the first Model A was sold to Dr. E. Pfennig, a Chicago physician, on July 15, 1903. This order came in none too soon, as the bank balance of the Ford Motor Company had dipped below $300. From then on in the American automobile industry, the Ford name was synonymous with success. In its first year, the company sold 1,708 Model As and took in over $1 million.

During that same summer of 1903, when the Wright brothers flew their powered craft at Kitty Hawk and Ford turned 40, the American automobile was gaining new respect. Three transcontinental crossings, in a Winton, Packard, and Oldsmobile, had shown that cars made in the United States could survive on the most wretched roads. Significantly, in its review of progress during 1903, *Scientific American* announced that U.S. car makers were in the "front rank," building cars fully as good "in design, workmanship, and beauty [as] . . . the very best of foreign makes." Since 1901 the United States had become a net exporter of automobiles.

To meet the growing demand, foreign and domestic, for U.S. gasoline cars, manufacturers were scaling up for larger production runs. In 1903 the Winton factory produced 700 cars; its 20-hp touring car, advertised as "Going Like the Wind," sold for $2,500. Even more impressive was the Olds output of 4,000 vehicles, still selling for $650.

As manufacturers of gasoline automobiles made halting progress toward mass production, the Electric Vehicle Company began to sue firms that had not taken out licenses under its Selden patent. Many entrepreneurs, including Winton and Olds, anxious to proceed without a legal cloud hovering over their enterprises, settled quickly and agreed to pay a royalty of 1.25 percent on each car. Undoubtedly, automobilists and automakers chafed at being taxed by the "Lead Cab Trust."

For whatever reason, Ford was not moved to obtain a license from the Electric Vehicle Company, and swiftly the fledgling firm was sued. As an important test case, the suit would drag on in the courts for many years; in the meantime, the Ford position was belligerent, as a 1904 advertisement in *Literary Digest* made clear:

The FORD has sounded the death knell of the Trust with its attempt to make a monopoly of the motor car industry and to charge exorbitant prices for inferior cars. . . . *The lowest price tonneau car with a double opposed motor sold by the trust is* $1,500.00. *The Ford saves you* $600.00.

We agree to assume all responsibility in any action the *Trust* may take regarding alleged infringement of the Selden Patent to prevent you from buying the FORD.

In this era of muck-raking and trust-busting, Ford's assault on the Electric Vehicle Company and Selden patent played well to the American public.

In court, however, Ford found the early going rough. To help make his case, Selden appeared with a working vehicle, of recent manufacture, but built largely in accord with the original patent specifications. Although the automobile did run, its ignition was of modern design. The Ford camp also had a busy workshop. One of the exhibits assembled by Ford craftsmen was a gasoline-powered vehicle based on pre-1876 technology, including a

Lenoirlike engine. It too ran. The U.S. Court of Appeals in 1911 decided that while Selden's patent was valid, Ford, using an Otto-type engine on his products, had not infringed it. And so vanished the short-lived automobile trust that had besmirched the reputation of the electric vehicle industry.

The Ford Motor Company brought out its 1905 automobiles in a range of body styles. The Model B was a $2,000 touring car, fancy by Ford standards, that had a four-cylinder engine. Also offered were Models C ($950), F ($1,200), and the $850 Doctors' Car. In the following year came the highly successful Model N at $600. Surprisingly, in 1907 Ford was selling the six-cylinder Model K, a 40-hp touring car, for $2,800. At this time, the average price of an American touring car, still bought mainly by affluent men, was more than $2,000.

Henry in 1907 was earning an annual salary of $36,000, nearly a king's ransom, so he and Clara began to indulge somewhat in luxury goods. One of their most noteworthy purchases was an electric car for Clara. Here, at last, was a personal transport technology, suitable for women, that could replace the trolley.

A prospective buyer of electrics in mid-decade was ill-advised to visit the auto shows, when the electric car was at its nadir of visiblity. In the 1905 show in Madison Square Garden, for example, fewer than thirty electrics were displayed by six manufacturers; and several of the latter, including Columbia, Studebaker, and Pope-Waverley, also exhibited gasoline cars. *Electrical World* noted that some progress was being made in vehicle design by "those steadfast souls who, battling against great odds, have carried the electric vehicle industry a step farther on the road toward its ultimate success," but the lack of standardization was deplored. Even at this late date, three styles of charging plug could be found among the vehicles.

Electrical World also carped that car designs were pretty much the same as in previous years, an invidious comparison with rapid changes in gasoline vehicles. Pricewise, electrics in 1905 and 1906 ran the gamut from $900 for a light runabout to several thousand dollars for a brougham. Not all manufacturers, of course, offered the complete range of models and prices. Runabouts and stanhopes (Fig. 26) were the most popular, but even they found few buyers. Fewer than 1,200 electrics were bought in 1905, less than 10 percent of all automobile sales. Not surprisingly, from 1903 to 1906 more firms dropped out of the electric car business than entered it.

One bright spot in the shows was commercial electric vehicles, which were

Figure 26. Pope-Waverley Model 27, stanhope. (*Harper's Weekly*, 8 July 1905)

beginning to attract attention because of their reliability. Some electric trucks were also capable of remarkable performance. In picking up or delivering its load, one model could climb 12-inch curbs, and the front and rear wheels steered independently, allowing it to turn on a dime and park virtually anywhere. These feats were facilitated by four-wheel drive, with each hub containing its own electric motor. The Vehicle Equipment Company of Long Island, though still making pleasure vehicles, enjoyed a prosperous business selling over 100 kinds of electric trucks and buses, with capacities ranging

Figure 27. An electric tour bus. (Collection of the author)

from 1 to 6 tons. According to *Scientific American,* "In the business and commercial vehicle line, for city work, the electric still reigns supreme" (Fig. 27).

In the three important New York shows of 1906, electric cars were scarce. Many manufacturers had declined to exhibit, perhaps believing that an out-of-the-way display was not worth the trouble and expense. Yet, the failure of car makers to show for the shows tacitly reinforced the perception held by auto aficionados, and perhaps much of the public, that the electric pleasure vehicle was no longer a factor in the industry.

Although the future of the electric automobile appeared bleak, Edison toiled to remedy the flaws in the nickel-iron battery. Solutions to some problems had actually been found before the end of 1904. To tackle the remaining problems—leaky cans and gradual loss of capacity—Edison and eighteen assistants began a new series of experiments. The leakage problems were solved within a few months; cans would have to be welded not soldered, and a new machine was installed for that purpose. The fall in capacity was caused by a balky positive electrode and proved more stubborn.

A common picture of the Wizard at this time shows him busy at a bench in

Figure 28. Thomas Edison toils at a laboratory bench. (U.S. Department of the Interior, National Park Service, Edison National Historic Site, 14.720/17, neg. 6397)

his chemistry laboratory (Fig. 28); in fact, Edison did many battery experiments himself. Preoccupied in the laboratory during early 1905, the Old Man was unable to take a winter vacation in Florida; however, he vowed in a letter to his friend, L. C. Weir, president of Adams Express Company, "I am bound to punish some touring machine next summer to make up."

The Adams Express Company was the largest user of the Edison battery, with eighteen delivery trucks so equipped in New York and Washington. A total of 144 vehicles were on the road with Edison batteries in early 1905, including those owned by Elihu Thomson and Andrew Carnegie (the latter had four electrics, including an opera bus). To keep these customers happy and to obtain crucial information on the state of the batteries, Edison designated an assistant, William G. Bee, as the official battery inspector. "Billy" Bee traveled from town to town, checking on the condition of batteries, responding to customer complaints, and effecting repairs. Defective cells were fixed or replaced at company expense or for a nominal rebuilding charge.

Bee's reports to Edison indicated that many problems were caused by improper battery installation or slipshod maintenance. Fortunately, most malfunctioning cells could be easily revived.

The Edison-equipped vehicles were giving surprisingly good service most of the time; business customers were especially pleased with the battery as well as the energy that Billy Bee and the Edison Storage Battery Company put into keeping them in working order. The big commercial customers, like Adams Express and Tiffany & Company, were eager to add Edison-equipped trucks to their fleets. Edison, however, did not want to sell more of the old batteries, claiming that he lost money on them.

By the middle of 1905, Edison had obtained excellent results on endurance tests of cells containing a redesigned positive electrode. He wrote with the good news to H. F. Parshall, a consulting engineer in London who had been helping to diagnose the battery's maladies: "I am certain now that the cell will remain constant for years & the mechanical part will be so perfect as to leave nothing to be desired." Sure that he had rooted out the battery's "bugs," Edison expected to scale up production by the end of the year.

Instead of commercializing the battery, however, Edison kept on experimenting with new positive electrodes, selling only a couple hundred batteries to Weir (and a few privileged others) in 1906. He also erected a new building for battery manufacture. Despite mounting pressure from customers and business associates, Edison refused to release the battery until it satisfied him; no doubt he felt compelled to create a breakthrough battery that could decisively still his critics and vanquish lead-acid. Edison wanted a battery that truly befit a Wizard.

If the electric car were ever to reach beyond small numbers of America's upper crust, it would need a vastly improved infrastructure for charging batteries at home and on the road. In the dark decade, however, electrification continued to spread slowly and unevenly, with mostly factories and businesses coming on line.

New factories were able to exploit the energy economies made possible by the endless variety of machines with built-in motors that were finally coming on the market. Although many installations continued to rely on tons of shafts and miles of belts, including the machine shop at Edison's West Orange laboratory, the adoption of the electric motor by American factories and mines had begun in earnest. Used steam engines glutted the market.

Electrification of the commercial world was also proceeding apace. Because many stores and businesses had power by 1910, they could take advantage of the flood of new electrical products. State-of-the-art barber shops and hairdressing parlors sported electric shoe polishers, nail polishers, and hair dryers. No bakery worth its salt could thrive without electric dough kneaders, biscuit cutters, and fans. And the well-appointed livery stable had its carriage elevators and electric horse clippers. The electrical conveniences worked reasonably well; but, above all, they conspicuously marked a business's commitment to modernity.

Gas lighting with its ever-present fire danger was on the retreat in industry, but in homes and many businesses gas (and kerosene) still reigned supreme. In some areas, like New York, gas producers had consolidated and lowered prices to stanch the flow of customers to electricity. What is more, the development of the Welsbach mantle, which efficiently produced a much brighter, whiter gas light, gave new energy to the gas industry just when it appeared that electricity might make a clean sweep in the lighting field. The rapid spread of the Welsbach mantle after 1890 was the main reason that gas companies were able to lower their rates, which for a comparable amount of light remained cheaper than electricity.

The electrical industry was not sitting still either. By the turn of the century new steam turbine generators, huge and efficient, were poised to take over power stations. As Thomas Hughes points out in *Networks of Power*, these humming behemoths provided such a jump in generating capacity that, when first installed in a central station, they were an enormous supply in search of demand. The trend toward larger generators and higher-capacity plants went hand-in-hand with the beginnings of consolidation. Small and relatively inefficient central stations were joined into larger regional operating companies (which detractors called electrical trusts). The greater efficiencies occasioned by larger power plants and larger systems meant that rates could drop, but not without the addition of new customers and new loads.

Other technological innovations also created problems and opportunities for the industry. Edison carbon-filament lamps had remained the standard into the new century, but inventors, especially in Europe, were working on improvements. By 1905 experiments with tantalum, osmium, and tungsten filaments had shown great promise. Tungsten quickly won out, and by the end of 1908 in the United States tens of thousands of tungsten lamps were being produced daily.

The new bulbs at first caused concern among station managers because, in giving off as much light as the old bulbs, they consumed less than half the power. *Electrical World* outlined the dilemma posed by high-efficiency bulbs. The metallic filament lamp, it stated in 1905, "carries with it a problem of the gravest import in connection with central station finances." The projected economies were so great that customers could be expected to replace company-supplied carbon filament bulbs at their own expense. The obvious solution—raise rates—would entail a messy battle "with all the risk from governmental ownership or control that such a contest would imply." Another solution would have to be found.

As the specter of better bulbs loomed on the near horizon, central stations did forge effective strategies to maintain income from lighting. To keep the lighting current flowing at the same level and to keep pace with the Welsbach mantle, central stations began to promote higher standards of illumination. Where a 16-candle-power bulb formerly had been deemed adequate for lighting a room, now it was claimed that only a 40- or 60-candle-power lamp would do. Consequently, some central stations at first introduced just the larger wattage tungsten bulbs. Another strategy was to push the new bulbs only to homeowners with gas lighting. The hope was that new users of electricity would offset revenues lost when the old customers finally converted to tungsten lamps. Tungsten bulbs did prove to be a decisive weapon in the tug-of-war with the gas companies.

Surprisingly, another threat to central station revenue was proposed legislation for daylight saving. The motivation behind these semi-annual clock adjustments was to reduce the amount of time that electric lighting was needed in the summer. *Electrical World* monitored these moves, but did not counsel central stations to oppose them; rather, it suggested that new summer loads be sought, such as refrigeration.

At night, electric advertising continued to grow in importance as a load. New signs—big signs—went up in downtowns, hawking everything from pickles to operas. One of the more impressive was erected in Kansas City to advertise the Owl cigar. In addition to a rocket that periodically shot up and burst into eighty colored lights, the sign boasted an owl 20 feet high whose green eyes constantly blinked. The words "Owl Cigar" flashed on and off as did "Now 5 Cents." People who could not afford a 5-cent cigar could at least enjoy the free electrical pyrotechnics.

Although most electric companies were profitable, the rate structure was a confusing mess. One of the major clarifying concepts to emerge early was "load factor," the percentage of total capacity in use at a given time. The load factor, it was found, not only varied seasonally but daily, with the peak in early evening and a deep valley in the middle of the night. The peak was of special concern because it determined the *minimum* generating capacity required to carry the station's load. As the peak increased, stations had to add new generators or banks of costly batteries. With generators getting larger and more expensive, the addition of capacity to meet the rising peak required ever more capital. At the same time, each increment of new capacity dropped the average load factor, sometimes below 30 or 40 percent. Needless to say, underutilized capacity was the bane of central station managers.

Gradually a consensus emerged that a station's profits could be increased by load-leveling, the addition of new kinds of loads during off-peak hours. Beginning in the late 1890s, for example, the motor load in factories was diligently cultivated because its peak differed from that of lighting. As more and more factories and businesses came on line, central stations relentlessly expanded, seeking new markets.

To encourage more business and, especially, to wean hotels, factories, and trolley companies away from their own isolated plants, central stations deeply discounted rates to huge and off-peak consumers of current. The fairness of discrimination in rates was debated, but strong dissenters were few; after all, the price of electricity to every category of consumer dropped almost continuously during the first decades of the twentieth century. Democratization of electricity was moving slowly, a by-product of decisions made for other reasons, but it was moving.

An obvious load builder and at times load leveler was the home appliance. Saddled with a reputation for being expensive and unreliable, electric appliances had languished. New designs were available in the new century, however, and central stations began to show fervent interest in them at the height of the better bulb scare. With electric rates now much lower than in the 1890s (ordinary prices in 1907 were 6 cents to 15 cents per kwh), the use of appliances was not egregiously expensive for a well-off family. Heating appliances, especially irons, were heavy users of power, and so central stations regarded them with delight.

Numerous promotions were devised to exploit these revenue possibilities. Perhaps predictably, electric appliances were claimed to be convenient, hygienic, and modern. Many central stations began to sell appliances, often at a discount; a few even gave their customers electric irons, quietly confident that a homemaker who tried one would never give it up.

One of the most ambitious appliance promotions was launched in 1908 by the Union Electric Light & Power Company of St. Louis. Several dozen electric appliances were available for short loans, the prospective customer merely choosing from a list that included total price and a payment plan. Items selected were "sent to the home of a customer accompanied by one of the company's lady demonstrators, who explains its use and advantages."

Firms proliferated new electric products for the home. Among the more interesting was the "vacuum massage vibrator and shampoo comb" made by Harvey & Hill, New York. The comb attachment was connected to a blower that allowed air (or shampoo) to emerge from holes in the teeth. The device also came with cups of three different sizes appropriate for applying suction to different parts of the body. Electric massage was the main purpose of the American Vibrator (Fig. 29), which claimed to develop "both neck and bust."

Another electric device, long neglected by central stations, at once began to appear more attractive as a load builder and load leveler. This, of course, was the electric vehicle, whose batteries could be recharged between midnight and 6 a.m. when there was little other call on current. Again in 1905 *Electrical World* flayed managers for overlooking electrics and urged their purchase for work around the station; some did follow the advice. New York Edison took the lead with more than fifty electrics by 1906, including runabouts, delivery wagons, and large trucks.

Getting a charge outside the home was still difficult in the first years of the twentieth century, but it gradually became easier, at least for people of means. By the end of the electric's dark decade, a respectable number of central stations had charging facilities and offered other services to electric car owners. A noteworthy case in point was the Rockford Edison Company. In this Illinois city of more than 30,000 people, conditions for the spread of the electric car were favorable: roads around Rockford were good and not too hilly, and homes still had DC power. In 1904, Rockford boasted 24 electric automobiles. To encourage further purchases, Rockford Edison offered a discount rate for off-peak battery charging (6 cents per kwh), which brought in monthly revenues of about $5 per car. In addition, the company charged cars at its station, furnished free inspections and routine maintenance, and of-

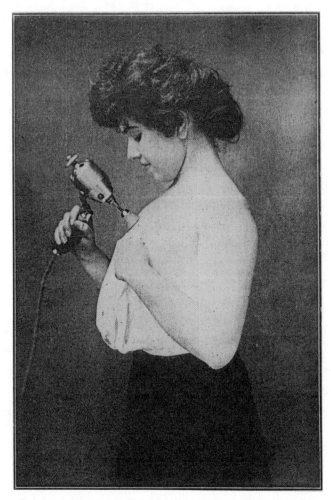

Figure 29. The American Vibrator. (*Electrical World*, 1906, vol. 47, p. 141)

fered a repair service. In short, Rockford Edison had taken the pains out of electric car ownership, and this translated directly into new car sales. With the blessings of Rockford Edison, two of its employees had become agents for Pope-Waverley automobiles. Early in 1906 the number of electrics in town had jumped to 60, more than one third of all automobiles. By then, the station's annual income from charging batteries alone was around $3,500. A year later the town had 82 electrics, and in 1909 there were 130.

In St. Louis, Union Light & Power Company established an electric car garage to foster the purchase of electrics. A monthly charge from $30 to $45, depending on the vehicle's weight, was levied for looking after electrics. This fee included battery charging, washing, and routine maintenance, but pick-up and delivery cost an extra $5. The garage had its intended effect: from 1906 to 1909 the number of electric cars in St. Louis soared from 17 to 300.

These success stories were highlighted in the pages of *Electrical World*. The intended message was quite clear: central stations could stimulate sales of electric cars that, in turn, would consume off-peak power. Apparently, the interests of the electric car industry and the power providers were one.

In a paper read at a meeting of the National Electric Light Association in 1907, Herbert H. Rice pointed out that "an electric carriage will use more energy in a day than most signs in a week, a fan in a month, a hot water bag in a year, or a curling iron in five years, and yet many dollars are spent in solicit-ing for and advertising the latter things and with few exceptions scarcely a cent is spent for the electric vehicle." He went on to observe that central sta-tions could expect a monthly income of about $6 for private automobiles, assuming a rate of 5 to 10 cents per kwh for charging. Other estimates of monthly earnings, based on actual garage experience, indeed ranged from $4 to $8. In mid-1907, *Electrical World* predicted "that the time will come—and not very far in the future—when electric automobiles will furnish one of the most important sources of income to the electric lighting companies."

In another article promoting the sale of electricity for charging vehicle bat-teries, *Electrical World* observed that some central stations could still make a profit on this off-peak load by charging only 2 to 4 cents per kwh. "Why not quote favorable rates and encourage the sale of electricity," counseled *Electri-cal World*, "when you can spare it at almost no additional cost?" This latter point was telling. Then, as now, the costs of generating off-peak power are so low—sometimes less than a cent per kwh—that it could be sold at deep dis-counts. In few central stations, however, did rates dip to the 2 to 3 cent level for home charging of batteries. Doubtless station managers had concluded, probably correctly, that the well-to-do owners of electrics could easily pay the higher rates.

Station managers may have shared Edison's vision of universal electric lighting, but economic realities still dictated a go-slow policy in the wiring of older homes. No central station in 1905 was about to launch a drive to electri-fy all working- and middle-class neighborhoods. Lighting of modest homes was thought to be unprofitable because such customers produced little revenue, added to the expense of doing business, and, worst of all, increased the peak load. Only slowly did the economics (and politics) of electrifying ordinary homes begin to change.

Looking ahead, *Electrical World* counseled central stations in 1908 to reduce their overhead and encourage small customers to sign on, adding that "No house or shop is too small to secure if one travels on the theory that electricity should be made a necessity instead of remaining a luxury." The pace of home electrification did begin to accelerate but, even in 1910, fewer than 10 percent of the residences in U.S. cities, towns, and villages were wired.

Although wiring of existing homes was still moving at a glacial pace, many new homes came with electricity. To encourage this trend, enterprising central stations gave contractors a financial inducement to put in power. By the teens, most new homes had current, and so electricity was no longer confined to the affluent. Indeed, construction booms in many cities of the far West had, by 1910, resulted in high levels of electrification. In Seattle, for example, an estimated 95 percent of the homes were wired; in Los Angeles, about 90 percent; and in Denver, 70 percent. Newly wired homes, of course, had AC current.

In homes with AC, battery charging became easier as a result of new technology. By the middle of the decade rotary converters were being replaced by mercury arc rectifiers. In these latter devices, invented in 1901 by the American Peter Cooper Hewitt and commercialized by Westinghouse and General Electric, AC was rectified (converted to DC) in a large bulb containing a pool of mercury. Cheaper (at around $200 to $250) and more efficient than rotary converters, mercury arc rectifiers were ideal for home or public garage. There was one problem though. The rectifiers were promoted as automatic, shutting off after the charging was complete, but in practice they had to be watched closely; sometimes the automatic cut-out failed, and the overcharge damaged the battery.

Although home-charging in areas with AC service was now more convenient, maintenance of lead-acid batteries remained a nuisance. In areas poorly served by garages familiar with electrics, car owners (or their servants) had to look after the batteries; too often, they were neglected or maltreated. The predictable result was cars with a range of 10 miles and expensive repairs. As Thomas Edison discovered when he queried all registered owners of electrics in New Jersey, many unhappy people had sold or abandoned their cars,

Figure 30. Mina and Thomas Edison take a ride. (U.S. Department of the Interior, National Park Service, Edison National Historic Site, album 17)

insisting that the batteries were just no good. Fortunately, Mina and Thomas Edison were able to take rides in an electric powered by the nickel-iron battery (Fig. 30).

Almost three decades after Pearl Street, the vision of electric lights in every American home remained far from fulfillment. Despite progress in the West, electricity's slow spread in the East and Midwest, home to nearly all carmakers, continued to dampen any expectation that the electric car could revive to a mass market. No matter if it were developed to perfection, the electric car could not be democratized until vastly more American homes were wired. In the meantime, the gasoline automobile, which required no revolutionary changes in infrastructure, began to find a mass market with Henry Ford's help.

9

THE ROAD TO REVIVAL

The same year that the Ford Motor Company was founded, 1903, *Munsey's Magazine* published an intriguing article on "The Low-Priced Automobile." Its author, W. E. Scarritt, president of the Automobile Club of America, predicted that:

Many a bright lad who is going to school to-day, the son of parents to whom the possession of an automobile seems as remote as the moon, will grow to manhood imbued with knowledge of the machine's value and determined to possess one for himself. And I predict that he will be able to realize his ambition.

This means that we shall develop lower-priced automobiles.

Like Scarritt, Edison, and many other Americans, Henry Ford believed that an inexpensive universal car would come to pass.

Slowly Ford began to formulate a plan for democratizing the gasoline automobile. If it were kept simple, he believed, the car could be operated easily by anyone and manufactured cheaply and in quantity. Moreover, by producing a standard model and reducing the price whenever possible through economies in the factory, the number of people who could afford the car would grow ever larger. Indeed, "it shall be so low in price that the man of moderate means may own one and enjoy with his family the blessings of happy hours spent in God's great open spaces." Henry Ford would make a touring car for the masses.

Ford and other inventors striving to build less expensive touring cars knew that middle- and working-class Americans were coming to expect that the miracle of mass production would eventually cause such elite products to "trickle down" to them as prices dropped. After all, by the turn of the century ordinary families owned items that had once been restricted to the well-to-do, like organs, fine china, clocks and pocket watches, sewing machines, and, of course, bicycles. Novels also spread visions of future societies in which all kinds of goods were inexpensive and plentiful; American industry, many people believed, could create this most American of utopias. Henry Ford was simply one among a multitude who shared this belief and applied it to his sphere of industrial activity, the motor car.

As of early 1907, the Ford Motor Company was trying to compete across a broad front, but the most able competitors, including Olds and Cadillac, had graduated to more expensive cars with higher profit per unit. Gradually, though, Ford began to regard the company's pricey models as distractions from his still-nascent vision of the people's automobile. The success of Ford's own Model N (a tiny runabout), doubtless the best $600 car in America, pointed the way.

But Ford also knew that purchase price was not the only deterrent to widespread adoption of the gasoline automobile. Expenses for maintaining a touring car ran into hundreds or even thousands of dollars a year. For example, one car owner's three-year record testified to annual expenditures averaging $2,300 for 3,000 total miles. According to *Scientific American*, the costs were incurred for tires, $500; gasoline, oil, repairs, $500; and chauffeur and garage rental, $1,300. Even without the latter expense, car maintenance was still $1,000 per year, far in excess of a working-class American's total annual salary and little less than the earnings of many a middle-class person.

Further information was furnished in a 1907 article in *Review of Reviews* on the upkeep of a gasoline touring car:

It may be possible for a man with a small car who motors modestly to get along with an expense of $20 or $30 a month if he has good luck and handles his car carefully and considerately, but the average cost of maintenance will be from $50 to $300 and even more a month.

Even the chief engineer of a central station would have struggled to keep a touring car running and support a family. Not until the reliability and maintainability of gasoline cars were vastly improved would their democratization be possible.

Curiously, in its retrospect of 1907 *Scientific American* observed that "the automobile has settled down to its approximate final type," adding that "Wonderfully rapid has been the development of this most complicated machine to its present perfection." The state-of-the-art touring car had a water-cooled, six-cyclinder engine capable of 40 hp; it could take its occupants over country roads at two or three times the speed limit.

After gaining controlling interest in his company in 1908, Ford bucked the industry trend by bringing out the Model T and, beginning in 1909, making only the Model T. Henry himself worked feverishly on the car with a host of capable assistants, and its elegant design, with the left-hand drive still used today, was quintessential Ford. Selling at first for $850 (plus extras like headlights and windshield), the Model T was still a long way from being the motor for the multitude, but it enjoyed critical acclaim and achieved a stunning popularity. In its first year, 10,607 were sold. Surprisingly, the Model T was initially available in colors, including red and blue; it was also offered in several body styles, but the touring car was by far the most popular.

Technological innovations, including components of vanadium steel for high strength and light weight, an engine block cast in one piece, planetary transmission, and built-in magneto, were among the reasons for the Model T's edge over the competition. Above all, though, the rugged Model T was easy and cheap to maintain.

Stephen W. Sears, in his *History of the Automobile in America*, lavished praise on the automobile that lived up to the advertising claim of being "High priced quality in a low priced car:"

In its price class . . . no other automobile on the market could touch Model T. Indeed, many cars costing twice as much—and a few costing three times as much—could not touch it. It was nimble as a jack rabbit, tough as a hickory stump, simple as a butter churn, unadorned as a farmer's boot. Plain the T may have been, but not unhandsome: it had the simple Shaker-like look of something designed exactly right for the job.

An important part of that job, of course, was to liberate the urban American on weekends and vacations.

The motor excursion was beginning to come within reach of the middle class. Some, whose reach exceeded their grasp, mortgaged their house to buy a car (and a few observers expressed concern about this alarming trend). Others scrimped and saved to come up with the cash. Unlike pianos and sewing machines, cars could not yet be bought on time; it was still a seller's market, with demand for automobiles far outstripping supply. In 1910, car registration in the United States approached a half million, which demonstrated that the automobile had already penetrated beyond the very wealthy.

As Flink shows in *America Adopts the Automobile*, cars had also been found indispensable for certain occupations. Doctors and salesmen, for example, were among the first to embrace the new vehicle as a necessity for work. Similarly, the farmer could take advantage of the automobile's flexibility and convenience in making trips to town, and power could be tapped off the engine, especially the Model T's, to run saws, cider presses, and so forth.

The sturdy T was designed perfectly to survive on America's rural roads. Of 2,151,590 miles of rural roads in the United States in 1904, only 153,662 miles had "satisfactory" surfaces. Satisfactory did not necessarily mean good, though. In fact, rural America did not get its first mile of concrete road until 1908, the same year as the Model T's debut; fittingly, that mile of concrete was laid down in Wayne County, Michigan.

Attracted by the sustained automobile boom, mechanics, entrepreneurs, and capitalists entered the car-making business. Most of these firms—there were hundreds by 1910—lacked adequate capital, a good product, manufacturing expertise, or a distribution network, and so vanished with little trace. A few upstarts, like Buick, would endure. Buick, in fact, was a leader in the use of electric motors in its factories. In 1910, for example, the company employed 185 motors to drive machines, the latter usually in groups. When in 1911 the *General Electric Review* had an article on "Electric Drive in the Automobile Industry," Buick and Cadillac, not Ford, were featured. But Ford would soon catch up, and then some.

As Edison toiled on the nickel-iron battery in his West Orange laboratory, he was aware that ESB was continuing to perfect the Exide. Seemingly, every year the Exide battery got just a little bit better. Exide batteries (there were several types) gave ESB unchallenged domination of the vehicle battery market and helped to establish, at least in some minds, the electric's practicality. In the media, the Wizard's revolutionary battery had become a backwater.

Had he waited too long to put it on the market? Perhaps the Old Man, puttering away with his chemicals, was now irrelevant to the electric automobile's fate.

Why was Edison unwilling to sell what was, already in 1907, an excellent battery? Of course he had high standards, but that wasn't all. Undoubtedly the Panic of 1907, serious surgery, and troubles with other projects had an effect. But Edison's dalliance was mostly a business decision that reflected his deep concern over the battery's reception. He had good cause to worry, as an unsigned article in *The Autocar*, which crossed his desk late in 1907, made clear:

[T]he common verdict of every impartial witness is that, while it [the Edison battery] is distinctly novel, it presents very little advantage over the older form of lead and lead oxide . . . for practical purposes it is no better than the older form of battery. . . . We appeal in the strongest terms . . . to Mr. Edison to consult his own dignity, and the dignity of the profession he represents, *and to cease giving childish statements to the world.*

Clearly, the advantages of the Edison battery over lead-acid were not perceived as decisive, and no one knew that better than the Old Man himself.

In early 1907, Edison believed that the nickel-iron battery lasted about two to three years, not phenomenally longer than a zealously maintained lead-acid battery. To Edison this meant that his battery, which was much more expensive than lead-acid (and cost more to charge because of a lower watt-hour efficiency), might not be competitive in electric cars, regardless of its higher energy density. Though providing excellent service, his battery was not yet a "commercial" proposition. If released to the general public, it might flop. Edison, who still wanted to deliver on his earliest promise to make a storage battery for electric automobiles that did not deteriorate, had little choice but to find a way to extend the battery's life still further.

During 1907 and 1908, while his factory cranked out small numbers of the improved cells, Edison perfected a radical design for the positive electrode. Conductivity was improved by using nickel flake, a material so thin that a bushel weighs less than 5 lbs. Hundreds of alternating layers of nickel flake and nickel hydrate (the active material) were tamped at high pressure into tubular electrodes. Another novel feature was small amounts of lithium hydroxide added to the cell's electrolyte, which somehow enhanced its operation.

In a letter to H. F. Parshall in June of 1908, Edison reported that "At last the battery is finished. . . . These cells will solve the problem in every respect, commercially and otherwise." After almost 50,000 experiments, Edison had finally declared success in the quest for the better battery. Small numbers of the new cells, A-4 and A-6, were sold late in 1908, and by mid-1909 production had risen to around 500 cells a week. The factory was running twenty-four hours a day, and neighbors complained about the noise.

Although the new battery still cost two to three times more than a lead-acid equivalent, Edison contended that it would be more economical in the long run because it lasted at least four years and its maintenance was largely trouble-free. But not everyone would agree with the Wizard's cost accounting.

Edison was uncharacteristically quiet about the new battery in 1908 and 1909, making few far-reaching claims to the press; he may have felt that its superiority over lead-acid was self-evident. Perhaps believing that customers would soon flock to West Orange, the Old Man did not immediately begin an advertising campaign, but he did provide particulars to the trade. In mid-1909 *The Commercial Vehicle* and *The Automobile* published reports of promising tests the Edison battery was undergoing in delivery trucks. The commercialization of Edison's new battery was announced in a January 1910 article in *Electrical World*. The three-page piece presented details of the battery's construction and performance, but otherwise made no comments. An equally reserved account appeared a few months later in *Horseless Age*.

Although the initial reaction was restrained, soon the Edison battery came to be appreciated as a technological triumph of the first order. Byron M. Vanderbilt, writing recently in *Thomas Edison, Chemist*, has labeled it "One of the outstanding developments in the history of applied chemistry." Not only could it withstand endless mechanical abuse, but even undercharging and overcharging did no harm. The battery could sit in a partially charged state for years with no adverse effect, and in use some lasted over three decades.

According to Edison, he spent $1,750,000 developing the nickel-iron battery; years would pass, however, before it would earn him much return on this investment.

In response to the threat posed by Edison's battery, ESB in 1910 announced the "Ironclad" Exide. The name, of course, was calculated to confuse; after all, the Ironclad contained no iron. Not surprisingly, the Ironclad's main selling feature was long life: with meticulous maintenance its positive plates now lasted at least two years. ESB introduced the Ironclad with a lavish promotional campaign intended to neutralize the favorable publicity Edison's new battery was finally receiving. The Ironclad, it was claimed, was perfect for use in electric vehicles. But so was the Edison battery, with its extreme longevity, higher energy density, exceptional mechanical durability, and ease of maintenance. Thus appeared two new batteries, each one capable (or so their makers hoped) of spearheading a revival of the electric vehicle. In fact, though, the electric revival was already well underway.

The year 1907 marked a turning point in the fortunes of the electric car. That the cars and their batteries were much improved was becoming generally appreciated; renewed interest in electrics was evident even in the auto shows. For example, in a Madison Square Garden show put on by the Association of Licensed Automobile Manufacturers, forty electric cars represented seven companies. *Electrical World's* write-up was effusive:

> in all that pertains to the comfort of the occupants, as well as the manner in which both the fitting and finish were executed, the electric vehicle surpassed any other type of automobile on exhibition. Couple with this the ease, simplicity and noiselessness of operation and the growing popularity of the electric vehicle especially for city use is accounted for.

The cars on display included all the familiar body styles as well as a few oddities. Refusing to yield the entire touring market to gasoline, Baker brought out an electric "roadster" that was a dead-ringer for the stereotyped gasoline touring car. At its top speed of 30 mph (another break from electric tradition), the car fell short of its advertised radius of action—an impressive 60 miles. With only a 60-mile range the Baker roadster could not really tour, but it did signal a renewal of optimism in the electric car industry.

Another unusual vehicle was shown by Columbia, a hybrid automobile that contained a four-cylinder gasoline engine, generator, and electric motor. By relying on electric drive, this vehicle avoided a mechanical transmission, the gasoline car's Achilles' heel.

Surprisingly, the electric was influencing the design of a few gasoline cars. Noting that the upper-income buyers of electrics seemed now to prefer enclosed bodies—coupés and broughams, several gasoline car companies were selling competitive models. The most successful clone, a one-cylinder coupé, was introduced by Cadillac in 1908. Competition from Cadillac would eventually prove significant, but in the meantime—1907 and 1908—the electric car began to show signs of life.

With a rosy future apparently ahead, the electric car attracted new firms to the industry, many of them carriage and wagon makers following Studebaker's lead. The most important entry was the Anderson Carriage Company of Detroit. The company, headed by William C. Anderson, was a respected manufacturer of "high-grade buggies." Long-term prospects for the carriage industry being bleak, Anderson began experimenting with automobiles. These projects yielded nothing until 1906, when George M. Bacon, an electrical engineer, came calling on Anderson, and said that he could design a fine electric carriage. Anderson gave him space, equipment, and supplies. Four months later, Bacon took Anderson for a spin in his first vehicle, which ran very well. Moving quickly into manufacturing, Anderson brought cars to market in 1907. The company's cars, and later trucks, carried the Detroit Electric brand; during the teens Detroit Electrics would outsell all others.

William C. Anderson, who became acquainted with Edison after taking a serious interest in using his battery, also knew Henry Ford. It was Anderson who arranged the fateful meeting in West Orange when Ford was reintroduced to Edison. The two inventor-entrepreneurs quickly became good friends and collaborated on several projects, including an anti-smoking campaign and an electric car (Chapter 11).

Mass-circulation magazines were now noticing, and drawing attention to, the new electrics' many virtues. *Harper's Weekly*, for example, in 1907 ran three favorable articles, which remarked that the car's mechanical construction and batteries had both been bettered since the turn of the century. Moreover, the electric now performed as well as the manufacturers' claims. Electrics, observed M. L. Goss, had "outlived prejudice" and were "here to remain." Even *Motor Age* in 1907 began to present progress in the electric art in a section called "Electric Vehicles."

Among the most noteworthy features of the new electrics was improved performance. For example, makers were consistently claiming a longer radius of action for their light vehicles, which in a few cases reached 100 miles (Fig. 31). Many cars had five or six forward speeds, and a top speed of 20 mph was no longer uncommon. The 1908 Baker roadster now boasted eight for-

Figure 31. The Baker runabout of 1909 was claimed to have a 100-mile range. (*The Outlook*, 6 March 1909)

ward speeds and peaked out at 40 mph; at a more conservative 14 mph, the car's range was nearly 100 miles.

Radius-of-action figures from before the turn of the century were sometimes on the optimistic side since trials had often been carried out, without many stops, on level and well-surfaced roads. The newer claims were more credible, and reflected improvements in lead-acid batteries, motors and running gear, and tire design and air-pressure management. In special publicity runs carried out by manufacturers, cars were exceeding 150 miles on a charge (see Figs. 34 and 35).

The electric's greater range led to a spate of articles and letters in *Horseless Age* on touring. Testimonials from electric tourists recounted pleasant trips through areas with a high density of central stations willing to charge visiting vehicles. Such areas, however, were rather uncommon outside the Northeast. Though electric cars may have been capable of leisurely touring, much as Woods had envisioned a few years earlier, for the most part there was still scant infrastructure to support it. Regardless, speeds of 20 to 40 mph and trips of 50 or 60 miles a day were too tame for the real touring impresario.

By the end of the decade, a 50–100 mile range could be taken as a reasonable expectation for an electric under ordinary conditions of use. (In very hilly cities, of course, the mileage would be much less; heavy stop-and-go driving and poor roads also took a toll.) With this range an electric car could, in effect, cruise the city all day long on one charge. After all, city speed limits were low, usually 12 mph or less, still geared to the pace of horse-drawn vehicles.

The electric car's revival was conspicuously marked by *Electrical World* in a long article on June 10, 1909. This was the first piece in many years to review the vehicles of major makers and to illustrate selected models. In addition to the old standbys, victorias, runabouts, stanhopes, and broughams, many 1909 lines of electrics included roadsters and coupés. By this time as well the automobilist magazines, especially *Motor Age* and *Motor World*, were carrying lengthy articles on the new electrics, explaining their technical features. Advertising in these magazines by electric car makers also picked up.

What markets did the makers of electrics expect their cars to conquer? The most perceptive people, in and out of the industry, had early on pondered the "sphere of action" of various motive powers and concluded that electrics would be confined to city use. The electric, many believed, was well suited for business purposes, "comparatively short pleasure rides," and delivery of parcels in city and suburbs. Because this sphere of action was identical to that of horse-drawn vehicles, owners of the latter were to become the electric's target market. Surprisingly, that market was still sizable.

Although trolleys had caused horse cars to exit most cities, horses remained essential for urban life in the early twentieth century. The vast bulk of goods, from beer and bread to light bulbs and brassieres, was still carried on carts, wagons, and trucks pulled by horses. The wealthy, of course, continued to employ horse-drawn coaches and carriages for getting around town.

As more and more automobiles appeared on city streets after 1900, sentiment against horses grew. Unsanitary and slow, horses had become a sweaty, smelly relic of a preindustrial age. What business did a horse have in the city, center of refinement and civilization? Above all, the hitched-up horse was an omnipresent reminder of man's brutality to beast; during heat waves and cold spells they died by the thousands. Buoyed by the rapid replacement of horse cars by trolleys, many people concluded that all city horses could soon be banished.

Technologically and ideologically, the electric vehicle was ready to make a run on the horse. *Electrical World* observed in 1907 that "The rapidly increasing output of electric vehicles from the various factories proves conclusively that as a substitute for the horse-drawn vehicle, the electric automobile is greatly in demand." Electric cars and trucks would play a role in helping to rid cities of the equine quadruped.

Although a stately electric brougham cost no more than a comparable horse-drawn rig (and could make four times as many miles in a day), owners of horse-drawn carriages in large cities were used to being pampered. In carriage houses, servants cleaned and varnished the coaches, repaired the harnesses, and tended the horses. Or the entire carriage outfit was taken care of by a livery stable, with the vehicle picked up by a servant as needed. For electric cars to appeal to the horsey set, then, they would have to be equally convenient to use. And in some cities they were.

Entrepreneurs set up a host of electric car garages, patterned after livery stables. Typical was the Denver garage that Oliver P. Fritchle opened in 1905. It was located in an exclusive neighborhood, to minimize pick-up and delivery distances for customers. Monthly charges were $25 for runabouts, $28 for medium-size electrics, and $30 for surreys, broughams, and four-passenger automobiles. The monthly fee covered one battery charge and one delivery daily; an extra charge cost 50 cents, while towing was $1 and up. Though quite competitive with the expense of boarding a horse and carriage in Denver, these rates were more than half the earnings of an ordinary worker.

In Toledo, Ohio, the Atwood garage maintained small electric cars for a monthly charge of $22.50. Of more interest was its extended service: for $50 a month the garage included battery refurbishing. That is, $50 a month covered every usual expense of owning an electric car; it was the ultimate in convenience for the urban elite.

By 1910 most large U.S. cities had at least a few garages that stabled electrics, usually for $30–40 a month for a small pleasure vehicle (excluding battery repairs). Washington D.C., with 600 or so electric cars, had nine garages in 1907. Using mainly off-peak power, garages often received discount rates from central stations.

The ability of the electric car to circulate on city streets all day long made possible a new lifestyle in which women enjoyed unprecedented freedom of action. Male automobilists may have disparaged the electric, but women paid them no heed. They held the electric in high regard because, without a coachman, a woman could go anywhere in town anytime she desired.

The electric had other virtues that endeared it to women (and some men). Above all, the electric was simple to drive—no cranking to start, no oil to turn on, no spark to advance manually, and no clutch and gears to change. The electric coupé or brougham was also an all-weather vehicle. In winter, the open-air gasoline touring car stayed in the stable; a horse-drawn carriage could venture out in the cold but might become paralyzed in deep snow. Neither cold nor snow slowed the electric on its appointed rounds to a tea or the theater. And lacking pungent exhaust fumes and oily grime, the electric was the clean car, especially appealing to women in dress or gown.

The electric's success as a town car was obvious to women of the urban elite, who saw their sisters in stylish coupés and broughams, taking children to school, dropping off husbands at work, shopping, and so on. In well-to-do neighborhoods, a long line of electrics was apt to mark a home hosting an afternoon reception, a gathering of women and their cars. The electric took up the liberation of the American woman where the bicycle left off, as long as she were rich (Fig. 32). In the years ahead, tens of thousands of wealthy families would buy into the new urban lifestyle wrought by the electric car. Not until after World War II, however, would that lifestyle be democratized.

In America of the Progressive Age contrasts in lifestyles were striking. Much as today, rich and poor lived not just in different neighborhoods but in different worlds. Reactions arose against this vast social inequality as well as the other evils of unbridled industrial capitalism. Reformers tackled the abuses of the trusts and widespread corruption in government, and champions for the downtrodden appeared. Sensitive to these issues, many women

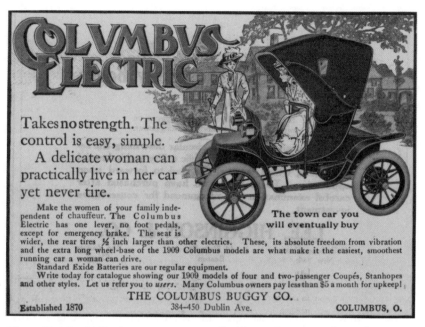

Figure 32. This 1909 advertisement promised to liberate the woman driver of a Columbus Electric. (*The Outlook*, 27 March 1909)

figured importantly in the Progressive movement, representing the interests of their oppressed gender.

One of the more flagrant gender inequalities was in the job market. Before the turn of the century, opportunities for women in the workplace were confined mainly to menial jobs—often in dingy factories—and low-paying, traditionally female occupations like nurse, maid, teacher, and social worker. More women were going to college, but careers that higher education opened up for men remained largely closed to the "fair sex." Even by 1910, among engineers, bankers, doctors, lawyers, and so forth there were precious few women.

Although perhaps 25 percent of American women above the age of sixteen held paying jobs outside the home in 1910, *married* women of the middle and upper classes were scarcely found in the workforce. As Claudia Goldin points out in *Understanding the Gender Gap*, many employers refused to hire married women and fired single women upon marriage. Upper-class women were sometimes wealthy in their own right (through business or inheritance, for example), or had huge allowances. As a result, they could indulge in a surprisingly liberated lifestyle, buying expensive products of their own choosing, from electroliers to electric cars, without necessarily having to seek a husband's approval. In sharp contrast, most middle-class women were, as consumers, entirely dependent on the earnings of their husbands, who doled out—not always generously—portions of their paychecks for household purchases. In the patriarchal family, what middle-class women lacked most, but in public utterances talked about least, was economic equality.

The women's movement of the Progressive Age had many facets and many agendas. Crusades against liquor and prostitution, protection of minors, securing a safe workplace, and suffrage were all central. Significantly, women's clubs and organizations founded to further these causes were composed mainly of middle-class members. Club activities took large numbers of middle-class women outside the home. For transportation they could turn to a generous friend with an automobile, but many women had to rely mostly on their feet, a cab, or the trolley. In their campaigns to obtain equal rights, however, new women increasingly exploited the touring car, which in only a few years had become the quintessential symbol of masculinity and male prerogatives. Wealthy suffragettes might own electrics, and middle-class women might covet them, but in the political arena it was the gasoline touring car—conspicuously driven by a woman—that publicly and potently expressed the quest for equality.

To dramatize their struggle, women sometimes organized their own automobile clubs and sponsored special events. One of the more colorful examples was a two-day endurance run, held in January 1909, from New York to Philadelphia and back, organized by the Womens' Motoring Club of New York. Nine gasoline touring cars with women drivers were entered, and all finished on time "without mishap." This event was described in *Motor World* as the "suffragette run," which highlighted its political aspect. Indeed, on the return trip, Governor Fort of New Jersey addressed the group at the capitol. That the "suffragette run" was deemed newsworthy and merited the attention of public figures along the way tells us today that it was unusual to see women driving touring cars in 1909.

In many quarters of the electrical industry there was, at the end of the decade, renewed faith in the electric vehicle's future. In some cities central station managers, garage owners, vehicle makers, and dealers were meeting together and outlining their common interest in pushing electric cars and trucks.

Countless papers with titles like "Relation of the Central Station to the Electric Automobile Business" were being delivered at meetings, and they underscored the benefits that could accrue to central stations that seriously encouraged electrics.

Some central stations were already giving operators of electric truck fleets big discounts on current. The electric truck itself was becoming a vigorous competitor of the horse, only feebly challenged at this early date by gasoline and steam vehicles.

Because people in commerce and industry pay close attention to dollars and cents, advocates of electrics employed comparative cost data in attempts to win over owners of horse-drawn wagons and trucks. Surprisingly, the numbers looked very good, and would continue to do so well past World War I.

Already in 1901 the U.S. Postal Service had gained valuable experience with electric vehicles in Cleveland. Covering a 22-mile route, a mailman with horse and wagon usually took six hours; the same work could be done with an electric vehicle in less than half the time, even in a snowstorm. Electric drive was clearly faster than the horse, but was it also cheaper?

One study showed that an electric delivery wagon annually saved $1,471 over the horse-drawn equivalent. In discussing these figures in *Electrical World*, Hayden Eames became almost ecstatic, proclaiming that "the electric automobile . . . is to-day the most economical and convenient means for the wholesale transportation of merchandise and retail transportation of people in cities."

Although a new electric delivery truck was often more expensive than a horse-drawn wagon, its upkeep and life-cycle costs were less per ton-mile of cargo hauled. Electrics, for example, were cheaper to garage because they took up much less space than horse-drawn trucks; they also had 25 to 50 percent lower maintenance costs. Most importantly, an electric truck and crew could easily do twice as much work in a day. The electric vehicle was also extremely long-lived, with some built before the turn of the century remaining in use for at least a decade. Finally, day after day an electric truck could be counted upon.

Data on the reliability of electric vehicles were furnished by C. F. Smith of Boston Edison's Automobile Department. According to Smith, in the first 10.5 months of 1909 not one electric in the company's sizable fleet was inoperable for as much as a day. Moreover, the electric automobile of Boston Edison's president ran 40,000 miles over a seven-year period without a single failure on the road.

In order to gauge central station activities in support of electric vehicles, *Electrical World* distributed a questionnaire to 4,000 stations, of which 1,500 responded. The results, published in 1909, were mixed. Because there were so few electric vehicles at that time—estimates range from 10,000 to 20,000—it is expectable that most stations would be indifferent to them. Indeed, many replies indicated not an iota of interest. Others explained away the absence of electrics in their service areas, mainly citing "Too many hills," terrible roads, or towns too small. A few expressed little confidence in electric vehicles themselves. Overall, the survey suggested that central station involvement in charging electric automobiles was still spotty, but interest was growing.

In places where electric car use had caught on, mostly large- and medium-size cities such as Cleveland, St. Louis, and Chicago, central stations were a major beneficiary. The total annual income from charging electrics around the country approached a half million dollars. In presenting these figures, *Electrical World* hoped that apathetic managers would conclude that catering to electrics could enhance their balance sheets. Impressed with the possibilities for profit, more central stations did begin to rally behind the electric.

Every indication now pointed to a harmonious and unified industry eager to push the clean and quiet town car. In recognition of their common cause, the Electric Vehicle and Central Station Association was established in 1909, and its meetings were covered prominently in *Electrical World*. In addition, the Electric Vehicle Association of America began to hold its annual meeting jointly with that of the National Electric Light Association, trade group of the central station industry. Alluding to these positive moves, *Electrical World* remarked that "The year 1909 has witnessed an awakening on the part of the electrical interests to the importance of the electric vehicle."

In the few years following 1909, the electric car would enjoy a brief renaissance. By then, the automobiles themselves as well as their batteries (both lead-acid and Edison) were mature and reliable technologies. Although it was hoped that electric cars might one day reach large numbers of Americans, in the meantime vehicle designs and the planned promotional blitz were targeted at wealthy consumers who owned horse-drawn carriages. Optimistic manufacturers had no inkling that the tenacity of touring, improvements in gasoline cars, and other factors would make the Classic Age of electrics a rather short era.

10

THE CLASSIC AGE

The year 1910 was a turning point, a convergence of circumstances that augured well for the electric car. Although neither the Edison nor the newest Exide battery revolutionized performance, both better batteries could be touted (in advertisements and articles) as technological breakthroughs responsible for the electric's apparently new-found practicality (Fig. 33). Electrics were being produced in many models by more than a score of capable manufacturers. Sometimes collaborating with central stations, these firms had forged a coherent strategy to promote town cars to the horsey set, and so the plush electric suddenly became much more visible in the mass media. Sales of electrics did surge in the early teens, sending tens of thousands of city horses back to the farm. The electric car was finally enjoying acclaim and a modest commercial success, no longer "the Cinderella of the automobile family."

During the first decade of the twentieth century, the rest of the automobile family began to experience spectacular sales. Car makers saw their customer base expand beyond wealthy aficionados, and responded with new advertisements in mass-circulation magazines, including *Colliers, McClure's, Life, The Saturday Evening Post, Harper's Weekly,* and *Literary Digest.* Not surprisingly, the most common model shown, usually without driver or passengers, was the gasoline touring car. Needless to say, articles in those same magazines continued to glamorize touring.

Although ads for electrics were sprinkled in these magazines throughout the dark decade, in most their visibility was low until 1910. For example, in

Figure 33. A 1910 advertisement for the Columbus runabout highlighted the Exide battery. (*The Literary Digest*, 19 February 1910, inside front cover)

the previous nine years, *Literary Digest* had published precisely thirty-one ads for electric cars, an average of three and a half a year; from 1910 through 1914, however, the annual average jumped to nearly twenty-four. Ads for gasoline cars, made by hundreds of companies, still dominated the magazines, but the electric automobile was no longer obscure.

The sudden spurt in ads for electrics in some magazines was no accident. Car makers, the larger central stations, and battery companies agreed that electric vehicles could have a bright future if the public were educated, through advertising, about their many advantages. Americans still harbored prejudices against electric vehicles, which clever promotions could overcome. Central stations contributed to an advertising pool that helped fund an ambitious campaign in mass-circulation magazines as well as in trade publications.

It was especially important that central stations—epitome of sound business sense—publicly endorse the electric, and many did. New York and Chicago central stations early on had taken a leadership role and now new firms followed with creative campaigns. In 1911, for example, Boston Edison, as part of a $100,000 promotion, published advertisements in forty-six local newspapers that featured the electric vehicle and emphasized that the company was sponsoring it. Boston Edison also organized a parade of sixty to eighty electric vehicles on Memorial Day, 1911. Through the auspices of Thomas Edison the parade was filmed and copies were made available for promotional purposes.

An even more important move would be for central stations themselves to use electric cars and trucks. At various meetings, vehicle makers pointed out often—and with considerable force—that horse-drawn and gasoline vehicles conspicuously carrying the central station's name hardly enhanced the electric's image. Emulating New York Edison, some of the larger central stations began to electrify their fleets. One industry observer estimated that central stations alone could provide a market for 50,000 to 70,000 electrics.

Several factors worked against a rapid conversion, however. Many managers were understandably reluctant to replace all trucks and cars at once. Surprisingly, though, stations bought new gasoline cars after 1910, even when electrics were perfectly suited for the work. Pressure to buy gasoline cars often came from deep within the company's ranks. Because electric companies sometimes allowed employees to use business vehicles on their own time for joy-riding, a meter reader or salesman would obviously advocate the purchase of a gasoline car because only in that vehicle could he, on the weekends, indulge in touring.

One purpose of the media blitz was to convince Americans of means that the new electric cars were technological marvels. So, in advertisements everywhere, technical virtues were loudly touted (Figs. 34 and 35). For example, Baker claimed that its system of shaft drive with bevel gears, available throughout the company's line, was "The greatest advance ever made in electric motor cars." Shaft drive with bevel gears was soon seen in the ads of other

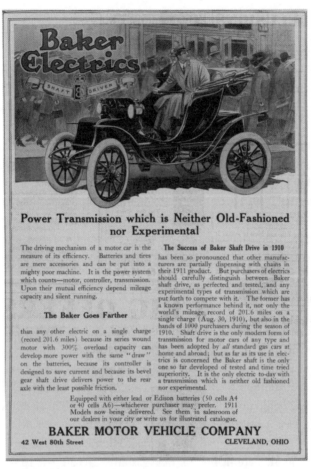

Figure 34. Baker Electrics were said to have high efficiency, enabling record long-distance runs. (*The Literary Digest*, 8 October 1910)

manufacturers, including the Detroit "chainless." The Waverley Company sung the praises of its "herring-bone gear," alleged to be the most efficient available, and its "full-elliptic springs." Almost every ad for electric cars at the beginning of the Classic Age made some mention of technical improvements and described them in superlatives, often implying that their vehicle embodied breakthroughs.

The hardware hype, though attenuated, continued into mid-decade. In writing about the 1913 models, William P. Kennedy noted in *Electrical*

Figure 35. The smooth-riding Baker sets another distance record, 1910. (*Life*, around December 1910)

World that little of significance had changed from the previous year. The main value of the new technical features, Kennedy observed, was to provide something that salespersons could point out while trying to influence consumers "likely to be swayed by the latest trend of fashion." He contended that some manufacturers had made the change from bevel gear to worm gear drive, not because the latter was better, but to avoid "the disadvantage they would suffer in marketing their otherwise 'old-style' product in the face of the flagrant advocacy of the 'new style'."

Better batteries also became a selling point. Boston Edison's ads, for example, claimed that the electric vehicle had achieved practicality because of "recent new and remarkable improvements in storage batteries." The perfected Edison battery had begun to receive more laudatory press coverage, including a glowing article in *Scientific American* in mid-1910, and so car makers were able to capitalize on the Wizard's latest wares. In a Detroit Electric ad of 1910, for example, Edison's visage appears in a cameo photograph above his signature along with a rosy description of the new battery's features. In large print, the ad reads, "This Battery Will Outwear Your Car." A Waverley ad of 1910 also traded on the Edison imprimatur, opening with the quote, "Now That's the Way to Build a Controller," said to be "the exclamation of the veteran wizard of the electrical science after carefully examining the Waverley patented No-Arc Controller." The ad also noted that "Mr. Edison himself is an owner and constant user of a Waverley Electric Carriage at his beautiful home." Late in the following year, though, Edison obtained a Detroit Electric for testing, and switched his loyalties to the latter firm.

In a 1911 ad, Detroit Electric asserted—in italics, no less—that

Thomas A. Edison has chosen the Detroit Electric exclusively as the one car properly made to use efficiently the tremendous capacity of the Edison battery. The Detroit Electric is the only electric pleasure car allowed to install his famous battery.

These claims were, to say the least, misleading. Detroit Electric did have an arrangement with Edison, in which the latter agreed "to sell the proportion of our output of batteries that we have reserved for pleasure vehicles for 1912 to you exclusively . . . reserving the right to supply from your quota batteries to Col. Bailey and General Healey." Nothing in this agreement, however, prevented other car companies from buying Edison batteries ostensibly intended for commercial vehicles. And Edison probably did not abide by it anyway. This curious agreement actually allowed Edison to put the best face on an unhappy situation: most car makers had no intention of adopting his battery.

There were several reasons for this surprising turn of events. Some car makers were obviously reluctant to redesign their vehicles to hold the larger Edison battery. Other firms resisted because the added cost per car ($200–600) gave them slight profit and caused prospective customers to gasp in disbelief, the battery's near-immortality notwithstanding. In addition, even in 1910 there was concern about whether Edison could actually deliver a large battery order in a timely fashion. Perhaps the most significant barrier was ESB's clever stroke of locking most car makers into contracts to buy Exide batteries exclusively. Nearly alone among car makers, W. C. Anderson, whose company built Detroit Electrics, refused to yield to ESB's strongarm tactics. To supply customer demand, he eventually began manufacturing lead-acid batteries.

In the early Classic Age, then, sales of Edison batteries for automobiles were a big disappointment to the Old Man. The battery's largest markets were in train lighting and electric trucks. In 1910, however, there were only a few thousand electric trucks on American streets—and more than a million horse-drawn wagons. Believing that the truck market would pump up if properly primed, in 1910 Edison began a project to create an electric delivery wagon that could replace the ubiquitous one-horse rigs used by most merchants. His plan was to make a rugged vehicle that would sell for around $750, considerably less than anything yet on the market. The Wizard would do for the small electric truck what Henry Ford was doing for the touring car.

Edison was not exactly a stranger to the world of electric trucks. In fact, since 1904 he had subsidized the Lansden Company of New York, and had given its president, John M. Lansden, Jr., advice on vehicle design. Edison bought the company outright in 1908 and took a more active role in management. Sales of the Lansden Company's line of large electric trucks were far from robust, and the firm was deeply in the red; by 1910 Edison's monthly infusion of cash sometimes ran to $4,000. In an effort to improve the firm's finances, Edison ordered Lansden to stop all experimental work and focus on making the standard vehicles. The Wizard himself would design the next new model.

Although Edison could have copied an existing electric delivery wagon, he had little confidence in them, and so decided to start from scratch—well, almost. He bought a standard Keystone wagon, made mostly of wood, and painstakingly electrified it. Even before the conversion was complete, Edison announced the project to the trade. His 1910 article in *Carriage and Wagon Builder* elicited letters from firms eager to mass-produce the vehicle. As word spread of the soon-to-be inexpensive electric wagon, merchants wrote to Edison, begging to buy one.

No. 1 Delivery Wagon rolled out of the West Orange laboratory in April 1911. It had cost $544.36 in materials (excluding battery) and $2,513.53 in labor. Believing that endurance tests needed to be rigorous enough to expose even the most subtle weaknesses of the wagon, Edison had a crew drive it heavily loaded over a 16-mile, circular route on "the worst roads around

Figure 36. Edison's No. 2 Delivery Wagon of 1911. (U.S. Department of the Interior, National Park Service, Edison National Historic Site, 06.116/40, neg. 221)

Orange," in one case towing a car weighing 2,435 lbs. Many flaws came quickly to light, as a wheel fell off, the front axle-brace broke, and so on. Wagon No. 1 was tested until early fall of 1911, and the many lessons learned from its travels of 4,000 miles were applied in building a new vehicle. A patchwork at best, No. 2 Delivery Wagon (Fig. 36) was ready for testing in October 1911. With three shifts of drivers, it was run over the torture course twenty-four hours a day.

By this time, inventor J. M. Lansden, Jr. had departed the company that carried his name. Perhaps tired of taking orders from Edison, now a meddling capitalist himself, Lansden had moved to General Motors, where he took charge of the new Electric Division of the GM Truck Company. There he could again design electric trucks. In its first electric truck brochure of 1912, GM traded heavily on Lansden's extensive experience in the business (partly gained, of course, at Edison's expense).

While Wagon No. 2 was rumbling through the New Jersey countryside, revealing new mechanical faults almost daily, Edison obtained quantitative data on horse-drawn wagons from merchants large and small. Carrying a letter of introduction signed by the Wizard, assistant W. H. Meadowcroft visited dozens of firms, administering a detailed, one-page questionnaire. The data looked good to Edison: monthly stabling alone was commonly $20-30 per horse, and the *average* distance traveled daily by a wagon was 15 to 40 miles—well within the range of a small electric truck. Some individual trucks, however, went farther. Thus, Edison worried about battery charging, remarking in some notes that "What is particularly needed in connection with the selling of the vehicles is a place where they can be charged quickly & economically, especially where the grocer has only one vehicle."

Edison soon had a plan to accomplish this. He had discovered that a nickel-iron battery run down to 60 percent of a full charge could be restored to 100 percent with a massive boost (a very high current charge)—in only 10 minutes. This would make it possible, Edison believed, for a merchant's lone truck to be recharged while being loaded for its next delivery. Frequent boosts would also allow use of smaller batteries in light delivery trucks.

Before this idea could be worked out (or even thought out) in detail, Edison, not surprisingly, made it public. At the convention of the National Electric Light Association on June 1, 1911, the Wizard divulged the scheme to an ever-eager press corps. The next day newspapers around the country ran articles with titles such as "Edison Perfects Storage Battery" and "New Battery Will Revolutionize Car Systems." The *Detroit Free Press* reported the development as follows:

Thomas A. Edison thinks he has now invented the storage battery that will overcome the three main objections to the one now in use: weight, bulk and length of time required to charge them. The new battery that he has been working on for months is so light that one large enough to run a butcher wagon can be put into a suit-case. It can be charged in four or five minutes, he says.

This account caught the eye of W. C. Anderson, the Edison battery's largest car customer, and he was not pleased. Immediately he fired off a pointed letter to Edison, requesting him to publicly deny the "report claiming you have perfected [a] new battery" because such a report "will stop sale of present battery." Edison replied to Anderson that, of course, he had made no such claim about a new battery, and took pains to explain that the proposition involved frequent boosts of standard Edison cells in a small delivery truck. The Old Man, however, was unconcerned about the garbled press coverage, pointing out to Anderson that he could not "deny every misstatement that appears in the paper."

As Anderson expected, in the weeks ahead both he and Edison had to explain why no new battery was imminent. The episode harmed Edison's credibility and, possibly, soured some potential customers on electric vehicles. Not long after the publicity abated, Edison seems to have dropped the boosting idea altogether, perhaps having realized that the charging equipment needed to supply big boosts for small merchants, especially in areas of AC service, would have been prohibitively expensive. (Surprisingly, the boosting scheme survived in the operation of some battery trolleys—Figure 37— another Edison enterprise intended to generate markets for his battery.)

Unfazed by the flap over the "suitcase battery," Edison continued testing Wagon No. 2 into the first months of 1912. By March the wagon was holding up a little better, but its power consumption was high. To solve this serious problem, Edison had his crew make change after change to reduce friction in

Figure 37. Edison shows off a battery trolley car. (U.S. Department of the Interior, National Park Service, Edison National Historic Site, 14.625/18, neg. 2204-A)

the drive train. This period of tinkering lasted more than two years, and involved at least one more wagon. Those who inquired in the interim about the wagon's progress were told the unvarnished truth, that it was "not ready yet." Perhaps this time the Wizard would fail to deliver the goods.

The new generation of electric cars, powered mostly by Exide batteries, was beginning to receive favorable attention in mass-circulation and even automobilist magazines. For example, *Collier's* observed in 1911 that "the once despised electric has amply proved its usefulness. Its sun is rising, not setting." Commenting on the design of the electrics in 1912, *Motor World* applauded the car's simplicity and reliability which make it "absolutely dependable." *Horseless Age's* "Electric Vehicles" section for a few years monitored progress in electrics. And a new magazine, *Electric Vehicles*, sung the praises of the car that had risen, Phoenixlike, from the ashes.

Gradually, through 1911, discussion of technical virtues—thought to appeal mainly to men—took a back seat to comfort, convenience, and luxuriousness. In focusing on such features, car makers were taking deliberate aim at women, whom they employed extensively in advertisements. L. D. Gibbs, superintendent of advertising for Boston Edison, in 1911 outlined the new advertising strategy at a meeting of the Electrical Vehicle Association:

In advertising the electric pleasure vehicle the use of illustrations showing a handsomely dressed and attractive lady operating her own car is far more convincing than a bald admonition to use such a vehicle. Such a picture at once conveys a notion of comfort, luxury, cleanliness, elegance and that indefinable element denominated "class."

The entire industry moved quickly to highlight women in this pictorial mode of persuasion (Fig. 38).

For example, among the people shown in and around the electrics throughout the Classic Age, women outnumbered men about three to one. Except in ads for electric roadsters, women were depicted as drivers more often than men, sometimes even chauffeuring their husbands. In contrast, only occasionally did women appear as drivers in ads for gasoline cars of the same period. Women were also shown transporting children and, especially, going out in groups, probably to a club meeting or other social event. In one fascinating Detroit Electric ad of 1912, a lone woman heads to her electric carrying a set of golf clubs (Fig. 39). Manufacturers clearly appreciated that the electric car appealed above all to the new woman.

Figure 38. Hupp-Yeats "electric coach." (*Harper's Weekly*, 12 August 1911)

A few women were even tapped to help market the cars. New York Edison's Automobile Bureau, founded in 1911 to promote electrics, employed a woman to demonstrate vehicles and give driving lessons. In 1912, Miss Virginia E. Aiken, age 16, became a sales representative for Babcock electric cars. According to *Electrical World*, "her saleswomanship has attracted much favorable comment in Boston circles."

The interiors of electric coupés and broughams were designed to dazzle women. Driver and passengers sat on lovely upholstered chairs, often in novel arrangements that suggested an intimacy appropriate for social intercourse

THE Detroit ELECTRIC

Society's Town Car

THE Detroit Electric can be depended upon for all-around service because dependability has been *built into it*. Not only great strength, but great mechanical and electrical principles are *inborn* in this superior motor car.

They are the foundation of your investment and will yield inestimable dividends of pleasure for yourself and friends.

The body designs of the 1912 Detroit Electrics have anticipated the style for years to come. They are dignified and have both character and correct taste. There is nothing "make-believe" or freakish either in the body designs, interior finish or mechanical construction of The Detroit Electric.

Let us tell you about the many *exclusive* features that have contributed to the ascendancy of the Detroit Electric as Society's Town Car.

We offer a selection of nine body designs. Illustrated catalog sent upon request.

Anderson Electric Car Co.
408 Clay Avenue, Detroit, U.S.A.

Branches:

Buffalo
Brooklyn
Cleveland

New York, Broadway at 80th Street   Chicago, 2416 Michigan Avenue
Altro Branch at Evanston, Ill.

Kansas City
Minneapolis
St. Louis

Selling representatives in all leading Cities

Figure 39. Detroit Electric, "society's town car," made a visual pitch to the new woman. (*The Literary Digest*, 20 July 1912, p. 115)

(Fig. 40). Manufacturers raced to outdo each other with luxurious appointments. For example, enclosed Ohio electrics were equipped with clock, reading lights, lady's toilet case, gentlemen's smoking set, flower vase of cut glass, and silk curtains. To ensure that its car's interiors represented the acme of parlor chic, the Baker Company enlisted the services of Frenchman Paul Poiret, designer of women's apparel. A 1913 Baker ad in *Collier's* exalted: "In the style of which he is the accepted master, Poiret has produced a variety of exquisite effects in self-toned harmonies of old gold, wine color and shim-

Figure 40. The Waverley limousine of 1911. (*The Saturday Evening Post*, 16 September 1911, p. 56)

mering greys, entirely unique in motor car interiors, which will appeal to the discriminating woman as unusually distinctive."

One of the most interesting woman-oriented publicity events was an electric "pleasure car salon," held in the ballroom of the Copley-Plaza Hotel in Boston. During this gala three-day affair in November of 1913, twenty-nine cars made by nine companies were on display. Invitations were issued to 10,000 "persons of recognized social standing," and the dollar entry fee—more than a half day's wages for the driver of an electric truck—ensured that only people of the proper class came. Amidst the cars were large bouquets of flowers on pedestals, and an orchestra provided music for the mood. The

2,500 visitors received an illustrated catalog, as if they had attended a showing in an art gallery. Apparently, a good time was had by all, including the car makers, who rang up $40,000 in sales.

Articles in *Colliers, Literary Digest, Country Life in America, The House Beautiful*, and other magazines read by women helped to spread the message that the electric car had been perfected and was ideal for use in city and suburbs, especially by women in carrying out their social duties.

The close association of women and electric cars, projected in advertising and articles in mass-circulation magazines, was a faithful reflection of reality. While electrics continued to find favor among some men, especially doctors and businessmen who made trips around town, most electrics were used mainly by women. G. N. Georgano, writing in *Cars, 1886–1930*, offers the following observation:

> The importance of the electric car to the well-off, urban American woman is clearly shown in a photograph of the cars assembled outside the Detroit Athletic Club in about 1914, when the members invited their wives to inspect the premises. Of about 35 cars visible in the picture, all but three are electrics.

America's wealthiest families often owned several cars, including an electric that the woman could drive. Thomas Edison's Detroit Electric, for example, was used mostly by Mina. Only a few suspected that the near-exclusive identification of the electric car with women might be harmful.

The snob appeal of the electric car was also reinforced endlessly in advertisements and brochures. Often, the owners of an electric were shown decked out in their most elegant evening attire, attending operas and concerts. In an electric coupé or brougham, with its plush upholstery and polished brass or silver fixtures, members of America's elite could travel in a style once reserved for royalty. Some ads made this connection explicit. For example, Rauch & Lang showed drawings of European royalty and their horse-drawn coaches, proclaiming that their "cars are built as staunchly and as ably as the famous royal coaches of history which have been handed down from generation to generation." By substituting money for pedigree, a Rauch & Lang customer could acquire a timeless symbol of social prestige and, in the bargain, dispense with horses.

Elitism was also blunt in a 1911 Baker brochure:

The Baker is pre-eminently a car for refined social uses. Its beauty of design and silent running appeal to women of taste. The car's social prestige is due to years of refined usage by people who want and will pay for the best. It has been repeatedly purchased abroad by foreigners of rank.

And, after all, the Baker "does everything that a gas car is called upon to do except touring."

In a 1913 brochure, Woods ended the introduction with a flourish, tying together its pitch to women and America's elite,

The Woods Electric, with its beauty, its ease, its convenience, typifies the civilization of our times, bearing testimony to man's conquest of the elements and to the constantly advancing status of the American woman, and the desire and intention upon the part of man to supply her with all the luxurious attributes of a real queen.

Competition between manufacturers to create ever finer metal coaches was, according to William P. Kennedy, leading to "extravagance in the finish and equipment of interiors," and this drove up the electric's price. He seemed resigned that this was all a prelude to the eventual appearance of a low-priced car that would make the elegant electric accessible to "the great mass of purchasers." Kennedy and others in the trade were still optimistic in 1913 that the rolling French parlor would eventually reach—and be embraced by—ordinary people. To this point, Kennedy argued, spartan electrics (mostly runabouts) had been shunned because they were not fashionable; a $1,000 coupé would have found a large mass market. What the electric town car obviously needed, then, was its own Henry Ford.

During the early teens, Henry Ford was struggling to keep up with orders for the Model T; soon the Ford works became too small. In 1910 operations were moved to a new factory, called Highland Park, designed by the Ford team and paid for by profits from automobile sales. Henry Ford no longer needed capitalists, for he could reinvest the wealth created by the Model T. In 1912 the 60-acre Highland Park works disgorged 82,388 Model Ts, which now sold for $600.

A key to Ford's success was building just one basic model. His fixation on this idea was indeed firm, as the Highland Park engineering crew discovered when, during Ford's first trip to Europe, they built a sleek red roadster. Finished just two weeks before Ford returned, the roadster "was a beauty . . . and everybody just admired it," according to the reminiscences of George Brown. Brown just happened to be in the garage when Ford entered and first spied the roadster. After five or ten minutes of small talk about the trip, Ford finally inquired, "What is that over there?" Brown told him that it was the new Ford car; in fact, the factory had already been tooled up and the bodies and other components ordered. Henry went over to take a closer look at the new Ford, walking around it several times. The rest of the story is best told in Brown's own words:

Finally he got to the left-hand side of the car that was facing me, and he . . . gets hold of the door, and bang! One jerk, and he had it off the hinges! He ripped the door right off! God, how the man done it, I don't know!

He jumped in there, and, bang, goes the other door. Bang, goes the windshield. He jumps over the back seat and starts pounding on the top. He rips the top with the heel of his shoe. He wrecked the car as much as he could.

After Ford finished "cussing out" the engineering crew for this unspeakable breach of Henry's Law, Thou Shalt Make Only One Model, George Brown had to cancel all the orders. This was the only time that Brown could recall seeing Ford *"real mad."*

The one-model mandate was clearly a crucial ingredient in helping Henry make a car for all people. Perhaps the Ford Company's most important innovation to streamline manufacturing, however, was the moving assembly line, experiments with which began at Highland Park in 1913. The movement of materials was precisely choreographed through a sequence of operations performed, along a line, by people and machines working as one. The results were dramatic. With the same labor force, for example, almost twice as many flywheel magnetos could be put together in a day. Within a year, the entire factory was converted into a series of tributary flows of parts feeding main flows of Model Ts—more than 200,000 in 1914, and nearly 400,000 in 1915. The time to produce a Model T dropped by a factor of eight. On December 10, 1915, Highland Park produced Ford's one-millionth car; the Ford Motor Company was now supplying almost half the automobiles in America. True to his word, Ford continued to lower the Model T's price, to $440 for the touring car of 1915, but by then it was available only in black.

While Ford factories in the mid-teens were putting out more than 1,000

Model Ts a day, the Good Roads movement, founded by the bicyclists, was also bearing fruit. At public expense American states were creating an infrastructure for the gasoline touring car. Millions and millions of dollars were being spent to pave country roads while city streets often remained unimproved. In a nation still heavily rural, a large constituency obviously favored this particular tilt in technology policy. And, significantly, city-dwellers bent on touring also wanted better country roads. Only in the electric vehicle industry did a few people utter ineffectual protests about the unfairness of this policy to the clean and quiet city car.

Sales of electrics did increase in the early teens, as many horse owners traded up to the new technology. Production of electrics, during the dark decade depressed at no more than 2,000 or 3,000 per year, ratcheted up to 4,500 in 1910. By mid-1911, *Electrical World* had proclaimed a "Boom in Electric Vehicles." More than 6000 electrics were sold in 1912, the majority being broughams and coupés. (Recall that in 1912 Ford produced 82,388 Model Ts.) The electrics were made by more than twenty companies, located mainly in the Midwest, offering eighty-plus models at prices ranging from the $850 Studebaker stanhope to the $5,500 Borland-Grannis seven-passenger limousine, with most costing between $1,800 and $3,600. The cheapest town cars sold for $2,200 to $2,500, four times the price of a Model T. In 1912 a very nice house in the suburbs could be bought for $5,000.

Electrics built in 1913 and 1914 were little changed in technology, price, and appointments from those of the preceding few years. By this time most coupés and broughams had aluminum panels for the body and roof, fixed upon wooden supports. Fenders were of aluminum, wood, or, in the case of the Baker coupé, patent leather. Body panels on the latter car were available in four colors, black, blue, green, or maroon, with striping and fenders to match. The Baker coupé cost a breathtaking $2,800, or $2,850 with a steering wheel. The larger firms made an assortment of body styles, and nearly all companies offered at least coupés and broughams.

Although fundamental technology remained the same, there were some technical embellishments designed to impress would-be buyers. Ohio Electrics, for example, had "the famous exclusive magnetic control." A fist-sized mechanism allowed the operator to change speeds, ring the bell, lock and unlock the controller as well as the car's doors, and energize the magnetic brake. The Ohio Model M had two controllers and two tillers so that the car

Figure 41. This Ohio Electric could be driven from front or rear seat. (*The Saturday Evening Post*, 25 January 1913, p. 52)

could be driven from a front or rear seat (Fig. 41). An electric heater was also available.

Sales of electrics were minute compared to the spectacular numbers being tallied by gasoline cars, but manufacturers had reason to retain their faith in the future. Pictures from the time show that, during the day, electric cars were hardly to be seen on busy city streets amidst the swarm of horse-drawn and gasoline vehicles. However, at night, beyond the photographers' reach, the electric town car took control. When popular plays ran at downtown theaters, for example, the curbs were crowded with shiny electric coupés and broughams. It is easy to appreciate the electric's appeal on those occasions.

After all, who would want to crank a gasoline engine while wearing a tuxedo or evening gown? Beginning in 1912, however, the urban elite began to have a real choice. In that year Cadillac brought out a gasoline town car with an electric self-starter.

Automobilists and people in the automobile industry had long appreciated that crank-starting was not a treat, especially in rain or snow. As *Motor World* observed in 1900, those who wrestled the crank around often got soiled with oil and scraped knuckles. And, if the engine "kicked," the result could be a broken arm (nicknamed by some doctors the "Ford fracture")—or worse. Women in their cumbersome costumes especially dreaded the starting nightmare. Not surprisingly, the automatic starter had become a holy grail for automotive engineers and inventors, who tried everything from injecting compressed air or acetylene into the cylinders to using strong springs to turn over the engine. For example, the driver of a 1910 Winton Six touring car, with its "self-cranking" engine, merely pushed a button to release compressed air into the cylinders, which moved the pistons. When the spark was turned on, the engine started.

Before any of these self-starters came into general use, another technology was rapidly adopted because it was part of an integrated starting-lighting-ignition system that at once brilliantly solved several persistent problems in gasoline cars.

Ignition batteries in gasoline cars at this time were small storage batteries or dry cells that had to be constantly refurbished or replaced. Because powering headlights with batteries was not usually feasible, prior to the early teens many automobiles employed chemical generators to make acetylene gas for their lamps, and others carried kerosene lanterns. Each lamp, front and back, had to be lit with a match, sometimes in rain or high winds. As automakers struggled with the self-starting problem, in the context of ignition and lighting systems that were somewhat less than convenient, new possibilities emerged.

It is ironic that the self-starter that prevailed would be part of an electrical system created by an electrical engineer. In fact, the view among electrical engineers, schooled in conservative design principles, was that gasoline engines could not be started with an electric motor. To develop the necessary horsepower, the starter motor would have to be enormous and would also require big batteries. Experiments that came to naught with electric starters, dating back to 1896, seemingly supported these pessimistic assessments.

Charles Franklin Kettering (1876–1958) was an electrical engineer who loved a challenge. He had begun his professional career working for National Cash Register in Dayton, Ohio. One of his earliest triumphs was to motorize the cash register; in so doing, he had defied conventional engineering wisdom. By all expectations, the motor he had designed was too small to get the job done. But it did. His innovative solution was to overload the motor for the brief period when it was engaged.

Kettering resigned from National Cash Register in 1909 to pursue electrical invention in automobiles, an area in which he and several National Cash Register co-workers had already been moonlighting. They founded the Dayton Engineering Laboratories Company, known simply as Delco, and their earliest product was an improved battery ignition system. The first order, for 8,000 sets, came from Cadillac (which was already part of General Motors, formed in 1908). By the spring of 1910, several other companies were also using Delco ignition systems. Prodded by Henry Leland, president of Cadillac, Kettering about this time began thinking about an electric "self-starter."

Kettering early on conceived the self-starter as part of a more encompassing electrical system that included starting, ignition, and lighting. The starter problem itself was easily solved: he simply applied the cash register solution to the car. A small electric motor, consuming vast amounts of power in short bursts from a lead-acid storage battery, would turn over a gasoline engine. Recharged by the starter-motor functioning as a generator, the battery could also supply electricity for lighting and ignition. The rest was a question of matching voltages and devising a regulator to keep the battery charged. Although in principle Kettering had solved the nagging electrical problems of the gasoline automobile, in practice it took another year to fine-tune the system.

Henry Leland and the Cadillac people were impressed with Kettering's work. In November of 1911, tiny Delco received an order from Cadillac for 12,000 starting, lighting, and ignition systems to be installed on their 1912 model. Within a year Delco had 1,200 employees and was producing electrical systems for other pricey gasoline cars.

With Kettering's system the automobile became the entire world of practical electricity writ small: like a central station, it had a generator driven by a prime mover along with a load-leveling battery; like a community, it distributed current through a network of wires; like homes and businesses and Great White Ways, it boasted electric lights; and like factories, it had a motor load. And so, thirty years after Pearl Street, Kettering had put into the playthings of America's elite a miniature electrical system of startling sophistication while most homes were still lighted by gas and kerosene lamps.

The triumph of Kettering's system was obviously welcomed in the electrical industry. In a curious twist, companies making gasoline automobiles had quickly become a huge market for motors, batteries, and so forth, instantly dwarfing the consumption of components by electric car manufacturers. *Electrical World* commented gleefully on this development but did not abandon the electric. After all, the latter was still a significant source of income to some central stations and the electric retained other advantages over gasoline town cars, like reliability, ease of operation, all-weather capability, and quietness, that appealed to the horsey set.

Nonetheless, the Cadillac and other gasoline town cars did chip away at the electric's market. Despite a prediction in *Motor Age* that 30,000 electric cars would be sold in 1913, the actual number was 6,000—around 1 percent of all passenger car sales. The "boom" had rapidly reached a rather low plateau. Apparently, the spread of electrification and charging facilities could stimulate electric car purchases only up to a point. Even the good press electrics were receiving in automobilist and mass-circulation magazines had little effect.

If gasoline town cars were getting better and taking away customers, then makers of electrics would simply have to work harder to get their message across. Electric car companies were already spending a higher percentage of gross income on advertising than their gasoline competitors, but in 1913 and 1914 they made even heavier investments in lavish magazine ads. The Electric Vehicle Association alone spent around $100,000 for magazine advertising in 1913 and 1914 (Fig. 42). The belief that people were unaware of the modern electric car and still needed to be educated was an obvious explanation for disappointing sales. Yet, members of the elite were already familiar with electrics, having seen them often at teas, the theater, and club gatherings; their friends owned electrics and talked about them. Undoubtedly it was this first-hand familiarity and praise from owners that was responsible in the first place for the electric car's revival, which began well before the major

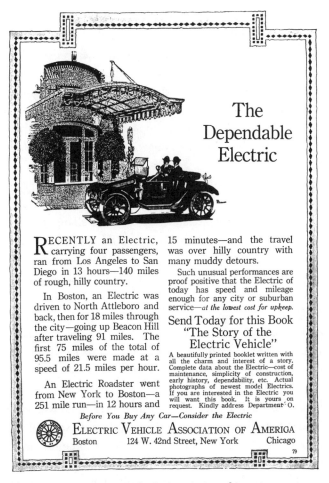

The
Dependable
Electric

RECENTLY an Electric, carrying four passengers, ran from Los Angeles to San Diego in 13 hours—140 miles of rough, hilly country.

In Boston, an Electric was driven to North Attleboro and back, then for 18 miles through the city—going up Beacon Hill after traveling 91 miles. The first 75 miles of the total of 95.5 miles were made at a speed of 21.5 miles per hour.

An Electric Roadster went from New York to Boston—a 251 mile run—in 12 hours and 15 minutes—and the travel was over hilly country with many muddy detours.

Such unusual performances are proof positive that the Electric of today has speed and mileage enough for any city or suburban service—*at the lowest cost for upkeep.*

Send Today for this Book "The Story of the Electric Vehicle"

A beautifully printed booklet written with all the charm and interest of a story. Complete data about the Electric—cost of maintenance, simplicity of construction, early history, dependability, etc. Actual photographs of newest model Electrics. If you are interested in the Electric you will want this book. It is yours on request. Kindly address Department O.

Before You Buy Any Car—Consider the Electric

ELECTRIC VEHICLE ASSOCIATION OF AMERICA
Boston   124 W. 42nd Street, New York   Chicago

Figure 42. The Electric Vehicle Association of America spent heavily on advertising. (*The Outlook*, 22 November 1913)

publicity campaigns. If America's elite failed to go electric, it was not from ignorance.

Advertisements in *Collier's, Literary Digest,* and so on were also intended to nurture a mass market beyond the very wealthy, which electric car makers hoped to cultivate. Indeed, some people in the industry believed that the electric car would be democratized, that middle-class Americans would soon tire of touring. In this view, the ability to tour was regarded as a temporary advantage of the gasoline car. When automobiling ceased to be a sport, thrifty citizens would select cars on the basis of economy and ease of operation. The touring fad would pass, like bikes and bloomers.

As the Model T was demonstrating more dramatically every day (182,809 were sold in 1913), the automobile had a mass market precisely because touring was not a fad; rather, for most urban Americans it was the *sine qua non* of automobilism. In responding to the mass demand for touring cars, America's automobile industry led the world; the top twelve producers in 1913 were all U.S. firms; number thirteen was Peugeot of France, which made about 5,000 cars.

With sales of electrics stalled, bickering broke out: central stations scored vehicle makers for not producing low-priced cars, and vehicle makers accused central stations of not establishing enough charging stations. Both groups were eager to fix blame so that action could be taken in time to save the electric. *Electrical World* chimed in, siding with vehicle makers in an editorial of June 1914. Echos of earlier themes are strong and clear:

> The central-station industry must make the electric car practicable by furnishing ample facilities for charging here, there and everywhere. . . . A foolproof automatic charging system available on one's own premises or operable from roadside taps as common as gasoline stations is the chief desideratum for the immediate future.

Other friendly outsiders criticized the car makers. Addressing the Electric Vehicle Association of America at its 1914 meeting in New York, Charles P. Steinmetz of General Electric, one of the nation's foremost electrical engineers, called upon manufacturers to build a cheap and light car, an electric equivalent of the Model T. His clarion call elicited prompt rebuttals by J. Crawford Bartlett and H. H. Doering. The gist of their papers was that the industry had already offered cheap electrics but consumers didn't buy them. That is why, they argued, few electrics in 1914 sold for less than $2000.

John H. Hertner of Rauch & Lang also insisted, in a letter to *Electrical World,* that car makers were building ever-more expensive electrics because that is what Americans wanted. Moreover, he argued, the man with $600 to $1000 to spend on a car "wants speed and mileage," which no electric—at any price—could provide. Hertner was emphatic that Americans of ordinary means, when buying their first car, would choose a gasoline vehicle to be able to "get out into the country." Another Rauch & Lang official observed that "the makers of the various 'low-priced' cars already brought out have all except one met with financial disaster. The single exception . . . is now in the hands of a receiver."

An obvious strategy for expanding the market was to promote the possibility, long a minority position within the industry, that the modern electric could tour. Although the electric did not reach speeds of 40 to 60 mph, as did gasoline touring cars of that time, a few car makers entertained the hope—fond though it was—that if rural speed limits were enforced (usually 25 mph or less), then buyers might emerge for electric cars capable of a more civilized kind of touring.

In 1911 the S. R. Bailey Company of Amesbury, Massachusetts, brought out an aerodynamic runabout designed for an 80- to 120-mile range using the Edison battery. Makers of sleighs and the famous Whalebone Wagon, the Bailey Company had special skills in building lightweight objects of bent wood. The wooden body on their first electric car, a victoria phaeton of 1908, weighed but 30 lbs. The electric runabout also had a body of bent, laminated wood. The firm enjoyed a long association with Edison, for whom it made wooden battery boxes. Edison, in turn, used a Bailey electric for testing batteries in 1909 and 1910.

Although Edison himself did not take long tours in an electric, he thought others could—and would—if only they were aware of the range that his batteries gave the modern car. In 1910 Bailey and Detroit electric vehicles took part in several publicity events orchestrated by Edison, including a 1,000-mile Ideal Tour (Fig. 43), a climb of Mt. Washington in New Hampshire (which came up a mile short from the top), and one-day tours around the New York area. The latter trips demonstrated that a stock electric car with two people aboard could travel 100 miles or more on ordinary roads with a single charge. Ads for the Edison battery played up these events to the hilt.

A relentless advocate of electric touring, Colonel E. W. M. Bailey himself drove a roadster on what was described in *Electrical World* as "perhaps the longest continuous trip ever made in an electric." The "tour" of 1913 lasted twelve days and racked up 1,300 miles from Boston to Chicago. The entire distance was covered at an average running speed of 17.8 mph. Even in rain the car was able to do better than 20 mph on paved roads. Despite near-constant rain or snow, there was only one mishap: the car ran off an embankment in the dark and had to be pulled out. Sometimes, however, it was necessary to make special arrangements with electric companies for charging along the route. In one case a 1,200 hp engine had to be fired up to furnish a

Figure 43. Thomas Edison poses alongside the Bailey roadster that survived a 1,000-mile run. (U.S. Department of the Interior, National Park Service, Edison National Historic Site, 14.625/12, neg. 214)

charge. *Electrical World's* commentary was telling: "The lessons of the journey seem to be that the electric vehicle is ready for touring, but that sellers of electricity should provide suitable charging means to meet the demands of electric tourists." Even the usually sober *Electrical World* had come to view touring in electrics as a realistic possibility.

In order to get greater distance in a touring electric, drivers would periodically stop along the way for a quick boost. The Edison battery survived boosting with no ill effects, but expert opinion was split on whether it harmed lead-acid batteries. In any event, by means of judicious boosts an electric could achieve unprecedented mileage. For example, on May 14–15, 1914, a Bailey car was driven from Boston to New York, a distance of 258 miles, in just over twenty-three hours. Actual travel time was only thirteen hours, the remainder was devoted to five boosts along the way. Only the true believer, facing a saturated—possibly declining—market for electric automobiles, could have regarded such a trip as touring.

Figure 44. The Detroit Electric's "aristocratic roadster." (*The Literary Digest*, 15 June 1912, p. 1265)

Although electric car makers staged carefully planned tours to showcase their cars' long-distance capabilities, and several mentioned touring in ads, only a few companies, like Fritchle of Denver, actually sold an electric "touring car." Many other firms offered "roadster" models that (like the earlier Baker) mimicked the style of the gasoline touring car (Fig. 44); they sold for a breathtaking $1,650 to $3,000 and were clearly aimed at wealthy men. In its description of Waverley's "Gasolenish Roadster," *Motor World* remarked that "the electric of the present is capable of making long runs, and looks the part to perfection."

The most knowledgeable people in the industry were wary of promoting electrics on the basis of touring. They counseled, for example, that if electric cars became stranded while on a long trip, their unhappy owners would doubtless trumpet the bad news far and wide, sullying the good reputation of the new electrics. But they need not have worried.

Although electric roadsters did find a small market among doctors and salesmen whose business required a reliable and economical city car, few men were taken in by the touring electric tease. After all, much of touring's allure was in careening over the countryside, oblivious to everything and everybody. Like the earlier bicyclists, tourists of the teens wanted to "scorch" the road, or at least travel as fast as a train; but high speed was not in the electric's repertoire of tricks. Once again automobile aficionados concluded that electrics, though vastly improved, were unable to tour.

11

DENOUEMENT

While Ford's innovative production methods were being discussed by industrialists around the world, the Dearborn-based company delivered a bombshell: the electric car industry would have a Henry Ford, and it would be none other than Henry himself. Interviewed at the New York automobile show, Ford announced that he and Thomas Edison were developing an electric car for the mass market; it would have a range of 100 miles, use Edison batteries, and sell for $600 to $1,000.

Beginning on January 10, 1914, the popular press and trade magazines reported on the proposed Ford-Edison car, mentioning that this enterprise would lead to "another great factory." Although newspaper coverage of this startling announcement was confined to tiny articles buried deeply, it caused a flurry of interest. The electrical industry in particular was abuzz. In announcing the news to its readers, *Electrical World* waxed enthusiastic: "At last . . . the electric vehicle is to have its chance under the long-denied advantages of a low price and quantity production." *Motor World* applauded the move, contending that "the demand for such a vehicle is very real and very large."

Inquiries began to pour into Ford headquarters from job seekers, parts suppliers, potential dealers and distributors, and people eager to buy the new car. Letters also arrived from *Electrical World*, seeking more details about the car's construction and performance; the Electric Vehicle Association, which invited Ford to join; and *Electric Vehicles*, which sought information as well as a subscription. *Electrical World* was given no information, the EVA was politely but firmly put off, and the invitation to subscribe to *Electric Vehicles* was undoubtedly declined.

An interesting letter was penned by Mrs. Bright of Columbus, Ohio, already an electric car owner. She was pleased that Ford was going to make an inexpensive electric since her old one was "giving out." Mrs. Bright urged Ford to "consider a suggestion from the standpoint of a woman." To retain its feminine appeal, she counseled, the car should be nicely finished with good quality upholstery, and "other little things in the way of dainty, and substantial 'trimmings' could be added," including upgraded tires. Ford spent most of his time in various company shops, and probably never saw Mrs. Bright's letter.

Nearly all of Ford's mail was dutifully answered by E. G. Liebold, his personal secretary. In the standard reply, Liebold emphasized that the Ford Motor Company itself "does not contemplate building an electric car." Rather, the electric was a personal project of Mr. Ford, who would eventually organize a separate manufacturing company that might "not be in operation for . . . a year or more." Who would head that company? The letters did not say, but in the original January interview Ford mentioned his only son Edsel, who at the time was just 21.

Taken together, Liebold's replies seem intended to dash hopes that a Ford electric would emerge in the immediate future. Such a cautious, take-it-slow approach was of course consistent with Henry Ford's engineering style. But this public posture also allowed the company to distance itself from the electric car project, perhaps so that it could be jettisoned later with no loss of face.

When electric cars were still riding high in 1913, Edison and Ford were working together on somewhat strange projects. With Edison's prodding and collaboration, Ford was making an experimental electric car, and Edison— commissioned by Ford—was building an electric lighting and starting system for the Model T. Actually, both projects were linked in the never-ending quest to expand the market for Edison's nickel-iron battery. Although increasing, sales did not yet reach the Old Man's expectations.

To meet the anticipated demand for the battery, which the new projects hopefully would stimulate, Edison needed fresh capital to enlarge the factory. He had already poured profits from his other enterprises into building up the battery company, but, as Edison wrote Ford in October of 1912, "this has a limit." What were his other options for raising capital? "Of course, I could go to Wall Street and get more," he cunningly continued, "but my experience over there is as sad as Chopin's Funeral March, [and so] I keep away." Henry took the hint. Between December 1912 and May 1915, Ford became the reluctant capitalist, loaning Edison $1.2 million at 5 percent interest. Although a million dollars was by this time pocket change to Henry Ford, it was a substantial sum to Edison. More than a decade later Edison would be four years behind in making the interest payments, and the remaining principal was $750,000.

To make room for a starting motor and generator in the Model T, Ford engineers moved the carburetor. The modified Model T was quickly dispatched to West Orange by Henry Ford, and Billy Bee, now manager of the Edison Storage Battery Company, was given authorization to start the project. In February 1912, a crew at the Edison lab began experiments. The results at first were discouraging, as the car would not start when the engine was cold. Adjustment of gear ratios, motor speed and power, number of cells, and so on brought but slight improvement over the next year and a half. Even the space inside the engine compartment turned out to be inadequate; the huge starter motor had to be mounted out front, just below the radiator, where it engaged a gear on the crankshaft. (The Edison crew had apparently learned nothing from Kettering and the Cadillac.)

The pace of development picked up at West Orange in late 1913. By January of 1914 an experimental system had been installed in twenty test Ts. Drivers reported countless problems, many mechanical, but some traceable to the Edison battery. The worst problem was that cars in cold weather at times failed to start because of low voltage. As word of this difficulty got out, Ford dealers threatened to substitute lead-acid batteries if they received Edison-equipped Model Ts. Eventually the Ford camp concluded, along with the rest of the industry, that the nickel-iron battery was unsuitable for starting gasoline cars. The project was allowed, mercifully, to die. When the Model T finally got a stock electric starter in 1919, as an option on the enclosed body styles, the battery that powered it was lead-acid.

The Ford electric car took shape in a shed in Highland Park during late 1913. In his reminiscences, E. C. Liebold claims that the project came under his direction. Actual work on the automobile was carried out by Fred Allison, an electrical engineer; Alexander Churchward, a designer and electrical engineer; and Samuel F. Wilson, a mechanic. Ideas also came from Ford and Edison, and in 1914 even Edsel. One could reasonably deduce that the project lacked the single firm hand needed for success.

Figure 45. Fred Allison and the 1913 Ford experimental car. (From the collections of Henry Ford Museum & Greenfield Village, neg. 0-1923)

Classic Age electrics embodied electrical and mechanical refinements that represented two decades of technological development. The Ford team could have exploited this experience but instead reinvented the electric car—with a peculiar Ford twist.

The experimental electric of 1913 (Fig. 45), which had been tested by the time of Ford's surprising announcement, incorporated a number of Model T parts, including rear end, front end, and suspension. Surprisingly, the entire battery was placed under the seat, a design seldom seen after the turn of the century. Like most electrics, it steered with a tiller. Although performance data on Ford's first electric are lacking, the design was unimpressive; the team at Highland Park was obviously groping, trying to master, mostly by trial and error, an unfamiliar technology.

During the years that the Ford electric was alive (at least on paper), the first era of electric cars in America entered its last stage. Gasoline town cars with

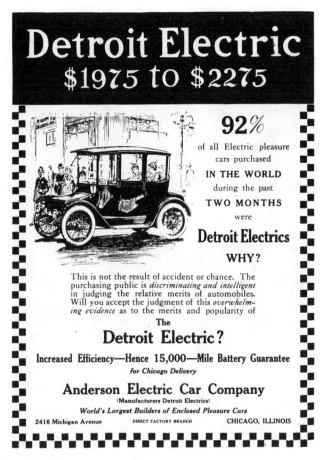

Figure 46. Detroit Electrics of 1915 were sold at lower prices. (*Electric Vehicles*, October 1915)

electric starters and many feminized features, being sold by a host of companies, began to make inroads into the electric's core of well-off women customers. Easily started and more reliable than earlier models, gasoline cars were also replacing electrics among the professional men who had preferred them for city work. In 1914 sales of electrics slipped from the golden years of 1912 and 1913, and, despite price decreases (Figs. 46 and 47), never rebounded.

The agony of the industry was played out on the pages of *Electric Vehicles* (which nonetheless still poked fun at its gasoline competitors—Fig. 48), with

Figure 47. Milburn Electrics were also a bargain in 1916.
(*Literary Digest*, 25 March 1916, p. 857)

blame generously apportioned among car makers and dealers, central station managers, an ignorant public, and even gasoline-car salesmen. But it was of no avail.

In response to relentlessly shrinking sales, the electric car industry also began to contract. At the peak of the Classic Age, more than twenty-seven companies were building electric cars; already by 1916 that number had dropped to around nineteen. Not all went immediately out of business, of course, for

Figure 48. Cartoon from *Electric Vehicles* pokes fun at gasoline automobiles. (*Electric Vehicles*, January 1917)

there was some consolidation. For example, Argo, Broc, and Borland joined forces as the American Electric Car Company; Baker and Rauch & Lang also merged and, under the Baker-Raulang brand, began to sell electric trucks. By the end of 1917, though, when the United States had entered the World War, fewer than ten companies remained; most did not survive the war's privations. In 1918 *Electric Vehicles* was itself forced to merge with another publication.

That any firms lasted past the war is testimony to the wealthy woman's loyalty to the electric car. This small group of satisfied customers, perhaps disdaining the gearshift and clutch of even the most refined gasoline town cars, continued to buy new electrics. In the twenties, this minuscule market allowed Detroit, Milburn, and Rauch & Lang (Baker-Raulang) to limp along. The last standard model electrics were the Detroit 97 and 99, which appeared in the late twenties; surprisingly, degenerate Detroit electrics with Dodge body parts could be special-ordered as late as 1940.

Ads for electric cars were rare in magazines of any kind after 1915. These few ads as well as articles in the automobilist magazines and *Electric Vehicles* indicate that post-Classic electrics were stylish and attractive (Fig. 49), the

Figure 49. The Ohio brougham of 1916 was a stylish automobile.
(*Literary Digest*, 25 November 1916, p. 1427)

last vestiges of the horse-drawn carriage lost in a sleekness unique to the automobile. Most design effort was devoted to appearances, which were sometimes inspired by the gasoline car (Fig. 50). Interiors of coupés and broughams remained fancy, little changed from Classic Age coaches. New roadsters also appeared, which *Electrical World* judged to be especially suitable for a man's use.

One of the few noteworthy innovations was the Woods gasoline-electric coupé, introduced in 1916. Selling for $2,700, it boasted a four-cylinder gas-

Figure 50. Styling of the Detroit Electric of 1919 shows the influence of gasoline cars. (*Literary Digest*, 20 December 1919, p. 107)

oline engine, electric motor, and a battery half the normal size. At low speeds in the city the electric drive was engaged, but in the country the engine took over (and charged the batteries). The huge demand that Woods anticipated for this extensively tested car did not come to pass.

Another novel car was the Dey, a cheap runabout manufactured in New York City. Charles Steinmetz, outspoken advocate of the low-priced electric, was intimately involved in designing the car. His ingenuity showed in the vehicle's compact double-rotor motor, which was an integral part of the rear axle. This move eliminated the need for a driveshaft and mechanical differential; as a result, the entire rear axle weighed only 200 lbs. With weight also shaved off body and frame, the entire car with battery came in at a noteworthy 1,400 lbs. The Dey was introduced at the start of 1917 for $985; despite a male body style, it generated an anemic consumer response. Before the year was over, the Dey had disappeared, failing to become, as *Electric Vehicles* had hoped, "A Start Towards a Million Electrics."

Other innovations were no more successful at jump-starting the electric. Beginning in the mid-teens, several auto companies teamed up with finance firms to make electrics more affordable. Typically, an installment buyer had to put down 25 percent of the selling price and pay 6 percent interest per annum. A few manufacturers also tried to ameliorate the ever-present charging problem by instituting a battery exchange system. In the Milburn electric of 1918, for example, a battery swap could be accomplished in just two and a half minutes. Despite finance plans and battery exchanges, sales of electrics continued to slump.

As the number of horses on city streets diminished during the late teens and twenties, traffic began to move more swiftly. To allow the electric car to keep up, manufacturers sacrificed some range in favor of top speed. For example, the Detroit Model 78 of 1920, a brougham, could reach 25 mph. Surprisingly, the Detroit Model 97 was capable of cruising at 30 to 35 mph when an optional shunt was installed; but at those speeds wind resistance would have pushed the range below 50 miles. Although a few electric cars kept pace with traffic in the twenties, most could not. Predictably, in the twenties and thirties the electric acquired its long-lived reputation for slowness, and, as its owners aged, for being an old lady's car.

Although cars found the going tough, other electric vehicles were still on the move. Cabs enjoyed renewed interest in several cities; in Detroit, for example, a twenty-seven-cab fleet was on the streets around the clock, their nonstop service made possible by curb-side charging facilities at many hotels. While cabbies gabbed and waited for customers, they could boost their batteries.

Electric trucks were also doing well—for a while. Outfitted in many cases with Edison batteries, trucks were being increasingly adopted by merchants, especially in New York City, during the mid and late teens. Large-scale tests demonstrated that the electric truck was more cost-effective than horse- or

Figure 51. The Ward Baking Company of New Jersey operated a fleet of electric delivery trucks. (U.S. Department of the Interior, National Park Service, Edison National Historic Site, 06.116/4, neg. 4375)

gasoline-powered equivalents. For example, an MIT study showed that for both light and heavy vehicles, electrics had lower costs per delivery as well as per mile. Some owners reported that the daily operating expense of an electric was half that of a gasoline truck. Data from Boston Edison also pointed out that, compared to the always cranky gasoline truck, electrics suffered negligible downtime. *Electrical World* put it concisely: "for short-haul, frequent-stop service the electric wagon has no competitor."

Not surprisingly, electric trucks were favored by owners of large delivery fleets, especially department stores, brewers, bakers (Fig. 51), and express and transfer companies. In the well-staffed garages of these firms, electric vehicles—the batteries in particular—were properly taken care of, and so furnished excellent service.

As Edison had anticipated, during the mid-teens small electric delivery wagons came into their own. In 1914, for example, thirteen manufacturers were selling trucks of a ½ ton or less, ranging in price from $1,400 to $2,350.

By the following year, the Ward Motor Vehicle Company of New York was offering a 3/8 ton electric wagon for only $875 on an innovative installment plan. After one year, the truck itself was paid off, but not its Edison battery, which was actually rented from the Edison Storage Battery Company for $10.50 per month. Such plans made electric trucks finally affordable to the small merchant.

With his own trouble-plagued delivery wagon now superfluous, Edison ceased experiments in mid-1914; after all, trucks from scores of companies were creating a substantial demand for his battery, and he had already unloaded the Lansden Company. By the late teens, the Edison Storage Battery Company, in its enlarged factory financed by Ford, was producing thousands of cells daily for electric trucks and countless commercial and industrial applications. Though a huge money-maker at last, Edison's better battery never conquered lead-acid in electric automobiles as he had originally intended.

Electric trucks gave yeoman's service, even climbing 20 percent grades in San Francisco, but not every buyer was satisfied. A brewery in Indiana complained that its vehicles were wearing out too quickly. At the suggestion of a central-station man, a speed-recording device was hidden on one of the company's trucks. It supplied evidence that the driver had been accustomed to loafing and drinking beer for half an hour at each stop, after which he raced flat out—above the speed limit—to the next stop. The offending driver was fired, and repair costs dropped appreciably. In other cases, troubles were traced to poor maintenance practices, a common affliction of firms having only one electric truck.

Despite the electric's many economic advantages, the bulk of small merchants, needing only one or two trucks, usually chose gasoline. Their reasoning was simple: a customer might require a delivery beyond the electric's range. To extend the range of electric trucks, a few companies in collaboration with central stations set up battery rental-exchange depots; this "Hartford Plan," however, did not become popular.

Large fleets of electric trucks were a significant presence in big cities well into the twenties, driving countless horses into retirement (or glue factories). Under the heavy demands of war-time work, however, gasoline truckmakers, especially General Motors, increased their product's reliability and enlarged their factories. Despite the belief held by some in the electrical industry that gasoline trucks would never be used in large cities for short-haul deliveries, in the late twenties and thirties electrics and the last horse-drawn vehicles were replaced by swift and well-made gasoline trucks.

That gasoline trucks were much improved does not entirely explain why they finally drove the electrics off the road; other factors were evidently at work. As always, of course, drivers preferred the speed and power of gasoline trucks, and many sympathetic managers—most of whom owned gasoline cars for similar reasons—gave in to this "prejudice." Ironically, by helping to rid the road of horses, all electric vehicles contributed to rising speeds in cities and suburbs, which put electric trucks at a particular disadvantage. Most large electric trucks, for example, were geared to a maximum of 7–15 mph. In addition, the ownership of millions of cars by ordinary Americans accelerated the process of suburbanization begun by the trolley. As cities expanded, sometimes coalescing into massive conurbations, the electric truck's range came to be regarded as too limited. Anticipating a mix of short and long trips, the majority of truck buyers chose a general-purpose gasoline vehicle despite its more frequent breakdowns and higher operating expenses. By 1922, electrics made up only 3 to 4 percent of the 800,000 motor trucks in large U.S. cities.

The electric truck's longevity would also be part of its undoing. The vastly outnumbered electric trucks, some ten to twenty years old by the mid-twenties, appeared to be antiquated, a dying breed. Merchants large and small flocked to gasoline trucks, which projected an up-to-date image. As home deliveries declined with the spread of the automobile and suburbs, even the great electric fleets gave way; some vanished altogether, while others were converted gradually to "modern" gasoline trucks. The number of electric truck-makers dwindled, leaving as survivors only a few companies, like Baker-Raulang, that made specialty trucks for materials handling in factories and warehouses.

Trolleys were also in trouble, and for some of the same reasons. The democratization of automobiles gave even working-class people an alternative for daily transportation. Increasingly, ordinary people turned to their speedy cars during weekdays and abandoned the trolley; the gasoline car was no longer used just for recreation. Automobile suburbs continued to spread, leaving trolleys far behind. Forced to retain their 5-cent fare in the face of rising operating costs, many trolley companies ran into serious financial problems. Predictably, with maintenance deferred, the old trolley systems became run-down and vulnerable. When GM and other firms moved on the trolleys, many transit companies and regulatory agencies were receptive to the pitch for modern, flexible, and allegedly cost-effective buses. Over the next decades, especially after World War II, most trolley systems were dismantled: overhead wires torn down, tracks paved over, and cars burned or turned into restaurants. In some cities today, the only vestige of their once-glorious trolley system is an ancient amusement park, emplaced originally at the end of a line to attract riders and consume off-peak current.

While the technology of commercial electric cars (and trucks) had stabilized in 1914 and appearances only were polished, efforts to refine the crude Ford electric went forward. Work on a new prototype apparently began early in 1914, and Electric Car No. 2 was finished on June 10, 1914 (Fig. 52). Henry gave it a test drive, and was pleased with its smooth ride and near noiseless-ness. The good news was conveyed a few days later to Edison, who was pro-vided with some technical particulars as well as pictures of the bodyless car.

The latest electric embodied a substantial redesign, including a new frame. As in other modern electrics, the batteries were now divided into two groups. In addition, both front and rear ends were modified, but retained traces of their Model T ancestry. Curiously, Electric Car No. 2 had a steering

Figure 52. Ford Electric Car No. 2. (From the collections of Henry Ford Museum & Greenfield Village, neg. 188.72082)

wheel (from a Model T); obviously it was to be a male-oriented electric, probably a roadster. However, the car could only reach a less-than-scorching 17 mph. Its longest run ("over average roads and grades"), completed at a crawl, was a pathetic 59.1 miles.

The Ford electric team had many ideas for perfecting the car's performance, and the toil continued during the rest of 1914. In November Edison himself visited the Ford plant and was, by Billy Bee's account, "delighted" with the little electric. Had he visited in a January or February, he might have been less pleased. According to Liebold's reminiscences, the car would not run in the dead of a Dearborn winter. (Doubtless they had improperly left the batteries directly exposed to the cold.) To get around this problem, the project team once outfitted the car with a complement of lead-acid batteries. When Henry saw their handiwork, he "raised the devil all over the place."

Although a new expense account for the electric car was opened at Ford in December of 1914, it is unlikely that much further development took place. Ford refused to exhibit the car at the Pan-Pacific Exposition in 1915, even though Edison supported the idea. Liebold was still answering inquiries in early 1915 with the pat response that production of the electric Ford was at least a year off. By mid-1915, however, the Ford Company's replies, now being signed by Liebold's assistant, G. S. Anderson, became even more cryptic: "the electric car proposition we have in mind is still in an experimental stage. When or how this car will be built we are unable to definitely state at this time." In a letter penned by Anderson in 1916, he admitted that "On account of the very extensive improvements and additions to the present factory . . . the electric vehicle has not received a great deal of attention."

Throughout this period the principals were preoccupied with other matters, not the least of which were new business opportunities presented by the World War. In addition, Ford was engaged in an important lawsuit with the Dodge brothers, was building new factories and the Fordson tractor, and in late 1915 set sail to Europe on his ill-fated peace ship; Edison's phonograph factory suffered a tragic fire; and young Edsel was often busy touring.

Well into 1917 the Ford Company's public posture was that the electric car project "was still in an experimental stage." With no hand on the wheel, the electric Ford was obviously on the road to oblivion; not surprisingly, Ford and Edison ceased issuing grand pronouncements on their joint venture. In view of the declining popularity of electric cars generally, the Ford project could be silently and understandably scuttled.

Creation of an electric car at Ford clearly had a low priority. The project's team was small, seemingly lacked first-hand expertise in electric car construction, and received sometimes conflicting charges from too many bosses. Had Henry really believed that a mass-market electric was in Ford's future, at the very least he would have ensured that the team had one strong leader. In his heart of hearts, Ford could not have seriously expected to be making millions of electric cars for the middle class.

Less than a decade had passed since the Henry Ford family had risen from the middle class to join America's nouveaux riches. In 1914 the Fords—one of America's wealthiest families—owned at least four automobiles in addition to sundry Model Ts: Henry's $7,000 1912 Rolls Royce, a Marmon and a Mercer (both mostly driven by Edsel), and Clara's 1913 Detroit Electric brougham. But they had not forgotten what life was like before the automobile. Henry would have clearly appreciated the aspirations of middle-class families to own cars as well as their financial limitations. A prosperous middle-class urban family could have afforded one of the less expensive electrics, but instead chose a gasoline car—even though the price of gasoline was rising while that of electricity was falling. The reasons for this choice are fascinating.

Undoubtedly both men and women of the middle class longed to own cars. Obviously, any automobile would eliminate the social discomfort felt by trolley riders, especially middle-class women. Above all the electric attracted women because it was the ideal city car—clean, quiet, economical to operate, and easy to drive—that could give them during daytime a freedom of action impossible with trolleys. And, of course, it was regarded as a requirement for the glamorous activities of elite women, a car designed for feminine tastes that, increasingly, were being molded by mass-circulation magazines. As *Electric Vehicles* stated in 1916, "There is hardly a woman living who would not like an electric." The middle-class man, on the other hand, mainly coveted the car that offered adventure and excitement. In ads everywhere and on city streets he could see that the real man's car was a gasoline touring car like the Model T. An electric roadster may have looked like a touring car, but everyone knew it did not perform like one.

In very wealthy families the conflict over cars could be settled by buying two, one a gasoline touring car, the other an electric coupé or brougham. Many of America's elite, like Thomas and Mina Edison and Henry and Clara Ford, owned "his" and "hers" gasoline and electric automobiles. This resolution attached importance to the activities of women and so embodied a certain gender equality. On the other hand, it must be stressed that the electric was a wealthy family's second or even third car; in the majority of cases, a gasoline touring car had been bought first.

Middle-class families at that time, however, lacked the wealth to purchase two cars, and so the decision about which one to buy did become a struggle. Most likely, the husband was able to convince his wife that a gasoline car could do more than an electric and was cheaper too, and so was the only sensible purchase; after all, women might also enjoy touring. A woman unswayed by this argument could always be reminded that the husband was entitled to make the decision because he was the family's breadwinner. One way or the other, the battle between the sexes in middle-class families was resolved in favor of gasoline cars. If such families had been wealthier or if middle-class women had enjoyed greater economic independence, the electric car in the teens might have found a market of millions.

This claim of course presumes that middle-class families could have charged electric cars at home. In fact, wiring of older homes picked up momentum in the mid-teens. Going increasingly under the name "public utilities," central stations saw the political virtue of reaching out to ordinary Americans. If the majority of homes remained without electric lights, they reasoned, people were likely to become restive and vote in "demagogues" who might threaten the utilities with government ownership. To attract more residential customers, some companies added special salespersons and expanded their collaboration with contractors to wire old houses in quantity. And, of course, they devised ever-more clever and sophisticated campaigns to push electric appliances. The latter now included a luxurious electric "lounging robe" and an electric bed with built-in heating pad, fan, and lamps. Irons, however, were still the staple.

After about 1912, the pace of home electrification hastened, especially in small- and medium-size cities of the East and Midwest. In these communities 10 to 50 percent of all residences were wired. The largest eastern cities continued to lag, with around 10 percent "saturation," but in the West (with its inexpensive hydroelectric power) a majority of homes—old and new— were on line by 1915. Because the price of power was still declining (by 1916 it was usually 5 to 10 cents per kwh), and minimum monthly charges had dropped below a dollar, more families were eager to sign up for service. Thus, although electricity was far from universal, millions of middle-class families had it by the end of the Classic Age and could, with a mercury-arc rectifier, have charged electric cars at home.

Even with electrification spreading, the market for electrics was still mainly upscale. The few inexpensive electrics available (in both male and female body styles) were simply not popular with consumers, a fact Ford would have known. After all, some of the cheapest electrics of 1914, the Columbia runabout ($785) and "coupette" ($985), were being manufactured in Detroit, but only in small numbers and not at a profit. Even on the West Coast, electric cars, though available from reputable dealers, were not selling well. No West Coast city was ever featured in *Electrical World* for having an abundance of electrics. Clearly, even when their homes had inexpensive electricity, members of the middle class were buying Model Ts and other gasoline touring cars. By the mid-teens, the most knowledgeable people in the automobile industry realized that the electric car—no matter how inexpensive—could not trickle down to middle-class families. The correctness of this belief was highlighted by the conspicuous failure of the Dey in 1917.

Henry Ford was no fool. Despite his loyalty to Edison, he would not have indulged in the folly of mass-producing a vehicle that utterly lacked a market. In the end, there was no Henry Ford of the electric car because there was no mass demand for inexpensive electrics. Had that demand materialized, on the West Coast or elsewhere, Ford as well as the major electric car companies —especially Detroit Electric—would have made vehicles to meet it.

All the while, Ford factories cranked out Model Ts. Although for nearly twenty years Ford made only this model, the car itself was not unchanged, as Ford tinkered with the T to reduce production costs and improve quality. The result was a subtle evolution in design that followed a trajectory almost oblivious to fashion. Ironically, in the late teens Ford was using the industry's most advanced production technology to mass-produce an antiquated, unsophisticated car.

Consumers, however, were beginning to pay attention to looks and to "conveniences." During the twenties when financing auto purchases was routine (except at Ford), many Americans turned to cars with bigger engines, loads of accessories, and stylistic embellishments. Eventually, using Ford's factory methods, other automakers brought down the price of more fashionable cars. Sales of the Model T—essentially a 1905 touring car—began to level off, then fall. Yet Ford was unmoved by those in the company who, beginning in the late teens, had counseled radical change. Not until 1927, when forced by Chevrolet's conquest of the low-priced market, did Ford relent and authorize a new model. With the demise of the Model T an era had come to an end. No longer were minor mechanical refinements enough to ensure growing sales; following trends in other industries, car makers had become habituated to annual model changes based largely on looks.

Though Ford improved the Model T each year, it was old-fashioned even while still in its youth, so fast was the pace of technological change in the automobile industry's first decades. Ford resisted the more radical innovations because they would have upset the delicate harmony of his assembly lines; and too many improvements would have raised the Model T's price, which was anathema to Ford. By the mid-twenties, the fossilized Model T sold for as low as $290, but it was no bargain.

Technological innovation in the auto industry began to slow down in the twenties from a cause most curious. In 1914, the National Automobile Chamber of Commerce, an association of automobile manufacturers, instituted a patent-sharing agreement. The purpose of this cooperative arrangement, which nearly all automakers signed (except Ford who abided by it anyway), was to prevent a William C. Whitney or a Henry Selden from monopolizing the manufacture of cars. The main effect of this agreement over the long haul, however, was to discourage technological innovation.

Because automakers knew that what they invented in one year could become industrywide practice in the next, incentives for invention were greatly reduced. Investing in new technologies simply did not pay because a company could gain no more than the most temporary advantage over competitors. Perhaps that is why the automobile industry became fat and complacent, underinvesting in research and relying on its suppliers for the few innovations that did come along. In this regard, the contrast between the U.S. automobile industry and the electronics industry, which had no patent-sharing agreement, was striking. In *The Portable Radio in American Life*, I recount a succession of stunning products, from plug-in radios in 1927 to transistor radios and color televisions in 1954, that flowed from electronics companies, large and small, during the same period that Detroit's products underwent their annual facelift.

As Flink wrote recently in *The Car Culture*, "most of the basic innovations that add up to the modern motorcar [had] been made by the late 1920s." He further points out that when styling took command of the industry in the mid-twenties, smaller companies were placed at a disadvantage. Not only did car makers require styling departments with artists, but the constant retooling was very expensive. The smaller firms, always looking for some edge in the marketplace, had remained relatively innovative. But they could not do it all—new styles each year and new technology. Most of the forty-four U.S. car makers of 1929 did not survive the Great Depression.

And what happened to the dream, shared by Henry Ford and Thomas Edison, that the inexpensive car would allow ordinary city-dwellers to spend happy hours in "God's great open spaces"? Beginning in the twenties it came true. As country roads were paved and motels and diners sprang up along well-traveled routes, touring—now tamed—became the family vacation.

Despite the failures of their joint projects, Ford and Edison remained close friends until the latter's death in 1931. Every year they exchanged birthday telegrams, and in the late teens took camping vacations together along with tire magnate Harvey Firestone and the near-ancient John Burroughs, esteemed botanist.

Henry Ford lived until 1947, his last years racked by power struggles over control of the industrial empire he built, and the untimely death of his successor Edsel in 1943. During the Depression the still-energetic Ford embarked on new engineering ventures, in one instance creating a car with a body of plastic partly derived from soybeans. The idea was to help out America's troubled farmers by finding new uses for their crops.

During the 1920s Edison pursued several challenging projects in the laboratory, including the extraction of rubber from goldenrod. He lived to witness the birth of radio broadcasting and the rise of the national networks, all made possible by the electric power system he brought into being and the vacuum tube, technological offspring of the light bulb. When Edison died in 1931, nearly every urban home in America had electricity; a half-century after Pearl Street was lit up, an infrastructure was finally in place for home-charging the electric automobile.

But Americans were not interested; they already had cars, countless gasoline cars. Everyone knew that America's mid-century prosperity was intimately tied to a robust gasoline automobile industry. After all, one-sixth of the U.S. workforce depended on that industry for their livelihood, from petroleum geologists, to assembly line workers in thousands of car and car-part factories, to service station attendants. And citizens of all social classes were enjoying the freedom brought by the gasoline car. It had become America's superartifact—the object that reflects and reinforces a society's most conspicuous concerns.

Electric vehicles, of course, did not completely die out. In countless warehouses and factories, electric trucks labor in American industry; on thousands of golf courses and in retirement communities, electric cars move elderly people and their toys; in homes and along streets, electrified wheelchairs allow the disabled to enjoy an enhanced quality of life; and in airport terminals, little electric cars beep obnoxiously and nearly run us over. Surprisingly, there are vastly more electric vehicles in America today than there were in the teens or twenties.

In addition, a great number of enthusiasts—some would say dreamers—kept alive the vision of the silent and reliable electric car. *Popular Science, Popular Mechanics,* and a host of other hobbyist and speciality magazines gave a voice to electric car experimenters and showcased their creations. In a few cases the inventors started up small firms to make their vehicles. Seeing opportunities in the field, especially after passage of the federal Clean Air Act of 1967, a number of high-tech firms also undertook electric vehicle and battery development, and a few brought cars or trucks to market. Even the Detroit Three built electric car prototypes in response to public concern over energy and the environment; despite public promises, however, none was commercialized. In 1976 the U.S. Congress enacted the Electric and Hybrid Vehicle Research, Development, and Demonstration Act, which attempted to advance electric vehicle technology and demonstrate its commercial feasibility. In support of these noble goals, however, Washington furnished only modest funding; yet progress was made. Beginning in the late 1970s, the Electric Power Research Institute (EPRI), mindful that electric vehicles could benefit its members (about 600 U.S. electric utilities), supported battery research and tested vehicle components, subsystems, and prototypes.

The activities of enthusiasts, battery and vehicle companies (large and small), EPRI, and federally supported researchers and developments in other industries have advanced electric car technology in the past two decades. As Mark DeLuchi and his colleagues concluded recently in *Transportation Research,* "the technology of EV batteries and powertrains has developed incrementally, and the cumulative result in a sense has been a 'breakthrough'."

Lead-acid batteries for traction now typically have lives of four to six years with a respectable energy density; a set suitable for an electric car costs between $750 and $1,500. Significantly, lead-acid batteries can now be built to endure the rigors of boosting. Motors are more compact and lighter per horsepower than ever before, while retaining high efficiency. Solid-state controllers reliably give electric vehicles continuously variable speeds. Advances in bearings and lubrication make it possible to reduce drivetrain friction to very low levels. And strong, lightweight materials allow cars to shed excess weight. The upshot, as G. A. Pratt remarked in a 1992 article in *Technology Review,* is that "electric vehicle technology has improved enough so that a viable car can be made today."

The need to transform AC to DC for battery charging remains, but new technology has decisively solved the old problems. Solid-state rectifiers are efficient, reliable, and compact; they can even be built into vehicles, making it possible to get a charge anywhere there is a standard AC outlet. What's more, solid-state electronics permit the use of cheaper, lighter AC motors.

Above all, interest in electrics today is widespread, and many believe we are poised on the threshold of a new era of electric automobiles. As *Newsweek* announced in April 1991, "electric cars are coming."

12

PROGNOSIS FOR THE ELECTRIC CAR

When I was last at Disneyland, a few years ago, my wife and I stood under the monorail track near the main entrance, waiting for our sons to finish their souvenir shopping. Pointing to the train passing almost noiselessly above, I remarked that this impressive technology was from the mid-1950s. How sad, I said wistfully, that no American city now boasts a monorail system. When first installed in Disneyland, the monorail pointed to the possibilities of "new" kinds of mass transit. Today it is just another big toy in an aging amusement park. During the fifties and sixties, Americans built freeways and widened streets to make room for more cars.

Not surprisingly, more cars are owned per capita in the United States than in any other large country. The price we pay for our freedom, for our "car culture," is considerable: tens of thousands die yearly in accidents; cities suffer perpetual rush hours and noise pollution; countless hours are wasted in commuting; nonrenewable resources, imported at enormous expense, are consumed at a frightening rate; and in many urban areas the air is, to say the least, unhealthful. The obvious prescription for these ills is more and better mass transit, such as buses, subways, and light rail—including trolleys and monorails.

The vision that our cities can become more habitable if they have fewer cars and more mass transit is very appealing. However, most Americans and most American cities (now mainly suburbs) grew up with the automobile, adapted to it, and in its absence would be paralyzed. Weaning U.S. urbanites from their cars will require, at best, several decades as well as huge outlays of capital that our depleted society seems incapable of supplying. Thus, while agitating for public transportation, Americans concerned about sick cities also see promise in switching over to alternative automobile technologies, especially the clean and quiet electric car. The electric does not solve every problem wrought by the automobile, but it solves a few problems well. That is why ordinary Americans have already brought into being a new era of electrics.

Tired of their smoggy air and decades of foot-dragging by Detroit, Californians decided in 1990 to force major automobile companies to commercialize electrics. The California Air Resources Board mandated that, in 1998, 2 percent of the new cars offered by manufacturers selling 3,000 or more cars in the state have *zero* emissions; now and for the foreseeable future only electrics can meet this stringent standard. In 2003 fully 10 percent of the cars sold by these companies in California must have zero emissions—an estimated 200,000 or more electrics. Under growing grass-roots pressure, a dozen other states, including New York, had by mid-1993 adopted or were considering similar codes. Assuming that oil company lobbyists and the Detroit Three do not succeed in getting the regulations gutted, it is forecast that automobile firms doing business in the United States will have to sell, in 2003, at least a half-million electric cars.

Needless to say, all large automakers want to do business in California, New York, and other states, and so they have reluctantly geared up programs to bring electrics to market. Interest in zero-polluting city cars is also emerging across the Atlantic, and this has provided a home-grown incentive for European automakers to commercialize electrics. At the 54th Frankfurt International Automobile Show held in September 1991, more than twenty electric car prototypes were displayed by American, Japanese, and European companies. The new era of electrics is beginning, then, around the world.

Firms in Denmark, Sweden, Italy, and France already sell, or are on the verge of selling, electrics at reasonable prices. The French-made Volta, for example, is a lightweight car (1,050 lbs) capable of reaching 45 mph; this two-seater is made in several utility body styles, including van and pick-up, and has a range of 50 miles. Commissioned by the city of Los Angeles to build $7 million in fleet vehicles, Clean Air Transport Svenska, a Swedish firm, is making hybrid vehicles. One model is a compact four-seater with a reinforced plastic body. The on-board, auxiliary gasoline engine can extend the

Figure 53. Solar Electric's Destiny 2000. (Solar Electric, Santa Rosa, California)

car's 60-mile range to more than 150 miles, and it has a top speed of about 70 mph.

Unknown to most Americans, several obscure U.S. companies already sell electrics. For example, Solar Electric Engineering of Santa Rosa, California, offers five models, ranging from a converted Ford Escort ($15,700) to the Destiny 2000, a two-seat sports car built on a Pontiac Fiero chassis. The electric Escort, with optional solar panels, reaches highway speeds and has a range of 25-60 miles. Noel Perrin's charming book, *Solo*, describes his adventures with a Solar Electric Escort station wagon. His conclusion: it is a superb commuter car but don't go touring because getting a charge on the road is still difficult. Solar Electric's Destiny 2000 (Fig. 53) comes in at $28,500, and includes an array of solar cells (which provides a tiny bit of power and extends battery life). With its lightweight fiberglass body, the Destiny 2000 can travel 40 to 60 miles on a charge and cruises at 60-70 mph.

Sebring Auto-Cycle, of Sebring, Florida, manufactures the Zzipper, a three-wheeler that runs around $9,000. The Zzipper has a top speed of 55 mph and a 50-mile range. Incidentally, Sebring Auto-Cycle and its predecessor companies at the same address have sold more than 4,000 electric cars since 1973.

A third U.S. firm is based in Melbourne, Florida. Solar Car Corporation markets an electrified Ford Festiva for $17,500 and a compact pick-up, based on a Chevrolet/GMC truck, for $19,500. The electric Festiva has a range of 25-60 miles and top speed of 65 mph. Other small U.S. firms are offering, or are soon planning to offer, electric cars or complete electric car kits.

The American companies that pioneered the new electrics have gained much practical experience and have shown that existing technology is adequate for making short-range commuter cars that some Americans will buy. These companies, however, are small, oriented to local markets, and do not advertise nationally in mass media. Thus, they probably will be shoved further into the background as the giants of the auto industry belatedly introduce electrics, later in the 1990s, with a great media blitz. Only the small companies that acquire adequate capital to scale up production and build world-class distribution networks and sales organizations will in any way be prepared for the cutthroat competition ahead.

Many electrics on American streets today are gas guzzlers that have been painstakingly electrified by their owners. Dozens of firms are springing up throughout the nation to do these conversions, which cost around $5,000 to $10,000. Using a several-year-old gas car with a nice body, a "new" electric can be created for much less than $15,000. Conversion kits are available off the shelf from many companies listed in *Why Wait for Detroit?* (edited by S. McCrea) and in Philip Terpstra's 1992 *Electric Vehicle Directory*. Countless electric car clubs also provide advice, and sometimes extra hands, to help out with conversions.

Ordinary Americans can now buy the clean and quiet city car from small U.S. companies or build their own. But they can't buy one yet from Detroit.

And what plans have the Detroit Three for commercializing the electric? One concern is that the Detroit Three eventually will bail out again, and import the electric cars they will have to sell in the states. In the meantime, however, GM, Ford, and Chrysler have once again established electric car programs. Actually, Chrysler has already released a full-size van with nickel-iron batteries, intended for fleets, selling in the neighborhood of $120,000, and it has brought other expensive vehicles to the prototype stage. Ford also has a full-size van being readied for market and cars in the works. Although

Figure 54. The Impact, GM's prototype electric car. (GM Electric Vehicles)

GM is some years away from commercializing an electric vehicle, its proto-type automobile has received a great deal of national attention.

In a move that took the automobiling world by surprise, General Motors unveiled, at the Los Angeles Auto Show in 1990, an electric car of stunning appearance and performance (Fig. 54). The car, which has the unfortunate moniker "Impact," was actually designed by an outside consulting firm, AeroVironment, headed by Paul MacCready. It was MacCready who sired the Gossamer Condor, the first person-powered plane to accomplish con-trolled flight, and the Sunraycer, GM's record-breaking solar-powered vehi-cle. In less than a year, MacCready's team created far more than the show car commissioned by GM. Designed as an electric from top to bottom, the im-pressive Impact is powered by lead-acid batteries. The Impact easily cruises at 70 to 100 mph, and its range is claimed to be 120 miles (at lower speeds, of course).

The heavily publicized Impact is having a beneficial effect by dispelling the electric car's dowdy image. Shaking loose the belief that the electric is but a slightly reformed golf cart is why the Impact has a high speed—a governor is needed to keep it *below* 75 mph—and snappy acceleration (0-60 in 8 seconds flat). With its *two* 57-hp AC motors, at least five times more horsepower than needed for a city car, the Impact is not your father's (or mother's) electric. Not only has the Impact shattered the perception that electrics must be slow, but it has been a public relations bonanza for GM as countless magazines and newspapers covered in detail the "revolutionary" electric car. Unfortunately, even if most people wanted an electric that performed almost like a Porsche, they could not afford the Impact at an estimated cost of $20,000–30,000. Although in 1992 GM claimed that it would commercialize the Impact in 1994, by early 1993 the company was backpedaling. It is doubtful that a cash-strapped and wary GM will put the Impact on the market before the end of the decade, if ever.

Is it realistic to expect GM, Chrysler, and Ford to offer inexpensive electric cars to the U.S. public? An obvious implication of the Ford-Edison car project is that we cannot count on a big U.S. automaker to mass-produce a cheap electric. Such a vehicle must always be anomalous, an orphan, in a company geared to the mass-manufacture and mass-marketing of gasoline cars. The many aborted electric-vehicle projects that these companies have undertaken since the mid-sixties, which mostly produced prototypes of pricey cars, also fuel the pessimistic conclusion that the people's electric will not roll out of Detroit—at least not right away.

Why the Detroit Three are reluctant to commercialize electric cars affordable to ordinary people is no mystery. Profit is, understandably, the Detroit automakers' foremost concern; and inexpensive cars, sold in small numbers, do not promise profit. Just as Henry Ford allowed his electric car project to die because he saw no mass market for an inexpensive electric, the Detroit Three will likely stall until convinced—probably by the success of foreign firms later in the decade—that such cars can attract a consumer following beyond a few yuppies and hard-core enthusiasts. GM, Ford, and Chrysler may be the last companies in the world to recognize when the time for the people's electric has arrived.

If the pricey Impact is actually introduced as promised and finds buyers, GM may expand its offerings, perhaps eventually trickling down electrics to a mass market. Foreign firms, however, are apt to take a more direct route to the masses with a "trickle up" strategy.

In the early 1960s, for example, Japanese firms began to export motorcycles and automobiles to the United States, at first offering only inexpensive subcompacts, much smaller than any car that the Detroit Three built in the United States. Despite jokes at the time that they had been made from recycled American beer cans, the imports sold by the millions in the 1960s and 1970s because they were inexpensive, well made, and fit with the lifestyles of many young Americans. Building on these successes, Japanese automakers developed technology to move to larger, more powerful cars in the 1970s and 1980s. Today, of course, these companies are selling luxury cars, often to the same loyal customers who bought their subcompacts in the sixties.

In a spasm of wishful thinking, the Detroit Three believe they now enjoy a lead in electric car technology over their foreign rivals, and so will be able to stave off, with better-performing cars, competitors that employ a trickle-up strategy. To maintain their supposed technological advantage, the Detroit Three have embarked on an unprecedented joint project targeted at what many people believe is the electric car's weak link: the battery.

In the fall of 1991, GM, Ford, and Chrysler announced that they had created, with the blessings of the federal government, the U.S. Advanced Battery Consortium to improve electric vehicle batteries. On the surface, this surprising and well publicized act signals that the Detroit Three are in the vanguard of efforts to commercialize the electric car. Drawing on an earlier campaign to make better batteries, we can subject the current project to closer scrutiny, seeking other meanings.

Thomas Edison's public proclamations in 1901 that he was working on a better battery for electric cars—and that it was almost ready for release— simultaneously sent several messages to would-be car buyers. The most transparent meaning was that Edison had committed his considerable energies and resources to perfecting the electric car; the Wizard had faith in its future. Another message, much less obvious at first, stemmed from Edison's identification of the battery as the bottleneck holding back electric vehicles. Americans no doubt concluded that the battery problem was not trivial if Thomas Edison had taken it up; and, evidently, the electric car could not achieve practicality until that bottleneck was removed. With Edison hard at work on a new battery, however, the electric's future might soon be bright.

In the meantime, which lasted from 1901 to 1909, people lost patience waiting for the Wizard's new battery and bought gasoline cars. The irony is that throughout the entire period that Edison labored on nickel-iron technology, lead-acid batteries were being used to power eminently serviceable electrics.

This historical case allows us to appreciate what publicity about the battery consortium is really telling most Americans: good batteries for electric cars are not yet at hand, and are probably a long way off. A typical assessment was included in an otherwise upbeat article on electric cars, published in March 1992, in *The New York Times Magazine:*

> batteries have a long way to go. In fact the phrase most used about batteries is "the Achilles' heel of the electric car." Right now, they provide too limited a range, take too long to recharge and have too short a life to make electrics fully competitive in cost and performance with gasoline cars.

This misleading statement would cause most readers to conclude that commercializing the electric car today would be premature. As in Edison's day, however, building a serviceable electric car does not require a battery breakthrough. As we have seen, commuter electrics with a range of 25 to 60 miles are on the market already.

When placed into historical perspective, faith in the imminent appearance of a revolutionary storage battery, capable of giving electrics the same performance characteristics as gasoline cars, seems misplaced. Nearly every year during the twentieth century inventors announced breakthroughs in storage batteries. With only the rarest exception, these inventions have not been successfully commercialized, for all have drawbacks in purchase price, performance, maintenance costs, life expectancy, recyclability, or safety. Tellingly, the three main storage battery systems important today, lead-acid, nickel-iron, and nickel-cadmium, were all developed before 1910. Nickel-iron and nickel-cadmium batteries can power electric cars, but they are expensive (at least $6,000 and $25,000, respectively). "Advanced" battery systems, such as sodium-sulfur, zinc-air, and zinc-bromine, have been worked on for decades, and more decades may pass before any are ready for the people's electric. As Michael J. Riezenman observed recently, in an issue of *IEEE Spectrum* featuring electric vehicles, "no dramatic improvements in . . . batteries are expected soon."

Although no breakthrough batteries are on the horizon, one new battery—the nickel metal hydride—is likely to be improving the performance of electric cars before the end of the century. Ironically, the new battery is a distant technological descendant of Edison's nickel-iron battery. Developed by scientists at Energy Conversion Devices of Troy, Michigan, the battery is an alkaline system with an electrolyte of potassium hydroxide (and a trace of lithium hydroxide). The positive electrode is sintered nickel, while the negative is a powdered metal alloy, fabricated by processes unknown in Edison's time. Already commercialized for laptop computers and cellular phones, the nickel metal hydride battery is being adapted for electric vehicle applications with generous funding from the U.S. Advanced Battery Consortium.

With an energy density at least twice that of lead-acid, the new battery should give present-day electric cars a range of 50 to 120 miles. The battery can be easily boosted—a 60 percent recharge in 15 minutes, a full charge in less than an hour. Significantly, the battery is expected to last ten years, which will more than make up for its high price, an estimated $4,000–5,000. Best of all, the nickel metal hydride battery is a sealed system, requiring no maintenance. Commercial production of the new battery for electric vehicles is likely to be underway by 1997.

Because of the higher upfront cost of the nickel metal hydride battery (like the Edison battery), there will still be a substantial market for improved lead-acid batteries for electric vehicles. One design, now in the testing stage, shows considerable promise. Developed by Electrosource, Inc. of Austin, Texas, the Horizon battery departs from traditional lead-acid batteries in virtually every feature, from a woven positive electrode to horizontal stacking of plates. Despite its radical design, the Horizon battery lends itself to continuous-flow manufacture processes, and should be comparable in cost to conventional lead-acid batteries. Happily, the Horizon battery is expected to double the electric car's range while also accepting boosts.

Somewhat better batteries are clearly in the electric car's immediate future, but for the rest of this century, at least, electrics will not have the range of a gasoline car.

As in earlier times, public discussion of the electric car's future has been unduly influenced by what I have called the "better battery bugaboo" because the media naturally air the opinions of technical people. The comments of these "experts" betray a poor understanding of the larger social and cultural contexts in which they work. A product regarded by the technical community as "perfected" may be a flop with consumers, and products judged technically imperfect may still enjoy healthy sales and a high level of consumer satisfaction. The electric car of 1912, though ideal for city use, could not be afforded by the middle-class women who made up its largest potential market. It failed to reach these consumers for social and cultural—not technological—reasons. Thus, discussions must now focus on factors, apart from the vehicle and its batteries, that in the end will determine the electric car's destiny.

It is clear that, by the late 1990s, showrooms across America will be offering a surprisingly varied selection of electric cars made in Europe, the Pacific Rim, and America. Even so, executives at the Detroit Three, as well as sundry industry pundits, are concerned that the anticipated demand for such vehicles might not actually appear. In their darkest dreams, Detroit bean counters visualize unsold electrics stretching as far as the eye can see. Will the electric car in fact find a market beyond Sun Belt retirees and California yuppies? To answer this question, we must think about the relationships that ordinary Americans may come to have with electric cars in the years ahead.

During the past three decades, while the Detroit Three have been coping so ineptly with the inroads made by imports, America has been undergoing profound cultural changes that work in favor of the adoption of electric cars. Perhaps Detroit's aging auto executives should be reminded of their predecessors' once-fervent belief, aired in the fifties and sixties with great authority, that "Americans will never buy small cars." Having grown up comfortably with gas hogs, most senior citizens of that time did detest minuscule motor cars, but members of younger generations turned to them with gusto. Supplied mainly by foreign firms, small cars found important places in the lives of tens of millions of ordinary Americans. Now, new generations of Americans with different social needs, attitudes, and lifestyle expectations have reached car-buying age; many of these people are apt to regard the electric city car as something quite desirable—at least in principle.

In many textbooks and curricula in elementary and secondary schools, colleges, and universities, a strong environmental emphasis has taken root since the sixties. Beginning with the baby boomers, generations of urban Americans have grown up green, hoping one day to be able to buy nonpolluting automobiles. Not every American born since World War II has an acute environmental awareness, of course, but national polls indicate that tens of millions do. These are the people most likely to consider seriously buying an electric car because it reduces smog in cities, emits no greenhouse gases, and lessens U.S. dependence on foreign oil. Being a green technology, however, is insufficient to ensure the electric car's widespread adoption. Potential middle-class purchasers must also judge the electric car compatible with their lifestyles.

Today, the lifestyle of many ordinary Americans includes taking long trips by car. Thus, some argue, success will elude the electric until it can tour. Let us place this issue into historical perspective.

Over the decades, touring has been a moving target for electrics; and they are no closer to hitting it now than they were in 1900. Electric cars of the Classic Age did have a touring capability of a sort. Traveling 50 to 100 miles on a single charge and reaching speeds of 25 mph or more, an electric roadster of 1912 would have been a very fine touring car—in 1900. In the passage of that dozen years, however, performance requirements of the touring car, plaything of wealthy men, had changed dramatically. The touring car of the teens had to achieve speeds of 40-60 mph and travel more than 200 miles a day. No electric came close. During the many decades following the Classic Age, the performance requirements of the touring car became even more demanding. A vacation-worthy vehicle now must cruise the highways at 70-plus mph and go 500 or 600 miles in a day. Needless to say, electric cars still cannot tour.

Advocates of the touring electric of the future pin their hopes on two lines of technological development. The first, of course, is the better battery. Better is too mild a term, for miraculous would be the battery that could bestow upon electrics a 500-mile range. While not inconceivable sometime well into the next century, such a breakthrough is, as already noted, most improbable in the next decade or two.

A second avenue to the touring electric is through creation of an appropriate infrastructure, such as depots along highways for rapid battery exchanges and trolley-like operation on interstates. Many of these ideas, of course, date back to the first era of electrics. As New York's electric cabs and Milburn cars demonstrated, rapid battery exchanges are technically feasible. A workable system today would entail large, mechanized exchanges at no more than 15-mile intervals along all interstates (and in all towns). Building such a system obviously would require vast amounts of capital. That electric cars can operate in a trolley-like fashion was shown in 1897 by W. G. Caffrey, of Reno, Nevada, whose handiwork was favorably reported in *Horseless Age*. Recent experiments have attempted to use connections to the roadbed. When appropriate modern technology is perfected, the problem of paying for highway modifications will have to be faced. My hunch is that public utilities, battery companies, and state and federal governments will be reluctant to build an infrastructure for touring until electric vehicles are decidedly common, which may not be until the first decade of the next century.

In the most optimistic scenario, however, the continued expansion of air travel may eventually make the touring function obsolete for most family cars. Already, wealthy Americans fly to their travel destinations and rent cars. Still others rent cars at home for weekend travel and vacations. D. C. Tiffany of Boston set an inspiring example in 1913. Owner of only an electric, he rented a gasoline touring car for long trips. In the not-too-distant future, perhaps the buyer of an electric car will receive a book of coupons redeemable for 10-30 days of car rental per year. This would be far more economical than maintaining a gas guzzler just for the occasional trip out of town.

Like the better battery bugaboo, the touring electric chimera will be employed by the electric car's enemies (and a few friends) to foster unrealistic expectations about electric car performance. Detractors and misguided advocates will burden the electric with the need to wait for technological breakthroughs that may never come. The touring electric chimera will gradually fade, however, as people discover that the electric has finally found its own "sphere of action" on the streets of American cities. Though it cannot tour, the electric will be gradually adopted as an economical and socially appropriate commuter car.

That the electric is economical will become more generally known in the years ahead. Many people familiar with today's electrics insist that operation and maintenance costs are already lower than those of gasoline cars. Such evaluations include the replacement of an entire set of batteries, perhaps every four years (happily, lead-acid batteries are completely recyclable). However, abstract calculations in the technical literature, divorced from real people using real electric cars, do not consistently give the electric an economic advantage yet. When the Horizon and nickel metal hydride batteries become available, however, the electric car is expected to achieve a decisive economic edge.

Even if the electric car is not now cheaper to operate, it is much easier to maintain: no oil changes, no tuneups, no radiator flushes, and no broken belts or hoses. An electric's upkeep merely requires occasional lubrication of a few points, regular checks of water levels in the batteries, and periodic washing of the battery cases. DC motors also need additional but infrequent maintenance. People who hate the aggravations of gasoline car ownership, from breakdowns at the worst possible time to the terrors of emissions testing, will come to view the simple and reliable electric as a pleasant alternative.

To enhance the economic attractiveness of electric cars and so hasten their spread, public utilities as well as local, state, and federal governments are providing (or will soon provide) financial incentives. For example, public utilities are beginning to offer discounts to users of off-peak current who charge vehicle batteries. A few states heavily discount registration fees for electric vehicles; in Arizona, for example, it costs only $5 to register an electric car. In California, a generous tax credit is given to electric car purchasers. In addition, pollution taxes on gasoline vehicles, state and federal tax credits for buying an electric, and higher gasoline taxes are in place or in the immediate offing. In the year 2000, it is doubtful that gasoline in America will still be cheaper than bottled water.

The electric city car's utilitarian function is necessarily confined to commuting and running errands in town. Will ordinary Americans, spoiled by the unfettered freedom they have enjoyed with gasoline cars, perceive the electric as a capable city vehicle?

In the Classic Age city speed limits were low, and so the electric with a single charge could be driven all day long. Wealthy women like Mina Edison and Clara Ford enjoyed the ultimate in personal, mechanized mobility. Since the Classic Age, however, demands on the city car have greatly increased. In southern California, for example, commutes to work of 30 to 50 miles *each way* are common, while those of 50 to 80 miles are by no means unheard of. Southern California, of course, furnishes extreme examples; the majority of round-trip urban commutes clearly fall within the range of the electrics that can be bought today.

Electric car proponents never tire of pointing out that an electric with a range of 25 to 60 miles is an adequate city car for most people. What they ignore is the single most important lesson that the history of the early electric vehicle teaches us: the choice of a car technology is influenced by the *extreme*, not the average, anticipated use. Middle-class Americans in the teens flocked to the gasoline car, even though electrics could meet all of their urban transportation needs, because they anticipated touring every once in a while. In the showroom, today and tomorrow, ordinary Americans will not be thinking about the 20-mile trek back and forth to work each day, but about those few uncommon occasions—retrieving a sick child from school, shopping for a birthday gift at lunch, getting a root canal—when an extra-long range is essential.

Keeping this decision-making criterion in mind, we can predict that only people who live in compact towns and tiny cities, as well as those whose commutes in sprawling metropolitan areas are very short, will judge the 50-mile electric adequate for their needs. Although that group furnishes a sizable market for the people's electric, far more Americans will regard use of an electric car as too risky. Many of the latter will change their minds, later in the decade, as electrics with ranges of 75 to 150 miles become available. The most mobile urbanites, who anticipate a maximum daily range of 100 to 200 miles, may still not find electrics appealing. These last holdouts, however, may be won over by hybrid vehicles carrying a small gasoline or diesel engine, much like the Woods gasoline-electric coupé of 1916.

A more general solution to the range problem will be found in furnishing the means for easy recharging of batteries away from home during the day. In California, some employers already provide outlets in their parking lots so that owners of electric cars can plug in at work. Predictably, the "electrant," a coin-operated charging hydrant designed at the turn of the century for installation along city streets, has already been reinvented and updated. When they come on line, later in the decade, electrants will probably be called charging meters. These meters doubtless will be operated by the insertion of a credit card, with rates that vary by time of day.

As in the first age of electrics, power companies will be slow to establish an infrastructure for charging outside the home. When electric cars become more common, however, public utilities wishing to project an image of environmental concern (and municipalities desiring to proclaim their modernity) will jump on the charging-meter bandwagon and subsidize their installation. In the most optimistic scenario, by early in the next century fields of charging meters will spring up in a sizable number of public and private parking lots and along streets in electric-friendly towns and cities. Although most commuters would do their charging overnight at home, the proliferation of charging meters (and special stations for boosting) will give all electric car owners an extra margin of security. The sense of well-being that comes from knowing that a charge—just like gasoline—is available nearly anywhere will remove an important impediment to the adoption of the electric car.

The spread of electric cars will also be accelerated by nonutilitarian factors. Americans are always eager to use cars for displaying their wealth and special expertise, and this social need will find expression in electrics. Indeed, the electric lends itself perfectly to a variety of high-tech accessories. For example, the yuppie version of the electric car will not be complete without large panels of solar cells, cellular phone, 400-watt stereo with tape deck and CD player, world-band radio, CB transceiver, facsimile machine, back-looking radar, and burglar alarm. The upscale buyer will also be offered a horn that puts out a variety of sounds and songs, and "smart" windshields that get darker during bright sunlight. The *pièce de resistance* will be a real-time video display of the car's precise location on a city map using the Global Positioning System, a satellite technology.

The electric car will also come to be regarded as a desirable symbol of widely shared values and beliefs. Carrying the cachet of modernity, it will mean freedom from dependence on foreign oil, a sentiment supported by Americans across the political spectrum. And, of course, because the total pollution (on a per mile basis) contributed by electric cars and the power plants that charge their batteries is less than that emitted by cars burning hydrocarbons, Americans will employ the electric as a mobile billboard to announce their concern for the earth's well-being. Small wonder that many of today's electric owners prominently paint the word "electric" on their cars.

Although no one can be certain that a huge mass market awaits the electric car, there are ample grounds for believing that the people's electric will not languish in showrooms. At least some industry observers now agree that, as the environmentally friendly city car, electrics will find at least a modest mass market. Even *Motor Trend* has recently acknowledged that electric cars, "as non-polluting secondary vehicles used for a daily 50-mile commute, just might be the ticket." When inexpensive commuter electrics become more common later in the nineties, owners will tout their virtues to friends. Impressed, the latter will buy their own, and so on; inexorably electrics will gain a foothold in the cities of America. Unlike their ancestors, electric cars of the modern era will not be a spectacular flop.

The electric car's time has clearly come. Not only does the technology for making inexpensive electrics exist today, but in cities there is an adequate and easily improved infrastructure for charging. And, significantly, the electric city car is ideologically perfect for an age seemingly obsessed with the environment. By early in the next century the electric's success in this realm seems highly probable. Even with no breakthroughs in technology, it is possible to envision the eventual replacement of most family cars with electrics. The main question mark that remains is which companies—the Detroit Three, today's U.S. makers of electrics, or foreign firms—will be the big winners in the marketplace. Regardless of corporate winners and losers, ordinary Americans will at last be buying, in more than token numbers, a vehicle that has been for nearly a century the car of the future.

QUOTATION CREDITS

Complete references to sources cited by author and date only are provided in the Selected Bibliography.

CHAPTER 2

7   "perpetual-motion-man": Davenport 1851.
7   "most extraordinary" and "the days of": *New York Herald*, 27 April 1837.
7   "the purse strings": Davenport 1851.
9   "magnetic power": *The American Journal of Science and Arts*, 20 (series 2, 1850):282–284.
11   "invention factory": Friedel et al. 1986:x.
13   "[Arc] lamps were": Foster 1979:67.
14   "electrical railway": *Scientific American*, 28 February 1880.
15   "Mary had a": Clark 1977:76.
16   "I have it now": *New York Sun*, 16 September 1878.
17   "Edison's laboratory" and "seem satisfied that": *New York Herald*, 1 January 1880, p. 5.

CHAPTER 3

22   "boneshaker" and "ordinary": Smith 1972.
23   "Getting on": ibid.:11.
27   "central stations": Passer 1953:89.
28   "isolated lighting plants": Friedel et al. 1986:200.

29   "home executive": Venable 1981:8.
29   "from a lady's": draft letter from T. A. Edison to J. Hood Wright. Edison National Historic Site, Experimental Notebook, N87.11.15.
31   "just as soon as": Edison, quoted in Schallenberg 1982:68.
33   "dog cart," "propel the vehicle," and "no great speed": *Scientific American*, 6 October 1888, p. 215.
34   "on good roads" and "the first electric": *Scientific American*, 12 January 1907, p. 23.

CHAPTER 4

35   "of the ordinary": *Scientific American*, 9 January 1892, p. 18.
35   "a well loaded": *Western Electrician*, quoted in Sears 1977:14.
35   "among the many," "practical inventors," and "from the satisfactory": *The Electrical World*, 19 December 1891, p. 453.
39   "streetcar suburbs": Nye 1990:10.
39   "trolley breeze": ibid.
40   "six-day bicycle race": Smith 1972:134.
42   "new woman": Walker 1967.
42   "The use of the": Trowbridge 1897:132.
43   "Young man": Ford and Crowther 1930:5.
45   "upon a good" and "a long stride": *Scientific American*, 6 April 1895, pp. 214–215.
45   "irrespective of their": Salom 1896:280–281.
46   "decidedly the best": ibid.:283.
47   "The announcement": *Scientific American*, 26 September 1896, p. 253.
47   "it would be" and "whereas, on an": Salom 1896:290.
47   "all the gasoline": ibid.:289.

CHAPTER 5

49   "The guests of": *Scientific American*, 22 May 1897, p. 331.
50   "Only Pope": Rae 1965:21.
51   "People stood": *Wabash Plain Dealer*, quoted in Nye 1990:3.
51   "more than a": Nye 1990:54.
51   "merchants immediately": ibid.:5.
54   "in that dark": *The Electrical World*, 24 June 1893, p. 457.
55   "that a laundress": Jackson 1897:123.
56   "The incandescent": *Scientific American*, 25 May 1895, p. 322.
57   "The prominent feature": ibid., 13 May 1899, p. 301.
60   "superbly finished": Hiscox 1900:311.

CHAPTER 6

64 "a set of": *Horseless Age*, 10 September 1902, p. 273.

65 "25-cent piece": *Electrical World and Engineer*, 10 November 1900, p. 754.

66 "automobile as a" and "Micawber-like attitude": ibid., 10 June 1899, p. 794.

66 "Not unlike many": ibid., 15 December 1900, p. 930.

67 "simplicity, strength": Olson 1963:97.

71 "The horseless cab": *Scientific American*, 7 January 1899, p. 4.

72 "loud-lunged": *Horseless Age*, 15 May 1901, p. 1.

72 "stock-jobbing schemes": ibid., 10 April 1901, p. 25.

72 "the Lead Cab": ibid., 1 May 1901, p. 95.

72 "never breaks down" and "the electric": ibid., 3 December 1902, p. 622.

73 "for physicians'": ibid., 7 January 1903, p. 6.

74 "represents the": *Scientific American*, 6 April 1901, p. 211.

74 "the batteries did": Palmer 1902:646.

75 "merits of the": Hawkins 1902:111.

75 "Electricity is": Sutphen 1901:197.

CHAPTER 7

77 "The final perfection": Edison 1902:1.

77 "Twenty-one cells": ibid.:2–3.

78 "Within the reach": ibid.:3.

78 "one of the world's" and "a featherweight": Betts 1902:392.

78 "Edison is reported": Whitney 1902:95.

80 "has been developed": Palmer 1902:647.

80 "The technical and" and "The Edison battery": *The Motor World*, 29 January 1903, p. 628.

81 "A racing car": Olson 1963:127–128.

83 "an electromobile": *Scientific American*, 30 November 1901, p. 347.

83 "frightful din": *Electrical World and Engineer*, 23 November 1901, p. 851.

83 "road torpedo": *The Motor World*, 5 June 1902, p. 293.

84 "Like a flash": *Electrical World and Engineer*, 7 June 1902, p. 1016.

85 "[T]he lack of" and "in touring the": ibid., 19 July 1902, p. 79.

85 "glass showcase cupola": ibid., 28 February 1903, p. 374.

87 "combination surrey and" and "pneumatic cushions": ibid., 21 March 1903, p. 497.

87 "That the electric": *Motor World*, 22 January 1903, p. 560.

CHAPTER 8

91   "the little 26-inch" and "The smallest": *Scientific American*, 13 July 1901, p. 26.

91   "At present gasoline": Whitney 1902:94–95.

92   "desirable points": Johnson 1902:168.

92   "between steam and": *Outing*, January 1902, p. 494.

92   "The automobile of": Holland 1903:175.

92   "The electric vehicle": Eames 1906:4.

92   "dark age": *Electrical World*, 21 November 1914, p. 989.

94   "front rank" and "in design": *Scientific American*, 30 January 1904, p. 74.

94   "Lead Cab Trust": *The Horseless Age*, 15 May 1901.

94   "The FORD has sounded": *The Literary Digest*, April 1904, p. 569.

95   "those steadfast souls": *Electrical World and Engineer*, 21 January 1905, p. 164.

97   "In the business": *Scientific American*, 13 January 1906, p. 23.

98   "I am bound to": Letter from L. C. Weir to Thomas Edison, with Edison's draft reply, 11 January 1905. On file, Edison National Historic Site.

99   "I am certain": Draft letter from Thomas Edison to H. F. Parshall, 26 July 1905. On file, Edison National Historical Site.

101   "carries with it": *Electrical World and Engineer*, 3 June 1905, p. 1003.

101   "with all the": ibid., 3 June 1905, p. 1004.

103   "sent to the home": *Electrical World*, 26 December 1908, p. 1402.

105   "an electric carriage": ibid., 15 June 1907, p. 1212.

105   "that the time": ibid., 15 June 1907, pp. 1230.

105   "why not quote" and "when you can": ibid., 3 August 1907, p. 240.

106   "No house or shop": ibid., 7 November 1908, p. 982.

CHAPTER 9

109   "Many a bright": Scarritt 1903.

109   "it shall be so": Henry Ford, quoted in Olson 1963:186.

110   "It may be possible": Haines 1907:75.

111   "the automobile has" and "Wonderfully rapid": *Scientific American*, 4 January 1908, p. 7.

113   "the common verdict": *The Autocar*, 23 November 1907, p. 891.

114   "At last the battery": Draft letter from Thomas Edison to H. F. Parshall, probably 12 June 1908. On file, Edison National Historic Site.

114   "One of the": Vanderbilt 1971:233.

115   "in all that pertains": *Electrical World*, 26 January 1907, p. 202.

116   "high-grade buggies": *Electric Vehicles*, January 1916, p. 3.

116   "outlived prejudice" and "here to remain": Goss 1907:1697.

118 "comparatively short": *Electrical World and Engineer,* 23 November 1901, p. 866.

119 "The rapidly increasing": *Electrical World,* 6 April 1907, p. 684.

122 "without mishap" and "suffragette run": *The Motor World,* 14 January 1909.

123 "Relation of the": *Electrical World,* 11 March 1909, pp. 635–636.

123 "the electric automobile": Eames 1903:69.

124 "Too many hills": *Electrical World,* 5 August 1909, p. 314.

124 "The year 1909": ibid., 6 January 1910, p. 11.

CHAPTER 10

125 "the Cinderella": ibid., 12 August 1909, p. 356.

129 "likely to be" and "the disadvantage they would suffer": Kennedy 1914:24.

130 "to sell the": Letter from Thomas Edison to W. C. Anderson, ca. 1911–1912. On file, Henry Ford Museum & Greenfield Village.

131 "the worst roads": Thomas Edison, undated notes entitled "Electric Delivery Wagon," p. 1. On file, Edison National Historic Site.

133 "What is particularly": ibid., pp. 3–4.

133 "Thomas A. Edison": *Detroit Free Press,* 2 June 1911.

133 "report claiming" and "will stop sale": Letter from W. C. Anderson to Thomas Edison, 2 June 1911. On file, Edison National Historic Site.

134 "deny every": Draft letter from Thomas Edison to W. C. Anderson, ca. 6 June 1911. On file, Edison National Historic Site.

135 "not ready yet": Draft letter from Thomas Edison to Wood & Schermerhorn, publishers, ca. 20 May 1912. On file, Edison National Historic Site.

135 "the once despised": Towle 1911:34.

135 "absolutely dependable": *The Motor World,* 8 August 1912, p. 41.

135 "In advertising the": *Electrical World,* 1 June 1911, p. 1374.

136 "her saleswomanship": ibid., 6 April 1912, p. 753.

138 "pleasure car salon" and "persons of recognized": ibid., 22 November 1913, p. 1044.

140 "The Baker is" and "does everything": 1911 Baker brochure. On file, Henry Ford Museum & Greenfield Village.

140 "The Woods Electric": 1913 Woods brochure. On file, Henry Ford Museum & Greenfield Village.

140 "extravagance in the" and "the great mass": Kennedy 1914:24.

141 "was a beauty," "What is that" "Finally, he got," "cussing out," and *"real mad"*: The Reminiscences of George Brown, vol. 2. On File, Henry Ford Museum & Greenfield Village.

142 "Boom in Electric": *Electrical World,* 22 June 1911, p. 1590.

142 "the famous exclusive": Ohio Electric brochure. On file, Henry Ford Museum & Greenfield Village.

144 "self-cranking": *The Literary Digest*, 6 November 1909, p. 779.

148 "The central-station": *Electrical World*, 27 June 1914, p. 1470.

148 "wants speed and" and "get out into": ibid., 21 February 1914, p. 435.

148 "the makers of": ibid., 31 October 1914, p. 848.

149 "perhaps the longest": ibid., 8 November 1913, p. 937.

150 "The lessons of": ibid., p. 938.

151 "Gasolenish Roadster": *The Motor World*, 8 August 1912.

CHAPTER 11

153 "another great factory": *Detroit Free Press*, 10 January 1914.

153 "At last . . . the electric": *Electrical World*, 17 January 1914, p. 125.

153 "the demand for": *Motor World*, 22 January 1914.

154 "giving out," "consider a," and "other little things": Letter from Mrs. Bright to Edsel Ford, 27 February 1914. On file, Henry Ford Museum & Greenfield Village.

154 "does not contemplate" and "not be in": Letter from E. G. Liebold to F. C. Fisk, 17 February 1914. On file, Henry Ford Museum & Greenfield Village.

154 "this has a" and "Of course, I": Letter from Thomas Edison to Henry Ford, 29 October 1912. On file, Henry Ford Museum & Greenfield Village.

162 "A Start Towards": *Electric Vehicles*, January 1917, p. 1.

163 "for short-haul": *Electrical World*, 10 January 1914, p. 69.

167 "over average roads": Memo, H. W. Jones to Thomas Edison, 11 June 1914. On file, Edison National Historic Site.

167 "delighted": Letter from W. G. Bee to Henry Ford, 4 November 1914. On file, Henry Ford Museum & Greenfield Village.

167 "raised the devil": E. G. Liebold, Reminiscences, p. 811. On file, Henry Ford Museum & Greenfield Village.

167 "the electric car": Letter from G. S. Anderson to J. D. Main, 7 July 1915. On file, Henry Ford Museum & Greenfield Village.

167 "On account of": Letter from G. S. Anderson to B. F. Burch, 3 February 1916. On file, Henry Ford Museum & Greenfield Village.

167 "was still in": Letter from G. S. Anderson to F. M. Peterson, 8 March 1917. On file, Henry Ford Museum & Greenfield Village.

168 "There is hardly": *Electric Vehicles*, September 1916, p. 98.

171 "most of the basic": Flink 1975:174.

172 "God's great": Henry Ford, quoted in Olson 1963:186.

173 "the technology of": DeLuchi et al. 1989:256.

174 "electric vehicle": Pratt 1992:55.
174 "electric cars are": *Newsweek*, 1 April 1991, p. 62.

CHAPTER 12

175 "car culture": Flink 1975.
180 "revolutionary": Freedman 1992.
182 "batteries have a": Hazleton 1992:39.
182 "Advanced" and "no dramatic": Riezenman 1992:22.
189 "as non-polluting secondary": Cogan 1991:77.

SELECTED BIBLIOGRAPHY

Allen, Frederick Lewis

1952   *The Big Change: America Transforms Itself, 1900–1950.* Harper & Brothers, New York.

Allen, James T.

1900   *Digest of United States Automobile Patents from 1789 to July 1, 1899, Including All Patents Officially Classed as Traction-Engines for the Same Period.* H. B. Russell & Company, Washington, D. C.

Anonymous

1887   Storage Batteries for Electric Locomotion. *The Electrical World*, 20 August, pp. 100–102.

1893   The New Hotel Waldorf. *The Electrical World*, 8 April, pp. 260–261.

1897a   The Columbia Electric Motor Carriage. *The Electrical World*, 15 May, pp. 614–617.

1897b   Electric Motor-Cab Service in New York City—I. *The Electrical World*, 14 August, pp. 183–186.

1897c   Electric Motor-Cab Service in New York City—II. *The Electrical World*, 21 August, pp. 213–216.

1898   The New Station of the Electric Vehicle Company. *The Electrical World*, 3 September, pp. 227–232.

1899a   The Electric Cab Service of New York City. *Scientific American*, 25 March, pp. 184–185.

1899b   Automobile Charging Hydrant. *Electrical World and Engineer*, 10 June, p. 815.

1901   Automobile Storage Batteries. *Electrical World and Engineer*, 5 October, pp. 538–545.

1902a   As to the "Soap Box" Battery. *The Motor World*, 5 June, p. 291.

1902b   Cost of Operating Automobiles. *Electrical World and Engineer*, 22 November, p. 819.

1902c   Some Modern Automobile Accumulators. *The Motor World*, 17 May 1902, pp. 351–352.

1902d   The Baker Electric Racing Automobile. *Scientific American*, 14 June, p. 419.

1903a   Cooper-Hewitt Static Converter. *Electrical World and Engineer*, 17 January, pp. 121–122.

1903b   Show Proves a Revelation. *The Motor World*, 22 January, pp. 541–563.

1905a   New Type of Electric Truck. *Scientific American*, 24 June, p. 505.

1905b   Effect of Load Factor on Cost of Power. *Electrical World and Engineer*, 11 February, pp. 303–305.

1905c   The Electric Automobile Exhibit at the New York Show. *Electrical World and Engineer*, 21 January, pp. 163–164.

1905d   Mercury Arc Rectifier for Charging Batteries. *Electrical World and Engineer*, 28 January, p. 214.

1905e   New Electric Garage in Denver. *Electrical World and Engineer*, 27 May, pp. 979–980.

1906a   The Electric Flat-Iron. *Electrical World and Engineer*, 3 February, p. 237.

1906b   Central Station Work at Rockford, Ill. *Electrical World*, 17 February, pp. 366–368.

1907a   Electric Automobiles in Washington. *Electrical World*, 1 June, pp. 1078–1080.

1907b   The Central Station and the Electric Vehicle. *Electrical World*, 6 April, pp. 682–684.

1909a   The Electric Vehicle Situation. *Electrical World*, 4 March, pp. 534–535.

1909b   The Relations between Central Stations and the Electric Automobile. *Electrical World*, 5 August, pp. 314–320.

1909c   Care of Electric Automobiles in St. Louis, Mo. *Electrical World*, 29 July, pp. 257–258.

1909d   Electric Vehicles and Central-Station Business. *Electrical World*, 10 June, pp. 1482–1483.

1909e   Automobiles in Cleveland. *Electrical World*, 22 April, pp. 974–976.

1909f   Development of Electric Vehicle Business at Toledo, Ohio. *Electrical World*, 4 March, pp. 571–573.

1909g   New Nickel-Iron Battery Withstands Tests. *The Automobile*, 15 July, pp. 101–102.

1910a   Convention of the Electric Vehicle Association of America. *Electrical World*, 20 October, pp. 925–926.

1910b   Electric Vehicles at Rockford, Ill. *Electrical World*, 24 November, pp. 1239–1240.

1910c   Cost of Running Electric Vehicles. *Electrical World*, 3 February, p. 294.

1910d   Ratio of Wired to Unwired Houses. *Electrical World*, 6 January, p. 52.

1910e   Electric Light in 700,000 Residences. *Electrical World*, 20 January, p. 155.

1910f   Edison Nickel-Iron Storage Battery. *Electrical World*, 20 January, pp. 175–177.

1911   Growth of the Electric Car Industry Well Illustrated in the Chicago Show. *Motor Age*, 26 January, pp. 42–46.

1912a   Little Known Features of Modern Electrics. *The Motor World*, 8 August, pp. 41–45.

1912b   Standardization of Electric-Vehicle Speeds. *Electrical World*, 2 March, p. 446.

1912c   The Boston Electric-Vehicle Campaign. *Electrical World*, 6 April, pp. 738–740.

1912d   Operating Cost Data of Electric Vehicles. *Electrical World*, 6 April, pp. 756–757.

1912e   Relative Reliability of Electric and Gasoline Vehicles. *Electrical World*, 10 February, p. 293.

1912f   Results of Motor-Vehicle Research at Massachusetts Institute of Technology. *Electrical World*, 18 May, pp. 1068–1070.

1913a   Electric-Vehicle Cost Data. *Electrical World*, 5 April, pp. 731–732.

1913b   Record Run by Electric Roadster. *Electrical World*, 27 September, p. 617.

1913c   Electric-Vehicle Salon at Boston. *Electrical World*, 22 November, p. 1044.

1914a   Detroit Concern to Market Low-Priced Columbia Electric: Roadster Will Sell for $784. *Motor Age*, 19 February, p. 26.

1914b   Dr. Steinmetz on the Electric as the Ultimate Car. *Electrical World*, 31 January, pp. 241–242.

1914c   Electric-Vehicle Interests Convene at Boston. *Electrical World*, 30 May, pp. 1205–1208.

1914d   Cost of Commercial Electric Vehicle Operation. *Electrical World*, 17 October, p. 765.

1915   Selling Vehicles on the Installment Plan. *Electrical World*, 16 October, p. 856.

1916a   The Unimportance of Touring Ability. *Electric Vehicles*, August, pp. 51–52.

1916b   Building the Detroit Electric. *Electric Vehicles*, July, pp. 5–11.

1916c   The Kind of Car a Man Wants. *Electric Vehicles*, June, pp. 173–174.

1916d   Manufacture of Automobiles. *Electric Vehicles*, March, p. 85.

1916e   Progress of the Electric Passenger Automobile. *Electric Vehicles*, January, pp. 13–16.

1916f   Installment Plan Boosts Electric Vehicle Sale. *Electrical World*, 14 October, p. 785.

1916g   Rates for Residence Lighting. *Electrical World*, 29 July, p. 243.

1917   Making Batteries as Available as Gasoline. *Electrical World*, 28 July, p. 162.

1920   Electric Vehicle Sessions. *Electrical World*, 29 May, pp. 1253–1254.

1925   Three Barriers that Hold Back Electric Trucks. *Electrical World*, 31 January, p. 236.

1928   Operating Costs of Electric and Gasoline Trucks Compared. *Electrical World*, 2 June, pp. 1150–1151.

1975   Two Electric Cars. *Consumer Reports* 40:596–599.

1989   Electric Cars Stage a Comeback; Lightweighting Makes Them Practical. *Modern Plastics* 66:44–45.

1991   The Clean Machine. *Engineering* 231:26–27.

1992   Electric Car Pool: Automakers Consort on Advanced Batteries. *Scientific American*, May, pp. 126–127.

Aronson, Robert, and Larry L. Boulder

1974   EV Performance: Road Testing the Electrics. *Machine Design*, 17 October, pp. 19–28.

Babcock, F. A.

1907   The Electric Motor of Yesterday and To-day. *Harper's Weekly*, 16 March, pp. 373–374.

Baker, Joseph B.

1910   New Edison Storage Battery. *The Horseless Age*, 15 June, pp. 882–883.

1911   Thomas A. Edison's Latest Invention: A Storage Battery Designed and Constructed from the Automobile User's Point of View. *Scientific American*, 14 January, pp. 30, 45–47.

Basalla, George

1988   *The Evolution of Technology.* Cambridge University Press, Cambridge.

Bates, Bradford (editor)

1992   *Electric Vehicles: A Decade of Transition.* Society of Automotive Engineers, Warrendale, Pennsylvania.

Baum, L. Frank

1901   *The Master Key: An Electrical Fairy Tale, Founded upon the Mysteries of Electricity and the Optimism of Its Devotees. It Was Written for Boys, but Others May Read It.* Bowen-Merrill, Indianapolis.

Baxter, William, Jr.
1900   Electric Automobiles. *Popular Science* 57:479–490.
Bearce, W. D.
1911   Electric Drive in the Automobile Industry. *General Electric Review* 14:340–344.
Bell, Louis
1897   The Wonderful Expansion in the Use of Electric Power. *Engineering Magazine* 12:630–642.
Betts, R. G.
1902   Faster than the Locomotive: The Flight of the Automobile. *Outing* 39:392–398.
Bijker, Wiebe E., Thomas P. Hughes, Trevor J. Pinch (editors)
1987   *The Social Construction of Technological Systems: New Directions in the Sociology and History of Technology.* MIT Press, Cambridge.
Bivert, Eugene
1908   Care of the Electric Automobile. *The Motor Way*, February, pp. 16–17.
Blood, W. H., Jr.
1913   Status of the Electric Vehicle. *Electrical World*, 4 January, pp. 22–23.
Booth, Thomas B.
1899   American Types of Electric Motor Vehicles—I. Columbia Automobiles. *Electrical World and Engineer*, 6 May 1899, pp. 575–579.
Bowers, Brian
1982   *A History of Electric Light and Power.* Peter Peregrinus Ltd., Stevenage, UK.
Bowker, R. R. (editor)
1896   Great American Industries. XII—Electricity. *Harper's Magazine* 93:710–739.
Braden, Donna R.
1988   *Leisure and Entertainment in America.* Henry Ford Museum & Greenfield Village, Dearborn, Michigan.
Brady, Dorothy S.
1964   Relative Prices in the Nineteenth Century. *Journal of Economic History* 24:145–203.
Branch, Lester M.
1925   A User's Appraisal of Electric Trucking. *Electrical World*, 29 August, pp. 415–416.
Bruce, Robert
1900a   The Promise of the Automobile in Recreative Life. *Outing* 36:81–85.
1900b   The Place of the Automobile. *Outing* 37:65–69.

Budlong, M. J.

1907   The Development of the Electric Automobile. *Harper's Weekly*, 16 March, pp. 381–382.

Burlingame, Roger

1955   *Henry Ford: A Great Life in Brief.* Alfred A. Knopf, New York.

Callon, Michel

1980   The State and Technical Innovation: A Case Study of the Electric Vehicle in France. *Research Policy* 9:358–376.

Cannon, William A., and Fred K. Fox

1981   *Studebaker: The Complete Story.* Tab Books, Blue Ridge Summit, Pennsylvania.

Carlson, W. Bernard

1988   Thomas Edison as a Manager of R & D: The Case of the Alkaline Storage Battery, 1898–1915. *IEEE Technology and Society Magazine* 7(4):4–12.

Cavenaugh, Burleigh

1915   Poor Man's Electric. *Illustrated World*, December, p. 541.

Chalfant, E. P.

1916   Electric Passenger Vehicle Problems and Activities. *National Electric Light Association, Thirty-Ninth Convention, Proceedings*, vol. 3, pp. 186–205.

Clark, Ronald W.

1977   *Edison: The Man Who Made the Future.* G. P. Putnam's Sons, New York.

Claudy, C. H.

1915   What Cars in the Country Home Garage? *Country Life in America*, October, pp. 80–86.

Clough, Albert L.

1913   The Motor Car and Its Owner To-day. *Review of Reviews* 47:310–320.

1916   Democratizing the Motor Car. *The Independent*, 1 May, pp. 177–180.

Cogan, Ron

1991   Electric Cars. *Motor Trend*, August, pp. 71–77.

Collie, M. J. (editor)

1979   *Electric and Hybrid Vehicles.* Noyes Data Corporation, Park Ridge, New Jersey.

Collier, Peter, and David Horowitz

1987   *The Fords: An American Epic.* Summit Books, New York.

Collins, A. F.

1906   Mercury Arc Rectifier for Charging Storage Batteries. *Scientific American*, 17 February, pp. 148–149.

Colvin, Fred H.

1911   The Mechanics of the Edison Battery. *American Machinist* 35:241–248.

Condit, Carl W.

1977   The Pioneer Stage of Railroad Electrification. *American Philosophical Society, Transactions*, vol. 67, part 7.

Conot, Robert

1979   *Thomas A. Edison: A Streak of Luck*. Da Capo Press, New York.

Cowan, Ruth Schwartz

1983   *More Work for Mother: The Ironies of Household Technology from the Open Hearth to the Microwave*. Basic Books, New York.

Cushing, H. C., Jr., and Frank W. Smith

1916   *The Electric Vehicle Hand-Book* (fourth edition). H. C. Cushing, Jr., New York.

Cutcliffe, Stephen H., and Robert C. Post (editors)

1989   *In Context: History and the History of Technology. Essays in Honor of Melvin Kranzberg*. Lehigh University Press, Bethlehem.

Davenport, William

1851   Autobiography. Manuscript on file, Vermont Historical Society, Montpelier.

Degler, Carl N.

1980   *At Odds: Women and the Family in America from the Revolution to the Present*. Oxford University Press, New York.

DeLuchi, Mark, Quanlu Wang, and Daniel Sperling

1989   Electric Vehicles: Performance, Life-Cycle Costs, Emissions, and Recharging Requirements. *Transportation Research: Part A*. 23A:255–278.

DeWaard, John, and Aaron E. Klein

1977   *Electric Cars*. Doubleday & Company, Garden City.

Diemer, Hugo

1911   *Automobiles: A Practical Treatise on the Construction, Operation, and Care of Gasoline, Steam, and Electric Motor-Cars, Including Mechanical Details of Running Gear, Power Plant, Body, and Accessories, Instruction in Driving, Etc.* American School of Correspondence, Chicago.

Duerksen, Menno

1977a   Cars that Go Buzzz in the Night. A History of Electrics, Part I. *Cars & Parts*, August 1977, pp. 9–16.

1977b   Running Out of Juice. A History of Electrics, Part II. *Cars & Parts*, September 1977, pp. 9–18.

Du Moncel, Th., Frank Geraldy, and C. J. Wharton

1883   *Electricity as a Motive Power*. E. & F. N. Spon, London.

Dunbar, Seymour

1937   *A History of Travel in America* (second edition). Tudor, New York.

Duryea, Charles E.

1907   A Historic Motor Vehicle Recently Reproduced—The Ford-Lenoir Car.
            The Horseless Age, 2 October, pp. 502–503.

Dyer, Frank L., and Thomas C. Martin

1910   *Edison: His Life and Inventions* (2 vols.). Harper & Brothers, New York.

Eames, Hayden

1903   Present Status of Electric Automobilism. *Electrical World and Engineer*,
            10 January 1903, pp. 68–69.

1906   Minutes of the Meeting of the Association of Electric Vehicle Manufac-
            turers, 6 December 1906, Manhattan, New York. Manuscript on file, Ed-
            ison National Historic Site.

1910   The Electric Vehicle Opportunity. *National Electric Light Association,
            Proceedings*, vol. 2, pp. 88–119.

Edison, Thomas A.

1902   The Storage Battery and the Motor Car. *North American Review*, July,
            pp. 1–4.

1911   Electric Delivery Wagons. *Carriage and Wagon Builder and American Ve-
            hicle* 24(12):11–12.

1948   *The Diary and Observations of Thomas Alva Edison* (edited by Dagobert
            D. Runes). Philosophical Library, New York.

Edwards, Charles E.

1965   *Dynamics of the U.S. Automobile Industry.* University of South Carolina
            Press, Columbia.

Electric Power Research Institute

1992a   Electric Vehicles and the Environment. *Electric Power Research Institute,
            Brochure* 100553.

1992b   Infrastructure Development: Utilities and the Electric Vehicle Challenge.
            Electric Power Research Institute, Brochure 101035.

1993   The Transportation Program: Advanced Electric Vehicle Lead-Acid Bat-
            tery Project. *Electric Power Research Institute, Brochure* 102246.

Espenschied, F. F.

1925   What's the Matter with Electric Trucks? *Electrical World*, 11 April, p. 769.

Feiker, F. M.

1917   The Customer's View-Point on the Electric Vehicle. *Proceedings of the
            National Electric Light Association*, vol. 3, pp. 71–77.

Fliess, Robert A.

1900   The Electric Automobile from a Commercial Point of View—I. *Electrical
            World and Engineer*, 6 October, pp. 516–523.

Flink, James J.

1970   *America Adopts the Automobile, 1895–1910.* MIT Press, Cambridge,
            Massachusetts.

1975   *The Car Culture.* MIT Press, Cambridge, Massachusetts.

Flower, B. O.

1907   The Coming Electrical Home for America's Millions. *The Arena* 38(217):591–600.

Ford, Henry, and Samuel Crowther

1926   *Today and Tomorrow.* Doubleday, Page & Company, New York.

1930   *Edison As I Know Him.* Cosmopolitan, New York.

Foster, Abram J.

1979   *The Coming of the Electrical Age to the United States.* Arno Press, New York.

Foster, George B.

1919   A Message from Electric Vehicle Users or the Proof of the Pudding. *Proceedings of the National Electric Light Association,* vol. 3, pp. 84–93.

Fox, Richard Wightman, and T. J. Jackson Lears

1983   *The Culture of Consumption: Critical Essays in American History, 1880–1980.* Pantheon Books, New York.

Freedman, David H.

1992   Batteries Included. *Discover,* March, pp. 90–98.

Friedel, Robert, Paul Israel, and Bernard S. Finn

1986   *Edison's Electric Light: Biography of an Invention.* Rutgers University Press, New Brunswick, New Jersey.

Georgano, G. N.

1985   *Cars, 1886–1930.* Beekman House, New York.

Gilchrist, John F., and A. J. Marshall

1915   The Electric Vehicle and the Central Station. *Proceedings of the National Electric Light Association,* vol. 3, pp. 325–330.

Glaab, Charles N., and A. Theodore Brown

1967   *A History of Urban America.* Macmillan, New York.

Goldin, Claudia

1990   *Understanding the Gender Gap: An Economic History of American Women.* Oxford University Press, New York.

Goss, M. L.

1907   Yesterday and To-day of the Electric. *Harper's Weekly,* 16 November, p. 1697.

Graves, Ralph H.

1935   *The Triumph of an Idea: The Story of Henry Ford.* Doubleday, Doran & Company, Garden City, New York.

Gross, Ken

1992   The Electric Car Question. *Automotive Industry* 172:17.

Haines, Harry B.

1907a   The Automobile and the Average Man. *Review of Reviews,* January, pp. 74–83.

1907b   How to Tour in an Automobile. *Scientific American*, 9 November, pp. 330–331.

Hall, R. S.
1914   Report of Committee on Wiring of Existing Buildings. *National Electric Light Association, Thirty-Seventh Convention, Proceedings*, pp. 308–322.

Hausman, William J., and John L. Neufeld
1989   Engineers and Economists: Historical Perspectives on the Pricing of Electricity. *Technology and Culture* 30:83–104.

Hawkins, C. A.
1902   Automobile Endurance. *Overland Monthly* (n.s.) 40:111–114.

Hazleton, Lesley
1992   Real Cool Cars. *The New York Times Magazine*, 29 March, pp. 34–39, 68, 73.

Hillman, H. W.
1906   Electricity in the Home. *Cassier's Magazine* 31:25–35.

Hindle, Brooke, and Steven Lubar
1986   *Engines of Change: The American Industrial Revolution, 1790–1860.* Smithsonian Institution Press, Washington, D.C.

Hiscox, Gardner D.
1900   *Horseless Vehicles, Automobiles, Motorcycles Operated by Steam, Hydro-Carbon, Electric, and Pneumatic Motors.* Munn & Company, New York.

Hofstadter, Richard
1955   *The Age of Reform: From Bryan to F.D.R.* Vintage Books, New York.

Holland, James P.
1903   The Future of the Automobile. *Munsey's Magazine* 29:171–177.

Holland, Walter E.
1910   The Edison Storage Battery: Its Pre-eminent Fitness for Vehicle Service. *Electrical World*, 28 April, pp. 1080–1083.

Homans, James E.
1902   *Self-Propelled Vehicles: A Practical Treatise on the Theory, Construction, Operation, Care, and Management of All Forms of Automobiles.* Theo. Audel & Co., New York.

Horowitz, Daniel
1985   *The Morality of Spending: Attitudes toward the Consumer Society in America, 1875–1940.* Johns Hopkins University Press, Baltimore.

Hounshell, David A.
1984   *From the American System to Mass Production, 1800–1932: The Development of Manufacturing Technology in the United States.* Johns Hopkins University Press, Baltimore.

Hughes, Thomas P.
1976   *Thomas Edison, Professional Inventor*. The Science Museum, London.
1983   *Networks of Power: Electrification in Western Society, 1880–1930*. Johns
            Hopkins University Press, Baltimore.
1989   *American Genesis: A Century of Invention and Technological Enthusiasm,
            1870–1970*. Viking, New York.

Hutchings, James T.
1911   Report of Committee on Electric Vehicles. *National Electric Light Asso-
            ciation, Proceedings*, vol. 1, pp. 584–615.

Iversen, Wesley R.
1991   Electric Vehicle Race Gathers Momentum. *Design News* 47:93–101.

Jackson, John P.
1897   The Economy and Utility of Electrical Cooking Apparatus. *The Electrical
            World*, 31 July, pp. 122–123.

Jakle, John A.
1985   *The Tourist: Travel in Twentieth-Century North America*. University of
            Nebraska Press, Lincoln.

Jehl, Francis
1937   *Menlo Park Reminiscences*, vol. 1. Edison Institute, Dearborn, Michigan.

Jenkins, R. V., L. S. Reich, P. B. Israel, Toby Appel, A. J. Butrica, R. A. Rosenberg,
K. A. Nier, M. Andrews, T. E. Jeffrey (editors)
1989   *The Papers of Thomas A. Edison*, vol. 1, *The Making of an Inventor, Feb-
            ruary 1847–June 1873*. Johns Hopkins University Press, Baltimore.

Johnson, L. H.
1902   The Anatomy of the Automobile. *Overland Monthly* (n.s.) 40:163–170.

Johnston, R. H.
1907   The Joys of Touring. *Collier's*, 26 October, pp. 9–12.

Jones, Francis A.
1924   *Thomas Alva Edison: An Intimate Record* (revised edition). Thomas Y.
            Crowell, New York.

Jones, Howard Mumford
1970   *The Age of Energy: Varieties of American Experience 1865–1915*. The Vi-
            king Press, New York.

Josephson, Matthew
1959   *Edison: A Biography*. McGraw-Hill, New York.

Kaempfert, Waldemar
1924   *A Popular History of American Invention*, vol. 1. Charles Scribner's Sons,
            New York.

Kennedy, William P.

1914   Electric Vehicle Progress during 1913. *Electrical World*, 3 January, pp. 23–25.

1915a Electric Vehicle Cost Accounting. *Proceedings of the National Electric Light Association*, vol. 1, pp. 74–89.

1915b Review of the Electric-Vehicle Field. *Electrical World*, 2 January, pp. 25–27.

Kennelly, A. E.

1890   Electricity in the Household. *Scribner's Magazine* 7:102–115.

Kent, Dorman B. E.

1927   Address at the 125th Anniversary of the Birth of Thomas Davenport. *Proceedings of the Vermont Historical Society for the Years 1926–1927–1928*, pp. 207–232.

Kimes, Beverly R., and Henry A. Clark, Jr.

1989   *Standard Catalog of American Cars, 1805–1942* (second edition). Krause Publications, Iola, Wisconsin.

King, W. James

1963   The Development of Electrical Technology in the 19th Century: 1. The Electrochemical Cell and the Electromagnet. *United States National Museum, Bulletin 228, Paper 28*, pp. 233–271.

Kobe, Gerry

1992   Electric Car Update. *Automotive Industry* 172:76–85.

Koven, Mrs. Reginald de

1895   Bicycling for Women. *The Cosmopolitan*, August, p. 386–394.

LaMarre, Tom

1989   Detroit Electric, Society's Town Car. *Automobile Quarterly* 27(2):160–171.

Lampton, William J.

1902   The Meaning of the Automobile. *Outing* 40:692–699.

Larrabee, Eric, and Rolf Meyersohn (editors)

1958   *Mass Leisure*. The Free Press, Glencoe, Illinois.

La Schum, Edward E.

1919   The Electric Truck in Modern Transportation. *Proceedings of the National Electric Light Association*, vol. 4, pp. 37–49.

1924   *The Electric Motor Truck: Selection of Motor Vehicle Equipment, Its Operation and Maintenance*. U.P.C. Book Co., New York.

Latham, George E.

1903   The Automobile and Automobiling. *Munsey's Magazine*, May, pp. 161–166.

Leslie, Stuart W.

1983   *Boss Kettering*. Columbia University Press, New York.

Levine, Gary

1974   *The Car Solution: The Steam Engine Comes of Age*. Horizon Press, New York.

Linford, H. B., H. P. Gregor, and B. J. Steigerwald (editors)

1967   *Power Systems for Electric Vehicles*. Clearinghouse for Federal Scientific and Technical Information (PB177706), Springfield, Virginia.

Little, Arthur D., Inc.

1969   *Prospects for Electric Vehicles. A Study of Low-Pollution-Potential Vehicles—Electric*. National Technical Information Service (PB194814), Springfield, Virginia.

MacLaren, Malcolm

1943   *The Rise of the Electrical Industry during the Nineteenth Century*. Princeton University Press, Princeton.

Madison, Ryland

1912   The Lady and the Electric. *Country Life in America*, 15 July, pp. 36, 44, 46, 48.

Mansfield, E. S.

1917   Report of the Electric Vehicle Section. *National Electric Light Association, Fortieth Convention, Proceedings*, vol. 3, pp. 2–5.

Marshall, A. Jackson

1917   The Electric Vehicle: A Resumé of the Year's Progress. *Electric Vehicles*, January, pp. 29–30.

Martin, Douglas S.

1913   Central Station Co-operation in the Electric-Vehicle Industry. *The Engineering Magazine* 46:45–52.

Martin, T. C.

1916   Report of the Committee on Progress. *National Electric Light Association, Thirty-Ninth Convention, Proceedings*, vol. 4.

Martin, T. Commerford, and Stephen L. Coles

1919   *The Story of Electricity*, vol. 1. The Story of Electricity Company, New York.

Marvin, Carolyn

1988   *When Old Technologies Were New: Thinking about Electrical Communication in the Late Nineteenth Century*. Oxford University Press, Oxford.

Matthews, C. P.

1893–1894   Lead Secondary Batteries. *Proceedings of the Electrical Society of Cornell University* 1:1–11.

Maxim, Hiram Percy

1899a   Electric Vehicles and Their Relation to Central Stations. *The Electrical World*, 28 January, pp. 116–117.

1899b   The Automobile Situation. *Cassier's Magazine* 16:599–610.

1937   *Horseless Carriage Days.* Harper & Brothers, New York.

McClure, J. B.

1879   *Edison and His Inventions.* Rhodes & McClure, Chicago.

McCrea, S. (editor)

1991   *Why Wait for Detroit? Drive the Car of the Future Today.* South Florida Electric Auto Association, Ft. Lauderdale, Florida.

McGuire, Patrick

1990   Money and Power: Financiers and the Electric Manufacturing Industry, 1878–1896. *Social Science Quarterly* 71(3):510–530.

McKelvey, Blake

1963   *The Urbanization of America (1860–1915).* Rutgers University Press, New Brunswick, New Jersey.

Meade, Norman G.

1911   *The Electric Vehicle: Its Construction, Operation and Maintenance.* Hill's Print Shop, New York.

Merrick, Rodney K.

1919   The Present and Future Status of the Electric Vehicle. *Proceedings of the National Electric Light Association*, vol. 3, pp. 57–68.

Meston, T. M.

1906   Shall Central Stations Sell Apparatus? *Electrical World*, 5 May, pp. 947–948.

Meyer, Herbert W.

1972   A History of Electricity and Magnetism. *Burndy Library, Publication* No. 27.

Meyer, Stephen III

1981   *The Five Dollar Day: Labor Management and Social Control in the Ford Motor Company, 1908–1921.* State University of New York Press, Albany.

Michalowicz, Joseph C.

1948   Origin of the Electric Motor. *Electrical Engineering* 67:1035–1040.

Millard, Andre

1990   *Edison and the Business of Innovation.* Johns Hopkins University Press.

Miller, Ray, and Bruce McCalley

1971   *The Model T Ford: From Here to Obscurity, "An Illustrated History of the Model T Ford."* Evergreen Press, Oceanside, California.

Moffett, Cleveland

1900   Automobiles for the Average Man. *The Review of Reviews*, June, pp. 704–710.

Mowry, George E.
1958   *The Era of Theodore Roosevelt and the Birth of Modern America, 1900–1912.* Harper & Row, New York.

Myers, F. C.
1918   How the Electric Truck Releases Man for Productive Work. *Industrial Management*, April, pp. 277–280.

Nerpel, Chuck
1979   20 Electric Cars You Can Buy. *Motor Trend*, September, pp. 94–97.

Newcomb, T. P., and R. T. Spurr
1989   *A Technical History of the Motor Car.* Adam Hilger, Bristol.

Nicholson, T. R.
1971   *Racing Cars and Record Breakers, 1898–1921.* MacMillan, New York.

Noble, David W.
1970   *The Progressive Mind, 1890–1917.* Rand McNally & Company, Chicago.

Nye, David E.
1979   *Henry Ford, "Ignorant Idealist."* Kennikat Press, Port Washington, New York.

1983   *The Invented Self: An Anti-Biography, from Documents of Thomas A. Edison.* Odense University Press, Odense.

1990   *Electrifying America: Social Meanings of a New Technology, 1880–1940.* The MIT Press, Cambridge, Massachusetts.

Olson, Sidney
1963   *Young Henry Ford: A Picture History of the First Forty Years.* Wayne State University Press, Detroit.

Ovshinsky, S. R., M. A. Fetcenko, and J. Ross
1993   A Nickel Metal Hydride Battery for Electric Vehicles. *Science* 260:176–181.

Page, Charles G.
1850   On Electro-Magnetism as a Moving Power. *The American Journal of Science and Arts* 20(series 2):343–349.

Palmer, W. H., Jr.
1902   The Storage Battery in the Commercial Operation of Electric Automobiles. *Electrical World and Engineer*, 12 April, pp. 643–647.

Passer, Harold C.
1953   *The Electrical Manufacturers, 1875–1900: A Study in Competition, Entrepreneurship, Technical Change, and Economic Growth.* Harvard University Press, Cambridge.

Payne, Harold J.
1926   How the Automotive Industries Have Put the Electric Industrial Truck to Work. *Industrial Management* 72:88–95.

Perrin, Noel
1992   *Solo: Life with an Electric Car.* W. W. Norton, New York.
Phillips, D. M.
1926   The Electric Motor Truck. *Electrical World,* 24 April, pp. 863–866.
Pope, Franklin L.
1890   The Electric Motor and Its Applications. In *Electricity in Daily Life: A Popular Account of the Applications of Electricity to Every Day Uses,* pp. 31–61. Charles Scribner's Sons, New York.
1891   The Inventors of the Electric Motor—I. With Special Reference to the Work of Thomas Davenport. *The Electrical Engineer,* 7 January, pp. 1–5.
Post, Robert C.
1974   Electro-Magnetism as a Motive Power: Robert Davidson's *Galvani* of 1842. *Railroad History, Bulletin* 130, pp. 5–22.
1976   *Physics, Patents, and Politics: A Biography of Charles Grafton Page.* Science History Publications, New York.
Pratt, Gill Andrews
1992   EVs: On the Road Again. *Technology Review,* August–September, pp. 51–59.
Prout, Henry G.
1921   *A Life of George Westinghouse.* The American Society of Mechanical Engineers, New York.
Pulos, Arthur J.
1983   *American Design Ethic: A History of Industrial Design to 1940.* MIT Press, Cambridge.
Rae, John B.
1965   *The American Automobile: A Brief History.* University of Chicago Press, Chicago.
1984   *The American Automobile Industry.* Twayne Publishers, Boston.
Randolph, F. Mason
1903   International Automobile Racing. *Outing* 42:711–715.
Rathje, William L., and Michael B. Schiffer
1982   *Archaeology.* Harcourt Brace Jovanovich, New York.
Riezenman, Michael J.
1992   Electric Vehicles. *IEEE Spectrum,* November, pp. 18–24, 93–101.
Riley, Phil M.
1913   What an Electric Can Do. *Country Life in America,* January, pp. 23–26, 70–75.
Roemer, Kenneth M.
1976   *The Obsolete Necessity: America in Utopian Writings, 1888–1900.* Kent State University Press, Kent, Ohio.

Rogers, Benjamin
1909   The Commercial Truck vs. the Horse. *Scientific American*, 16 January, pp. 42–43, 63.
Rosanoff, M. A.
1932   Edison in His Laboratory. *Harper's Magazine*, September, pp. 402–417.
Rowsome, Frank, Jr.
1956   *Trolley Car Treasury: A Century of Horsecars, Cable Cars, Interurbans, and Trolleys*. Bonanza Books, New York.
Salom, Pedro
1896   Automobile Vehicles. *Journal of the Franklin Institute* 141(4):278–296.
Scarritt, W. E.
1903   The Low-Priced Automobile. *Munsey's Magazine*, May, pp. 178–180.
1906   The Future of the Automobile. *Cassier's Magazine*, March, pp. 427–430.
Schallenberg, Richard H.
1982   Bottled Energy: Electrical Engineering and the Evolution of Chemical Energy Storage. *American Philosophical Society, Memoirs* 148.
Scharff, Virginia
1991   *Taking the Wheel: Women and the Coming of the Motor Age*. The Free Press, New York.
Schiffer, Michael Brian
1991   *The Portable Radio in American Life*. University of Arizona Press, Tucson.
1992   *Technological Perspectives on Behavioral Change*. University of Arizona Press, Tucson.
Schoop, M. U.
1905   The Edison Iron-Nickel Accumulator. *Scientific American Supplement* 1564, pp. 25064–25067.
Scott, Robert F.
1966   Does Mourning Become the Electric? *Automobile Quarterly* 5:194–207.
Sears, Stephen W.
1977   *The American Heritage History of the Automobile in America*. American Heritage Publishing Company, New York.
Shacket, Sheldon
1979   *The Complete Book of Electric Vehicles*. Domus Books, Chicago.
Silliman, Benjamin
1837   Notice of the Electro-Magnetic Machine of Mr. Thomas Davenport, of Brandon, near Rutland, Vermont. *The American Journal of Science and Arts* 32, Appendix A, pp. 1–8.
Smith, Frank W.
1914a   The Electric Vehicle of To-day. *The House Beautiful*, April, pp. 56–57.
1914b   The Electric's Progress. *Collier's National Weekly*, 10 January, pp. 26–28.

Smith, G.
1980   *Storage Batteries, Including Operation, Charging, Maintenance and Repair*. Pitman, London.
Smith, Harold H.
1913   The Edison Storage Battery: Elements Entering into Construction, Service Tests, and Uses. *Engineering Magazine* 45:91–94.
Smith, Robert A.
1972   *A Social History of the Bicycle: Its Early Life and Times in America*. American Heritage Press, New York.
Sochen, June
1974   *Her Story: A Woman's View of American History*. Alfred Publishing, New York.
Society of Automotive Engineers, Electric Vehicle Committee
1991   *Electric Vehicle Design and Development (SP-862)*. Society of Automotive Engineers, Warrendale, Pennsylvania.
Sperry, Elmer A.
1899   Electric Automobiles. *American Institute of Electrical Engineers, Transactions* 16:509–527.
St. Clair, David J.
1986   *The Motorization of American Cities*. Praeger, New York.
Sutphen, Henry R.
1901   Touring in Automobiles. *Outing* 38:197–202.
Terpstra, Philip
1991   *1992 Electric Vehicle Directory*. Spirit Publications, Tucson, Arizona.
Thompson, Elihu
1894   Electricity in 1876 and in 1893. *Engineering Magazine* 6:442–455.
Thompson, Stephen G.
1913   Electric versus Gasoline Motor Vehicles: Comparison of Operating Speed and Maintenance Data in City Service. *The Engineering Magazine* 46:112–114.
Towle, Herbert L.
1911   Electric Vehicles—To-day and To-morrow. *Collier's*, 7 January, pp. 32–34.
1915   The Woman at the Wheel. *Scribner's Magazine*, February, pp. 219–223.
Traister, Robert J.
1982   *All about Electric & Hybrid Cars*. Tab Books, Blue Ridge Summit, Pennsylvania.
Trawick, S. W.
1923   The Status of the Electric Vehicle. *Electrical World*, 28 July, pp. 205–206.

Trowbridge, John
1897   Motor Carriages. *Living Age* 213:131–132.
Turner, Dawson
1900   Some Experiences with Modern Motor-Cars. *Littell's Living Age* 255: 636–642.
Unnewehr, L. E., and S. A. Nasar
1982   *Electric Vehicle Technology.* Wiley-Interscience, New York.
Vanderbilt, Byron M.
1971   *Thomas Edison, Chemist.* American Chemical Society, Washington, D.C.
Venable, John D.
1981   *Mina Miller Edison: Daughter, Wife, and Mother of Inventors.* Charles Edison Fund, East Orange, New Jersey.
Voigt, David Q.
1974   *America's Leisure Revolution: Essays in the Sociology of Leisure and Sports* (revised edition). Albright College, Reading, Pennsylvania.
Volti, Rudi
1990   Why Internal Combustion Engines? *American Heritage of Invention & Technology* 6(2):42–47.
Wachhorst, Wyn
1981   *Thomas Alva Edison: An American Myth.* MIT Press, Cambridge, Massachusetts.
Wagner, Herbert A.
1916   Public Service and the Consumer. *Electrical World*, 1 July, pp. 7–9.
Wakefield, Ernest H.
1977   *The Consumer's Electric Car.* Ann Arbor Science Publishers, Inc., Ann Arbor, Michigan.
Walker, Robert H.
1967   *Life in the Age of Enterprise, 1865–1900.* G. P. Putnam's Sons, New York.
Warner, Sam Bass, Jr.
1972   *The Urban Wilderness: A History of the American City.* Harper & Row, New York.
Waters, Theodore
1896   Electricity in Private Houses. *The Electrical World*, 8 August 1896, pp. 161–164.
Watts, E. M.
1925   Advantages of the Electric Vehicle. *Electrical World*, 28 March, pp. 665–668.

Wells, David T.
1907   The Growth of the Automobile Industry in America. *Outing*, November, pp. 207–219.
Whitener, Barbara
1981   *The Electric Car Book*. Love Street Books, Louisville, Kentucky.
Whitney, George F.
1902   The Automobile as an Aid to Business. *Overland Monthly*, August, pp. 93–96.
Williams, Arthur
1921   The Electric Vehicle. *Proceedings of the National Electric Light Association*, vol. 1, pp. 96–101.
Willson, R. Thomas
1953   *The First Hundred Years, Baker-Raulang*. The Baker-Raulang Company, Cleveland.
Woods, C. E.
1900   *The Electric Automobile: Its Construction, Care, and Operation*. Herbert S. Stone & Company, Chicago.
Young, Rosamond
1961   *Boss Ket: A Life of Charles F. Kettering*. Longmans, Green and Co., New York.

INDEX

A

AC. *See* Alternating current
Adams Express Company, 98, 99
Advertising, 101; automobile, 125–30; electric car, 135, 146–48, 159–60; elitism in, 139–40; lighting used in, 51–52; women-oriented, 135–39
AeroVironment, 179
Aiken, Virginia E., 136
Allison, Fred, 155, 156(fig.)
Alternating current (AC), 37–38, 63–64, 106, 174
American Association of Edison Illuminating Companies, 43
American Battery Company, 36
American De Forest Wireless Telegraph Company, 85
American Electric Car Company, 159
Anderson, G. S., 167
Anderson, William C., 116, 130–31, 133, 134
Anderson Carriage Company, 116
Appliances, 54–55, 100, 102–3, 169
Argo company, 159
Arizona, 187
Association of Licensed Automobile Manufacturers, 115
Atwood, William Hooker, 50, 79
Atwood garage (Toledo), 119–20
Autocar, The (magazine), 113
Automobile, The (magazine), 114
Automobile Club of America, 84

Automobile Club of France, 72
Automobile clubs, 72, 84, 122
Automobile Bureau, 136
Automobiles: advertising of, 125–30, 135, 159–60; American-made, 93–94; costs of, 109–10, 142, 148–49, 170–71; early, 24–25; electric, 33, 35–36, 44–45, 57–60, 72–73, 91–92, 106–7, 116–18, 119–20, 143–44, 146–48, 156–57, 158–59, 161–62, 170, 173–74, 176–80, 186–89; gasoline, 43, 44, 75, 79, 81, 87, 110–11, 115–16, 172–73; maintenance of, 186–87; production of, 66–67
Automobile shows, 1, 56–57, 78, 86–87, 95, 138–39, 176, 179

B

Babcock electric cars, 136
Bacon, George M., 116
Bailey, E. W. M., 149–50
Bailey, Company, S. R., 149
Baker, Walter C., 83, 84
Baker Motor Vehicle Company, 83, 127, 159; electric cars of, 115, 116–17, 128(fig.), 129(fig.), 137, 139–40, 142
Baker-Raulang, 159, 165
Bartlett, J. Crawford, 148
Batteries, 19, 72–73, 80–81, 106–7, 144, 181–82; alkaline, 69, 77; charging, 50, 63, 64–65, 106; Edison, 87–90, 98–99, 129–30, 133, 149, 150, 153, 154–55, 164; Electric

Batteries (*cont.*)
Vehicle Company, 79–80; Exide, 112, 114–15, 126(fig.), 135; Horizon, 183, 186; lead-acid, 32–33, 173–74; nickel-iron, 77–78, 97, 113–14; nickel-metal hydride, 182–83, 186; refurbishing, 119–20; storage, 30–31, 45, 68, 117, 124, 125, 130–31, 134
Baum, L. Frank: *The Master Key: An Electrical Fairy Tale*, 55–56; *The Wizard of Oz*, 38
Beach, Alfred, 15
Bee, William (Billy) G., 98–99, 155
Benz, Karl, 24–25, 26
Berlin, 14
Betts, R. G., 78
Bicycles: development of, 22–24; use of, 40–42
Bloomers, 24
Borland Company, 159
Boston, 39, 138–39
Boston Edison, 123, 135
Bright, Mrs., 154
Broc company, 159
Broughams, 57–59, 160
Brown, George, 141
Bryant, Clara. *See* Ford, Clara Bryant
Buffalo (N.Y.), 91
Buick, 112
Burroughs, John, 172
Buses, 32, 61, 85–86, 97

C

Cabs, 69–71, 72, 73–74, 79–80
Cadillac, 82, 110, 116, 144, 145, 146
Caffrey, W. G., 185
Caffrey Company, Charles S., 46, 70
California, 187
California Air Resources Board, 176
Carnegie, Andrew, 98
Carriage and Wagon Builder (magazine), 131
Carriages, 24–25, 33, 49–50
Centennial Exhibition (Philadelphia), 11–12
Central Railway and Electric Company, 65
Central stations, 124, 164; and appliances, 55, 102–3; and automobiles, 66, 123, 127; development of, 27–28, 33, 56; operation of, 51–52, 101, 105, 106
Charging hydrants, 65–66
Charging meters, 188
Charging stations, 65, 69–70, 74, 103–4
Chicago, 40, 46, 124, 127
Chiquita, 91
Chloride Manchester batteries, 80

Chrysler, 178, 180, 181
Churchward, Alexander, 155
Cities: cars in, 120, 124, 127, 164, 187–88, 189; lighting of, 51–52; mass transit and, 175–76; mechanization of, 39–40; transportation in, 5–7; trolleys in, 38–39
Clean Air Act, 173
Clean Air Transport Svenska, 176
Cleveland, 123, 124
Coaches, 7–8
Collier's (magazine), 125, 135, 137, 139, 147
Columbia, 28
Columbia Automobile Company, 71, 79, 95, 115
Columbia Electric Phaeton, Mark III, 49–50, 60
Columbian Exposition, 35, 36–37, 38
Columbia ordinary, 23
Columbus Electric, 121(fig.), 126(fig.)
Commercial Vehicle, The (magazine), 114
Consumerist theory, 1, 2
Conversion kits, 178
Copley-Plaza Hotel, 138
Country Life in America (magazine), 139
Coupés, 116, 142, 160–61
Couzens, James, 93

D

Daumon Victoria Mark VI, 60
Davenport, Thomas, 7
Davidson, Robert, 7–8
Daylight saving time, 101
Dayton Engineering Laboratories Company (Delco), 145
DC. *See* Direct current
De Forest, Lee, 85
Delco. *See* Dayton Engineering Laboratories Company
Denmark, 176
Denver, 106, 119
Denzler, C. E., 83
Destiny 2000, 177
Detroit, 67
Detroit Automobile Company, 67, 81
Detroit Edison, 26–27
Detroit Electric, 116, 130, 135, 170; cars by, 137(fig.), 151(fig.), 157(fig.), 159, 161(fig.), 162
Dey, 161–62, 170
Dick, Herman E., 77

Direct current (DC), 18–19, 30; and lighting
systems, 31, 37, 38, 63
Doctors' Car, 95
Dodge brothers, 93
Doering, H. H., 148
Dog carts, 33, 34(fig.)
Dowe, Frank, 73
Drexel Building, 28
Durant Sugar Refinery, 29
Duryea, Charles E., 42, 64, 75
Duryea, J. Frank, 42, 46
Dynamos, 9, 12, 13, 14, 33, 85, 86

E

Eames, Hayden, 50, 80, 92, 123
Edison, Mary Stillwell, 11, 28
Edison, Mina Miller, 28–29, 68, 107, 139
Edison, Nancy, 10
Edison, Sam, 10
Edison, Thomas Alva, 1, 3–4, 9, 15, 32, 38,
127, 150(fig.); on central stations, 27–28; ear-
ly career of, 10–11; and electric automobiles,
83, 107, 181; and electric lighting, 16–19, 37;
and electric trucks, 131–35, 164; and Ford,
43–44, 153, 154–55, 166, 167, 172; and stor-
age batteries, 68–69, 77–78, 80, 87–90, 97–
98, 106, 112–14, 130
Edison Electric Illuminating Company, 65
Edison Illuminating Company. *See* Detroit
Edison
Edison Storage Battery Company, 77, 99, 155,
164
Electrants, 65–66, 188
Electrical Exhibition, 56–57, 58
Electrical World (magazine), 35–36, 61, 103,
123, 163; on battery charging, 65, 66, 74; on
central stations, 105, 106, 124; on electric
cars, 114, 115, 118, 119, 128–29, 136, 142,
146, 148–49, 150, 153
Electric and Hybrid Vehicle Research, Devel-
opment, and Demonstration Act, 173
Electric Automobile, The (Woods), 65
Electric Car No. 2, 166–67
Electric Carriage & Wagon Company, 45, 70
Electric companies, 101–2
Electricity, electrification, 9, 54; of cities, 27–
28, 39–40; exhibits on, 11–12; home, 105–6,
169–70
Electric lighting, 56, 100–101, 154; development of, 9–10; Edison's work on, 16–18; systems of, 18–19, 31, 37–38

Electric Power Research Institute (EPRI), 173
Electric Storage Battery Company (ESB), 45,
70, 71, 72, 130–31; battery development by,
78, 112, 114–15
Electric Vehicle and Central Station Associa-
tion, 124
Electric Vehicle Association of America (EVA),
124, 146–47, 148, 153–54
Electric Vehicle Company (EVC), 45, 50, 71,
74, 84; batteries used by, 79–80; and Selden
patent, 94–95
Electric Vehicle Directory (Terpstra), 178
Electric Vehicles (magazine), 153, 154, 157–
58, 159(fig.)
Electric World (magazine), 170
Electrobats, 45–46, 47, 48, 70
Electrosource, Inc., 183
Elitism: in advertising, 139–40
Energy Conversion Devices, 183
Engines, 12, 24; gasoline, 43, 95; power of,
81–82; steam, 11, 13
England, 31–32, 33
EPRI. *See* Electric Power Research Institute
ESB. *See* Electric Storage Battery Company
Europe, 21, 33. *See also various countries*
EVA. *See* Electric Vehicle Association of
America
EVC. *See* Electric Vehicle Company
Excursions, 111–12. *See also* Touring
Exide batteries, 78, 80

F

Factories, 53–54, 102
Farmer, Moses G., 9, 16
Faure, Camille, 30–31, 33
Filaments, 16, 17, 18(fig.)
Firestone, Harvey, 172
Fischer Motor Vehicle Company, 85–86
Fliess, Robert A., 61
Following the Equator (Twain), 21
Ford, Clara Bryant, 25–26, 43, 95
Ford, Edsel, 155
Ford, Henry, 3, 4, 12–13, 19, 95, 170; on af-
fordable automobile, 109–10, 111; and auto-
mobiles, 43, 67, 81–82, 92, 93, 107; court-
ship of, 25–26; early career of, 26–27; and
Edison, 43–44, 153, 154–55, 166, 167, 172;
and electric cars, 154, 168; and Model T, 140,
141, 171
Ford Company, Henry, 81–82
Ford Escort, 177

Ford Festivas, 178
Fordmobile. *See* Model A
Ford Motor Company, 92–93, 110, 140–42, 154; and electric cars, 155–56, 166–68, 178, 180, 181; suits against, 94–95
Fort, Governor, 122
Foster, Abram, 13
France, 11–12, 14, 22, 24, 31, 42; electric automobile development in, 44–45, 176
Frankfurt International Automobile Show, 176
Franklin Institute, 47
Fritchle, Oliver P., 119, 151

G

Galvani, 7–8
Garages, 105, 119–20
Garrett, Henry, 72
"Gasolenish Roadster," 151
General Electric, 106, 148
General Electric Automobile Company, 58, 65–66
General Electric Review (magazine), 112
General Motors (GM), 132, 145, 178, 179–80, 181
Germany, 24, 31, 42
Gibbs, L. D., 135
Glenmont, 28–29, 63
GM. *See* General Motors
GM Truck Company, 132
Good Roads Magazine, 23
Good Roads Movement, 142
Goss, M. L., 116
Gould, Jay, 29

H

Harper's Weekly, 116, 125
"Hartford Plan," 164
Hayes, Rutherford B., 15
Hertner, John H., 148
Hewitt, Peter Cooper, 106
Highland Park, 140–41, 155, 156
Horseless Age (magazine), 42, 48, 66, 72, 74, 135; on storage batteries, 89, 114; on touring, 118, 185
Horses, 118–19
Hotels, 54
House Beautiful, The (magazine), 139
Houses: electrification of, 54–56, 105–6, 169–70
Hunt, R., 9
Hupp-Yeats: car by, 136(fig.)

I

Ideal Tour, 149
Ignition systems, 144, 145
Immisch & Company, 33, 34(fig.)
Impact, 179–80
Italy, 176

J

Jackson, J. P., 55
Japan, 181
Jeantaud, M., 45
Jenkins Automobile Company, 91
Jungner, Waldemar, 69, 87

K

Kammann Manufacturing Company, 87
Kelvin, Lord. *See* Thompson, William
Kennedy, William P., 128–29, 140
Kettering, Charles Franklin, 145, 146
Kruesi, John, 15

L

La Force et La Lumière, S. A., 31
Lamps: electric, 100–101
Lander (Wyo.), 51
Lansden, John M., Jr., 131, 132
Lansden Company, 131, 164
Lead Cab Trust, 72, 94
League of American Wheelmen, 23
Leland, Henry, 82, 145
Leland Avenue Railway (Philadelphia), 32
Lenoir, Étienne, 24
Liebold, E. G., 154, 155, 167
Life (magazine), 125
Light bulbs, 100–101
Lighting, 9–10, 51, 100; arc-, 13–14. *See also* Electric lighting
Literary Digest, 125, 126, 139, 147
Lloyd, R. M., 92
Locomobile, 67
Locomotives, 8
Long Island Automobile Club, 83
Los Angeles, 106, 176
Los Angeles Auto Show, 179
"Low-Priced Automobile, The" (Scarritt), 109

M

McClure's (magazine), 21, 125
McCrea, S.: *Why Wait for Detroit?*, 178
MacCready, Paul, 179
McKinley, William, 84

Madison Square Garden, 52; automobile
  shows, 56–57, 86–87, 95, 115
Magazines, 16, 21, 42, 139. *See also by name*
Malcomson, Alex, 92
Marketing, 35, 181, 183–84; for bicycles, 22–
  23; for electric cars, 170, 180, 189
Mark III, 49–50
Mark VIII, 79
Mass production, 110, 141
Mass transit, 175–76
Master Key: An Electrical Fairy Tale, The
  (Baum), 55–56
Maxim, Hiram Percy, 50, 72, 79
Maybury, W. C., 67
Meadowcroft, W. H., 133
Media, 15, 16
Medicine, 52
Menlo Park, 11, 15, 17
Merriam, J. B., 64
Metropolitan Traction Company, 71
Middle class, 21, 23, 168, 169
Milburn Electrics, 158(fig.), 162
Miller, Mina. *See* Edison, Mina Miller
Model A, 92, 93
Model B, 95
Model C, 95
Model F, 95
Model K, 95
Model N, 95, 110
Model T, 111, 112, 140–41, 148; electric start-
  ers for, 154, 155; sales of, 170–71
Morgan, J. Pierpont, 28
Morris, Henry G., 45, 46, 47, 48, 69
Morrison, William, 35, 36
Motor Age (magazine), 116, 118, 146, 151
Motors, 7, 14, 33, 99, 112
Motor Trend (magazine), 189
Motor World (magazine), 72, 87, 118, 122,
  135, 153
Muncie, 56
Munsey's Magazine, 109

N

National Automobile Chamber of Commerce,
  171
National Cash Register, 145
National Electric Light Association, 105, 124,
  133
National Geographic, 21
Newark, 11
New Britain (Conn.), 65

New England Electric Vehicle and Transporta-
  tion Company, 79
New Haven Carriage Company, 50
New Jersey, 106–7
Newspapers, 15, 16, 17
New York Automobile Show, 78
New York City, 6, 7, 58, 100, 127; automobile
  shows, 1, 95, 97, 115; cabs in, 69–71, 72,
  73–74; lighting in, 27–28, 54; trucks in, 162–
  63
New York Edison, 136
New York State Prison, 37
New York Times Magazine, 182
999, 82

O

Ohio Electric Car Company: vehicles by, 137,
  142–43, 160(fig.)
Oldfield, Barney, 82
Olds, Ransom E., 67
Oldsmobiles, 67, 93, 94, 110
Olson, Sidney, 81
Omnibuses, 61, 85–86
Oregon Railway and Navigation Company, 28
Otto, Nikolaus, 24
Outing (magazine), 21, 75, 78
Overland Monthly (magazine), 75, 78, 91–92
Overman Company, A. H., 24, 40

P

Packard, 93
Page, Charles, 7, 8
Palmer, W. H., 74
Pan-American Exposition (Buffalo), 91
Panhard et Levassor, 25
Paris Exhibition, 30
Parshall, H. F., 99
Patents, 72, 94–95
Patent-sharing, 171
Pearl Street District, 27–28
Perrin, Noel: *Solo*, 177
Peugeot, 25, 148
Pfennig, E., 93
Phaetons, 49–50, 60, 61(fig.)
Philadelphia, 11–12, 32, 45
Planté, Gaston, 30
Poiret, Paul, 137
Pope, Albert A., 22, 40, 50
Pope Manufacturing Company, 49–50, 58, 71
Pope-Waverly automobiles, 95, 96(fig.), 104
Popular Mechanics (magazine), 173

Popular Science (magazine), 173
Power stations, 64, 65, 100
Progressive Age, 120–22
Providence (R.I.), 46–47

R

Racers, 82–84
Races, 40, 46–47, 74–75, 81, 83–84
Radios, 85
Railroads, railways: electric, 14, 15(fig.), 29;
  technological changes in, 6–7; touring by, 21,
  22. *See also* Trolleys
Rauch & Lang, 139, 148–49, 159
Reckenzaun, Anthony, 31–32
Review of Reviews (magazine), 110
Rice, Herbert H., 105
Richmond (Va.), 29
Riker, Andrew L., 34, 50, 82–83
Riker Electric Motor Company, 46–47; vehi-
  cles of, 60(fig.), 61(fig.), 62(fig.), 75
Roads, 23, 112
Roadsters: electric, 149–50, 151, 160, 168
"Road torpedo," 83, 84
Rockford Edison Company, 103–4
Runabouts, 57, 79, 161–62

S

St. Louis, 103, 105, 124
Salom, Pedro, 45, 46, 47–48, 69
Saturday Evening Post, The, 125
Scarritt, W. E.: "The Low-Priced Automobile,"
  109
Science fiction, 55–56
Scientific American, 56, 57, 71, 81, 83, 91,
  129; on American automobiles, 94, 110, 111;
  on electric vehicles, 33, 34, 35, 44–45, 79, 97
Seattle, 106
Sebring Auto-Cycle, 177–78
Selden, George B., 12
Selden patent, 72, 94–95
Self-starters, 144–46
Services: for electric cars, 103–4, 105
Shaft drive, 127–28
Siemans, Werner, 14
Siemans and Halske, 14, 15(fig.)
Smith, C. F., 123
Social class, 5–6. *See also* Middle class; Upper
  class
Social History of the Bicycle, A (Smith), 23–24
Solar Car Corporation, 178
Solar Electric Engineering, 177

Solo (Perrin), 177
Sprague, Frank Julian, 29, 39
Sprague Electric Railroad & Motor Company,
  29
Stanhopes, 60
Starters, 154, 155, 157
Steam engines, 11, 12–13
Steamships, 21, 22, 28
Steinmetz, Charles P., 148, 161–62
Stillwell, Mary. *See* Edison, Mary Stillwell
Studebaker, 88(fig.), 95, 116
Sturges electric, 46
Suburbs, 39
Sutphen, Henry, 75
Sweden, 176

T

Technological constraint theory, 1, 2–3
Technology: changes and innovations in, 127–
  29, 171–72; embellishments in, 142–43;
  green, 184–85
Telegraphy, 10–11
Terpstra, Philip: *Electric Vehicle Directory*, 178
Thompson, William (Lord Kelvin), 31
Thomson, Elihu, 98
Three-wheelers, 24, 177–78
Tiffany, D. C., 186
Tiffany & Company, 99
Times-Herald Motorcycle Contest, 45, 46
Toledo, 119–20
Touring, 21–22; automobile, 84–85, 118, 122;
  by bicycle, 41–42; electric car, 149–52, 185–
  86
Touring cars, 84–85, 95, 125, 151, 168; costs
  of, 109–11
Trains, 9, 14, 15(fig.)
Transportation, 5–6; personal, 22, 40
Travel. *See* Touring
Tricycles, 24, 26(fig.), 34, 68
Trolleys, 40, 165–66, 185; battery-powered,
  31–32, 134(fig.); electric, 14, 29–30, 38–39
Trucks: electric, 61, 96, 98, 123, 131–35, 162–
  64, 178; gasoline, 164–65
Twain, Mark: *Following the Equator*, 21

U

Union Electric Light & Power Company, 103,
  105
U.S. Advanced Battery Consortium, 181, 183
U.S. Court of Appeals, 95
U.S. Postal Service, 123

Upper class: automobiles and, 42, 58, 67, 139, 168–69; traveling by, 21–22; women in, 121–22

V

Van Vleck, John, 65
Vehicle Equipment Company, 96–97
Vested interest theory, 1–2
Victor bicycle, 24
Victoria, 60
Villard, Henry, 28
Volk, Magnus, 33
Volta, 176

W

Wabash, 51
Wabash Plain Dealer, 51
Wagons: delivery, 35, 36(fig.), 59(fig.), 61–62, 123, 131–35, 163–64
Waldorf, Hotel, 54
Wallis, L. R., 66
Ward Baking Company, 163(fig.)
Ward Motor Vehicle Company, 164
Warren, Fiske, 34
Washington, D.C., 120

Waverly Company, 60, 128, 130, 138(fig.), 151
Wayne County (Mich.), 112
Weir, L. C., 98
Western Electrician (magazine), 35
Westinghouse, George, 37, 38
Westinghouse Company, 106
West Orange (N.J.), 28, 29
Whalebone Wagon, 149
Whitney, William C., 70–72, 73
Why Wait for Detroit? (McCrea), 178
Wilson, Samuel F., 155
Winton, Alexander, 81
Winton automobiles, 93, 94
Wireless Auto No. 1, 85
Wizard of Oz, The (Baum), 38
Women, 157; and bicycles, 23–24, 25(fig.), 41–42; and electric cars, 135–39; and Progressive movement, 120–22
Women's Motoring Club of New York, 122
Woods, C. E.: *The Electric Automobile*, 65
Woods Company, C. E., 50, 140, 160–61

Z

Zzipper, 177–78